Raves for Judy Gethers'
ITALIAN COUNTRY COOKING

"I am thrilled to have Judy's wonderful Italian book—
I want to make every recipe from cover to cover."
Maida Heatter

"Judy's creamy desserts and ice creams would tempt
any child's sweetest fantasy, as they do mine. The
pizza recipes are authentic. They will prove surprisingly easy to execute due to Judy's explicit step-by-step
directions. The informed wine list is inventive, with
some true finds to complement the joyful country
foods that fill these pages. I love this cookbook."
Wolfgang Puck, Owner and Chef of Spago

"The recipes in this book are a genuine expression of
research and feelings of what Italian cuisine is all
about. It is a feast of flavors and a great achievement
of what we would like Italian gastronomy to be. *Dulcis
Dulcis infundo:* to finish with a mouthful of flavor. The
chapter on desserts is filled with wonderful pastries, ice
creams and fruit desserts that will tempt one and all."
Piero Selvaggio, Owner of Valentino's Restaurant

ITALIAN

COUNTRY COOKING

For the American Kitchen

JUDY GETHERS
Illustrations by Susan Gaber

Ballantine Books   New York

Library of Congress Catalog Card Number: 85-90889

ISBN 0-345-30300-8
This edition published by arrangement with
Villard Books

Manufactured in the United States of America
First Ballantine Books Trade Edition: June 1986
10 9 8 7 6 5 4 3 2 1

For the men in my life—
Steve, Eric and Peter

Thanks to:

Piero Selvaggio, owner of Valentino restaurant in Los Angeles, for permitting me the freedom of his kitchen, for the many hours sharing with me his philosophy on food in general and Italian food in particular and for his superb suggestions of wines to complement *il pasto*.

Antonio Orlando, Valentino's chef, for allowing me unlimited access to his kitchen and his recipes.

Joan Hoien, my good friend, who traveled through Italy with me in search of culinary "plums." She tested many of the recipes that we tasted in our travels.

Beth Lefft, who diligently deciphered and then typed the recipes for this book.

Symbols

Throughout the book the following symbols
have been used to indicate which recipes
require the use of an ice cream maker
or for which the use of a food processor
is recommended:

Food Processor

Ice Cream Maker

Contents

List of Recipes

Preface

The basic ingredient in the lifestyle of an Italian is passion. It colors his art, chisels his sculpture, arranges his music.

It seasons his food.

Deceptively simple, characteristically robust, today's Italian cooking is a symbol of *la dolce vita*. However, each dish can vary, depending upon the mood of the chef. An Italian meal is as diversified as it is unique, since the ingredients are heavily flavored with an attitude. A peasant may sit down to a simple dinner of grilled fish, risotto with butter and grated cheese, and sliced fruit in syrup, savoring every bite. If it has been prepared for him, it will taste different from the same meal he experienced the week before, although the same hands may have stirred the sauce or cooked the rice. If he has prepared it himself, it will be spicier this time than the last, or less, depending upon his feelings at the moment.

Italians have championed the cause of their *cucina* since the days of the early Romans. Contrary to popular belief, it was the French who learned from the Italians. Today, farmers of all regions still take advantage of knowledge that dates back to those ancient times. Coupled with their indigenous produce, they have experimented with foods from other countries—tomatoes, corn, and rice—and made them their own. Today, these delicacies are thought of as native Italian.

Italian cuisine has long been my favorite. When my editor asked me to write this book, I was delighted. It offered an opportunity to explore more

deeply the secrets behind this extraordinary way of cooking. To share the results with you, I traveled widely through most of Italy, observing, conversing with the experts, assisting when possible, feverishly taking notes. As a result, this book is an eclectic collection of recipes, most adaptations of dishes I have eaten in Italy, still others from the minds and hands of the best Italian-American restaurant owners and chefs.

At first, it was to be called "Italian Country Cooking." But somewhere along the way, I discovered that tastes and American ingredients are not always the exact equivalent of the Italian. There are certain products which cannot be imported to the United States from Italy. Parma ham, for instance, comes primarily from Canada because of the restrictions imposed upon Italian exports. Tuscan beef, some of the Mediterranean fish . . . the list of unobtainable ingredients is considerable. Fortunately, with a little help from our farmers, cattle raisers and fishmongers, we can enjoy many authentic Italian dishes using local ingredients. Therefore, "Italian Country Cooking for the American Kitchen." Quality and freshness are still key words, as important to the American cook as the Italian. Whether prepared by a professional or an amateur, home cooking (*la cucina casalinga*) must be a labor of love.

The wines of Italy (every region boasts its own vineyards) are almost as popular in the United States as they are in Italy. Soave, Verdicchio, Orvieto and Valpolicella are just a few of the well-known varieties. Throughout the book I have suggested wines which will best complement a particular food or meal. In keeping with the Italian-American feeling, I have listed some excellent American wines as well. I have also tried to include selections that are not always familiar but are well worth sampling.

On my last trip to Italy, I rediscovered the pleasures of drinking red wine. I had sworn off reds since even a sip or two left me feeling ill the next morning. In Florence, Arthur Schwartz, a prominent food and wine writer and connoisseur, offered me a glass, promising no ill effects. (Because of different production methods, Italian reds are free of the histamines that can cause discomfort.) He was right. Now I can enjoy a glass of red *vino . . .* as long as it's Italian.

What will you find within these pages? We start with light, delicious appetizers in anticipation of what's to come. Then, on to hearty soups and stocks. Sauces, which can be served with pastas and vegetables as well as main dishes, follow. There is a generous chapter on pastas, rice and polenta, often referred to as the Italian national dishes, and another on very special country-style breads and doughs. You'll find interesting ways to prepare fish, which seems to have replaced beef in the kitchens of many Americans. We go on to poultry, which has found a new audience after years as the culinary poor relation, and game, gaining in popularity. The meat chapter includes familiar as well as newer methods of preparing veal, lamb, pork and beef. Vegetables, in many instances, become meals unto themselves. In Italy, salads are never dull. For a light meal, try the marvelous frittatas and egg dishes. And last, but never least, a round of Italian desserts including luscious *gelati* and light fruit concoctions.

Buon gusto, amici!!

The Italian Kitchen

Equipment

I consider this list of equipment essential for a well-functioning kitchen, a kitchen that will make your work easier. You can add to the equipment as your experience and kitchen space dictate. I feel that you should buy the best quality that you can comfortably afford, the material durable enough to give you long-lasting service.

2 sets dry measuring cups
3 liquid measuring cups—1-, 2-, and 3-cup
2 sets measuring spoons
1 portable timer
2 skillets—10- and 12-inch, of non-stick material
1 6-inch crepe pan
2 sauté pans—8- and 14-inch
4 saucepans—1½-, 2½-, 4-, and 6-quart
1 double boiler
1 stockpot—12-quart
1 flameproof casserole or Dutch oven, 6-quart
2 roasting pans, to fit your oven
2 nonstick baking sheets, to fit your oven

1 9-inch-square baking pan
1 13 × 9 × 2-inch baking dish
1 9 × 5 × 2-inch loaf pan
1 8-inch pizza pan
1 lasagne pan
1 springform pan, preferably 8- or 9-inch
1 8- or 9-inch pie plate
1 6-cup soufflé dish
8 ½-cup soufflé or timbale cups
1 8-inch tart pan with removable bottom
3 stainless steel mixing bowls—small, medium and large
3 knives—3- or 4-inch paring knife, 6- to 8-inch knife, and 10- to 12-inch chef's knife
1 boning knife

1 pair kitchen shears
   Food processor
   Electric mixer
   Pasta machine, hand-cranked
      model
   Potato ricer

Mandoline, optional
Mezzaluna, a crescent-shaped
   chopper with one handle at
   each end, optional
Vegetable peeler

I prefer a carbon steel blade for knives as opposed to stainless steel. Carbon steel keeps its edge, will last longer and is less expensive. But it does require care; it should be washed and dried after each use, and should never be put into a dishwasher.

Knives should be sharpened professionally once or twice a year and then kept sharp with a sharpening steel or stone. Dull knives are far more dangerous than sharp ones.

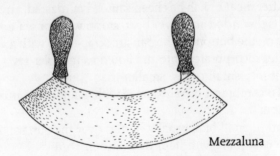

Mezzaluna

Cooking Terms

It is important to become familiar with cooking expressions when reading a cookbook, so I have compiled and defined a list of kitchen terms for a better understanding of my recipes.

Al dente Describes the cooking of pasta or vegetables to the "almost cooked" stage, but still slightly crisp.

Bagna cauda To make a bath of hot sauce for dipping raw vegetables.

Bain-marie A French term. To cook food in a bain-marie is to cook it *over* simmering, not boiling, water on top of the stove, or *in* a hot-water bath in the oven.

Blanch To partially cook food in boiling salted water and then plunge into ice water to stop the cooking process.

Cube To cut into ¼- or ½-inch pieces.

Deglaze After meat or fish has been sautéed or roasted, any fat remaining in the pan is discarded and, over heat, stock, wine or water is added. All the particles on the bottom of the pan are scraped up with a whisk or wooden spoon and incorporated into the liquid as it cooks.

Dice To cut into small cubes, smaller than ¼ inch.

Dissolve To combine a dry substance with a liquid and mix or stir until it is in solution.

Dot To scatter small bits, usually butter, over the surface of food.

Dredge To coat food with flour or crumb mixture.

Dust To sprinkle with flour, crumbs or sugar until lightly coated.

Filet Meat, chicken or fish that has had the bone(s) removed.

Fold A delicate over-and-under motion used to incorporate whipped egg whites or cream into a heavier substance to lighten.

Fry To cook in shallow hot butter, oil, or fat, or a combination; also known as sautéing.

Garnish A decorative touch added to prepared food to make it visually attractive.

Glaze To cover with a shiny coating; for example, to brush with egg wash. To "reduce to a glaze" is to reduce until there is very little liquid left in the pan—just a thin, shiny layer.

Grate To shred a food (cheese, carrots, potatoes, etc.), producing fine, medium or coarse pieces. This can be done with a grater or food processor.

Grease To coat a pan or bowl with butter or oil.

Grill To cook on a grating, griddle or rack over hot coals or fire.

Hull To remove the leafy sprout from fruits or vegetables, such as strawberries.

Julienne French term meaning to cut into uniform strips, ⅛ to ¼ inch thick.

Knead To work dough with a pressing motion, folding and stretching at the same time, making it smooth and elastic. Kneading may be done by hand, with an electric mixer or with a food processor.

Mandoline A rectangular apparatus used for cutting fruits and vegetables into slices, julienne strips, etc. An inexpensive plastic model can be purchased that is very satisfactory.

Marinate To soak food in a liquid to add flavor or to tenderize.

Melt To liquefy by heating.

Mince To cut or chop into very small pieces.

Mix To incorporate a combination of ingredients.

Mound To pile into a heap.

Peel To remove the outside skin or covering of a fruit or vegetable with a knife or peeler.

Pipe To push food through a pastry bag.

Pit To remove seeds or pits.

Pith The white, bitter layer between the rind and flesh of citrus fruit. If some of this white pith remains after peeling, it should be scraped off with a knife.

Poach To cook foods in a simmering liquid such as stock, wine or seasoned liquid.

Preheat To bring the oven to the desired temperature at least 20 minutes before baking, roasting or broiling.

Reconstitute To restore the original water content to dried foods by soaking.

Reduce To evaporate liquid by boiling, thus concentrating the volume, flavor and texture.

Refresh To plunge hot cooked food into ice-cold water to stop the cooking process.

Rice To press cooked food, such as potatoes, through a perforated apparatus, forming small ricelike particles.

Rind The outer peeling of citrus fruit.

Roast To cook in an uncovered pan.

Sauté To cook food in an open saucepan or skillet. For best results, there are three basic rules to follow: 1. heat pan before adding fat; 2. make sure food being added is thoroughly dry; 3. do not overcrowd pan.

Simmer To cook liquid just below the boiling point.

Skim To remove scum or fat layer from the surface of a liquid.

Steam To cook food on a rack over boiling water in a covered vessel.

Truss To use skewers or string to keep the legs and wings of a fowl close to its body as it roasts.

Whip To incorporate air into a food, giving increased volume and lighter texture.

Zest The outer peeling or rind of citrus fruit cut into tiny pieces.

Cooking Techniques

The following section, devoted to an explanation of techniques, is as important as the recipes themselves. The purpose is to clarify directions for those not familiar with them, and to suggest some shortcuts I have learned from the many chefs I have worked with during my years as a cooking teacher at Ma Maison's cooking school, Ma Cuisine, in Los Angeles.

CUTTING—If right-handed, hold the knife handle comfortably in your right hand. Place the food to be cut on the work table with your left hand on top, fingertips curled under. The flat side of the knife should be against your knuckles, the blade perpendicular to the work table. Cut down through the food, using the knuckles of your left hand as a guide.

TO CUT INTO JULIENNE SLICES—*Chef's knife* Cut food into 2-inch-long pieces. For rounded vegetables, cut away a thin sliver lengthwise and lay the vegetable on the cut side. Cut the vegetable lengthwise into thin slices. Stack a few of the slices and again cut thin slices lengthwise.

TO DICE OR CHOP FINE—*Chef's knife* First julienne the food. Stack the thin strips together and then cut across into small pieces. Hold the point of the knife on the work table and just lift the handle, allowing your left hand to move back slowly as the food is diced.

TO CUT LEAFY VEGETABLES OR HERBS—*6- or 8-inch knife* Stack a few of the leaves to be cut and roll tightly. Cut into thin slices and lift to unravel. This can be done with spinach, basil, etc.

TO CUT CHICKEN OR OTHER FOWL INTO EIGHT PIECES—*Chef's knife* Place the whole chicken on your work surface. To cut, start with the legs. Pull the leg away from the body and cut through the loose skin, exposing the joint. Cut through the joint, separating the thigh and leg from the body. Cut apart the leg from the thigh. Repeat with the other leg and thigh. Cut each wing off at the second joint, keeping the first joint (the "drumette") attached to the breast.

Turn the chicken on its back. Separate the back from the breast by cutting through where the breast ribs attach to the back ribs.

Lay the whole breast on its back and slice down the center, leaving two halves. If you have trouble cutting through the center, lay the knife on top and press down with your hand or with a mallet. Cut each half into two pieces.

TO BONE CHICKEN BREASTS—*Boning or small paring knife* Place whole chicken on the work surface, breast facing up. Feel for the breastbone and lightly outline either side of the bone with the tip of the knife. Then make a cut on one side of the bone and, using your fingers, start pushing the meat away from the bone. The flat side of the knife should scrape against the bone as the knife point aids your fingers in gently removing the breast meat from the bone. Repeat on the other side. With the point of the knife, cut away the white tendon running through the filet. Lightly score each filet, first in one direction, then the other, crossing the first lines, to tenderize.

TO PEEL TOMATOES, PEACHES, ETC.—*Small paring knife* Core stem end. Lightly score other end with a cross, using the tip of a knife. Drop into boiling water for 10 seconds and transfer immediately to ice water. Skin will peel off easily.

TO SEED TOMATOES—*Small paring knife* Cut tomato in half horizontally. Gently squeeze the tomato, discarding the seeds. You may have to use your fingers or a knife tip to gently pry out seeds.

TO CLARIFY BUTTER—Melt butter over very low heat. Remove from heat and let rest for a few minutes. Spoon off and discard the residue that accumulates on the top. Pour the clear liquid into a clean container. Stop pouring when you reach the milky residue in the bottom of the pan. Clarified butter will not burn as quickly as whole butter and is better to use for sautéing.

BEATING EGG YOLKS TO A RIBBON—Beat egg yolks with a wire whisk or a rotary beater or electric mixer. Gradually add sugar, continuing to beat until the mixture is pale yellow and forms a slowly dissolving ribbon when the whisk or beater is lifted. At this point, other ingredients can be incorporated.

BEATING EGG WHITES—For best results, have the egg whites at room temperature. Place whites in a clean bowl and whip with a balloon whisk or the whip of an electric mixer. Gently beat until the whites form soft peaks. If sugar is to be added, it is added gradually at this point and then the whites are beaten until shiny and slightly stiff. Do not overbeat.

Special Ingredients

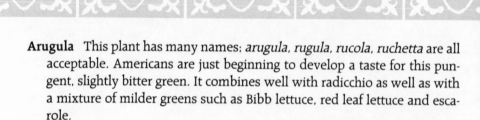

Arugula This plant has many names; *arugula, rugula, rucola, ruchetta* are all acceptable. Americans are just beginning to develop a taste for this pungent, slightly bitter green. It combines well with radicchio as well as with a mixture of milder greens such as Bibb lettuce, red leaf lettuce and escarole.

Artichokes *(Carciofi)* Artichokes are available all year. The smaller the artichoke, the more tender it will be. If cooking a few at a time, try to select artichokes of the same size to ensure even cooking. When cooking the bottoms, rub with a lemon half immediately after turning to prevent discoloration. Place in pan with lightly salted water to cover and a lemon half. Arrange a double thickness of paper towel over artichoke bottoms to help steam the artichokes.

Asparagus *(Asparagi)* Asparagus can be bought almost year round, but the price is prohibitive during the off-season. It is at its best from the middle of February through June. Canned or frozen should never be substituted for the fresh stalks. Asparagus should be cooked slightly al dente, never soft.

Beans *(Fave)* Cannellini are small white beans which are probably used more often than any other bean in Italian dishes. They are available dried or already cooked and canned. Other beans familiar to Italian cooks are chickpeas, dried lima beans, navy beans and lentils. To cook dried beans, first sort through them, discarding the discolored or shrunken ones. Rinse under cold water, then let soak in cold water to cover 3 to 4 hours. Do not salt in the early cooking stage, since salt tends to toughen the beans. Season during the last half hour of cooking. Cook beans in a heavy-bottomed

pot on top of the stove, over low heat, or in a 300°F oven, gently stirring occasionally.

Bouquet garni A French term used to describe a bunch of herbs tied together or enclosed in a cheesecloth bag and placed in a soup or stew. The herbs are easier to remove at the end of the cooking time if tied together. A basic bouquet would include a few parsley sprigs, 1 thyme sprig, 1 bay leaf and a few whole peppercorns.

Breadcrumbs *(Briciole)* An excellent way to use leftover bread, crumbs are used to coat food to be sautéed, or to thicken soups and stuffings. Crumbs are easily made by drying bread in a low oven, cutting into small pieces and then grinding in a food processor or blender. They can be used immediately, refrigerated in an airtight container, or frozen until needed.

Butter *(Burro)* I recommend unsalted grade AA butter. When used for sautéing, it is usually combined with a good-quality oil to prevent burning, since butter has a low burning point.

Capers *(Capperi)* Capers are closed flower buds found on a small bush that grows wild in many Mediterranean countries. Preserved in vinegar, the buds can perk up the flavor of meat and fish dishes.

Fennel *(Finocchio)* This licorice-flavored bulb can be eaten raw or cooked. The seeds can be kept in an airtight packet for a year. Fennel is used to flavor fish, sauces (such as mayonnaise) to be served with fish, and potato salad. The seeds also add flavor to sausages and other pork products.

Figs *(Fichi)* Fresh figs are a delicacy and very perishable. They can be found from early July through October, eaten raw or sautéed lightly.

Italian Seasoning A blend of dried herbs—sage, marjoram, oregano, thyme, basil, rosemary—to be used when the fresh herbs are not available.

Mushrooms *(Funghi)* Porcini, or any other dried mushrooms, should be soaked in warm water 20 to 30 minutes to replace the moisture taken from them during the drying process. They are convenient to use, since they can be kept on the shelf until needed. Only a small amount is necessary to flavor a dish. If cooked too long, the mushrooms toughen and lose flavor and aroma.

Oil *(Olio)* In most of Italy olive oil is one of the basic cooking ingredients. Good olive oil is essential to the good taste of the food. Each region presses its own oil, and oils vary from one region to another. There are big differences among the hundreds of varieties of olives from which the oil is taken. The olive, the picking and the method of pressing all determine the quality of the oil. The best should be delicately fragrant, with a delicious taste. Extra-virgin olive oil is cold-pressed without additives and has only 1% acid. It is a thick, greenish-colored oil. Not only are we now importing olive oils from Italy, but we are crushing our own olives in the Napa Valley, and the resulting oil is excellent. There is no substitute for olive oil to flavor salads or vegetables or to drizzle over beans, turning an ordinary dish into a gourmet's delight. To keep olive oil fresh after opening, remove the cork or bottle top and lightly stuff gauze or cheesecloth into the opening, allowing air to circulate without contaminating. Do not refrigerate.

Throughout the book I call for olive oil where necessary; otherwise I specify cooking oil. Good for all-purpose cooking are safflower, peanut and almond oils. They have a high burning level with no distinctive flavor of their own.

Peppers *(Peperoni)* Brought to Italy from the New World, sweet peppers have become an Italian staple. They can be eaten raw, roasted, steamed or sautéed. Yellow, green and red peppers are now available in markets.

Radicchio A red lettuce with a white strip through the middle, radicchio is grown in Treviso and comes in small or large heads. It is a great delicacy and should be used sparingly, usually combined with another green.

Rice *(Riso)* The Italian rice is short-grained and has its own special taste. It can never be confused with the dry, fluffy rice most Americans are familiar with. Arborio is the generic name of the imported Italian rice available in the United States; it can be found under many brand names.

Sun-dried tomatoes *(Pomodori secchi)* These flavorful tomatoes are dried in the sun and then packed in oil. They come in small or large jars and will keep, refrigerated, for months.

Tomatoes *(Pomodori)* Tomatoes are at their best during July, August and September, though they are available all year round. Very ripe, soft tomatoes produce the best tomato sauce. When these are not available, canned, peeled plum tomatoes can be substituted. Canned tomato paste or purée should be used sparingly.

Truffles *(Tartyfi)* In my opinion, the white truffles of Piedmont are by far the most delicious. Truffles can be preserved by submerging them in vodka until needed. But first try refrigerating them in a closed jar with uncooked, unshelled eggs for two or three days. Then scramble the eggs—they will be the best you have ever eaten.

ANGEL HAIR—A long, thin round pasta called angel hair because of the fineness of the noodle.

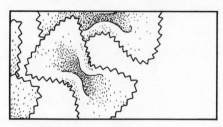

CANNELLONI—A large, tubular pasta that can be stuffed with a number of fillings—spinach, ricotta, meat or a combination.

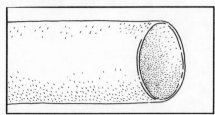

FARFALLE—Shaped like a bow tie, this pasta can have straight or curly edges.

FETTUCCINE—A long, flat noodle, the Roman version of tagliatelle, fettuccine combines well with most sauces. Yellow and green fettuccine are most commonly found.

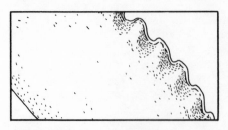

LASAGNE—Flat, wide sheets of pasta, lasagne comes straight or curly edged. If the pasta is homemade, make the noodle slightly smaller than the size of the pan being used. Yellow or green lasagne is most commonly used.

LINGUINE—A long, thin flat noodle that is wider than angel hair and thinner than fettuccine.

PENNE—A tubular pasta, penne comes plain or ribbed. The ends are cut at an angle.

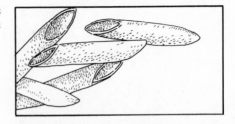

RIGATONI—A short, tubular macaroni, usually ribbed.

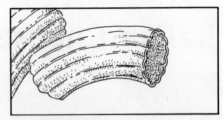

SPAGHETTI—The most familiar form of pasta, spaghetti is a long, round noodle that can be thin or thick.

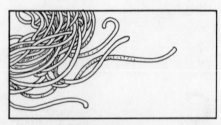

STUFFED PASTA—Ravioli, Cappelletti, Tortellini Ravioli can be square or round; cappelletti are shaped like little peaked hats; tortellini are stuffed rounds of dough that are folded in half and the ends brought together to form a circle of dough with a hole in the center. The stuffing can be fish, cheese, chicken, meat, vegetables or a combination of the above. They can be served with a sauce of your choice or with melted butter and Parmesan cheese.

TAGLIATELLE—A long, flat yellow or green noodle, this is the Bolognese version of fettucine. It is extremely versatile, combining well with meat or cream sauces.

VERMICELLI—This is a thin spaghetti, thicker than angel hair.

Italian Cheeses

Cheese is a staple in the Italian diet. It is served as a separate course and is an important ingredient in many dishes. I have included a small list to familiarize you with some of the Italian cheeses available in the United States.

Bel Paese A semisoft, very mild cheese made from cow's milk. It is used as a table cheese as well as in cooking.

Fontina A fairly firm cheese, similar to Gruyère in texture, with tiny holes on the surface. Not only is it indispensable in preparing *Fondue* (page 30), but it is an excellent table cheese. Do not confuse this with Danish fontina, which in no way compares in flavor or texture.

Gorgonzola A rich, creamy, blue-green veined cheese made from whole cow's milk. It can be mild *(dolce)* or sharp *(piccante)*, is used as a table cheese and is particularly tasty over pasta.

Mascarpone A rich fresh cream cheese that spreads easily. It can be eaten just sprinkled with sugar and/or cocoa powder.

Mozzarella A bland, smooth cheese that is used on lasagne, pizza, sandwiches, etc. Fresh buffalo mozzarella, a great delicacy, is now available in gourmet Italian food shops. Fresh mozzarella is very perishable and should be used within two or three days after purchasing. Smoked mozzarella keeps a bit longer.

Parmesan *(Parmigiano)* A firm cow's milk cheese. The best and most expensive is Parmigiano-Reggiano. Aged Parmesan is grated and served in

pasta, soups, salads, etc. and is best when freshly grated. In Italy, when the cheese is very fresh and moist, it is eaten as a table cheese.

Pecorino A medium-sharp cheese made from sheep's or goat's milk. Aged pecorino is used alone in dishes or combined with Parmesan.

Provolone A hard but creamy cheese made from cow's milk. It can be mild or sharp, fresh or smoked. It melts easily and can be grated or sliced.

Ricotta Made from either cow's or goat's milk, ricotta resembles a smooth cottage cheese. Fresh ricotta is generally used in cooking but can be served as a table cheese.

Romano A sharp, firm cheese made from goat's milk. It is grated and can be substituted for Parmesan in most dishes.

Herbs and Spices

Herbs and spices are basic to Italian cooking. As in any good kitchen, the fresher the herb, the better the flavor. But our garden-less, window-box-less, green thumb-less friends may find it difficult to grow fresh herbs, and at certain times of the year fresh herbs are just not obtainable.

In some recipes only the fresh herb will do, but in many, dried herbs may be substituted. A general rule to follow is to use twice as much of the fresh herb as you would the dried. As with any flavoring, your taste should determine the amount, remembering that the purpose is to enhance rather than to overpower your food.

Basil *(Basilico)* A member of the mint family, basil has a distinctive and spicy aroma. Fresh, it may very well be the best of all herbs, used to flavor tomatoes, tomato sauce, soups, salads, and of course the irreplaceable pesto. It retains the most flavor when cut and added at the last moment. Leaves can be preserved by covering with oil (preferably olive oil) in a lidded jar and refrigerating or freezing.

Bay leaf *(Lauro)* A stiff green leaf used to flavor soups, casseroles, stews and roasts.

Cinnamon *(Cannella)* Used primarily in sweet dishes, it is occasionally added to meat and game.

Fennel *(Finocchio)* A member of the carrot family, the bulb of this plant has an anise flavor and is used whole or sliced, as a cooked vegetable or raw

in salads. The leaves are used in sauces, mayonnaise, and egg and fish dishes. The seeds flavor sausages, cooked meats, dried figs and cookies.

Garlic *(Aglio)* Used properly, garlic adds just the right flavor to meats, sauces, casseroles and vegetables. When browned in oil or butter and then discarded, just the faint taste remains. The pungent flavor that can be overwhelming is not typical of Italian cooking (pasta with oil and garlic, and pesto are exceptions).

Italian parsley *(Prezzemolo)* Notably different from the curly parsley familiar to most Americans, this is a flat-leafed variety used to flavor soups, stews, salads, and serves as a garnish to these and many other dishes.

Marjoram *(Maggiorana)* Available fresh during the summer, this aromatic herb is used in soups, stews, vegetables and fish dishes. This is the sweet variety.

Mint *(Menta)* Used with vegetables, soups, salads, fish and fowl, mint should be used sparingly since it is very aromatic.

Nutmeg *(Noce moscata)* Used to flavor spinach, ravioli, cheese dishes, etc., nutmeg is always freshly grated in Italian food. The packaged ground nutmeg cannot compare in flavor and aroma to fresh nutmeg.

Oregano *(Origano)* The wild variety of marjoram is what we know as oregano. The unmistakable flavor of oregano is found in pizza, sauces and casseroles.

Pepper *(Pepe)* Peppercorns were used as far back as the Greek and Roman periods. Black and white peppercorns come from the same berry, the white picked when the berry is almost ripe, the black when it is unripe. Both are then dried. Black peppercorns have the stronger flavor, but white is preferable for some dishes. Whichever you use, use the whole peppercorn and grind as needed.

Rosemary *(Rosmarino)* Lamb and pork are often flavored with rosemary, as are some breads. However, this is an overwhelming herb and must be used very sparingly, the fresh as well as the dried.

Saffron *(Zafferano)* Saffron is very expensive and used sparingly. The most economical way to use saffron is to steep threads in tepid water for a few minutes, strain and add the liquid to the dish for color and taste.

Sage *(Salvia)* Once established in your garden, this herb will bloom year after year. A member of the mint family, sage is used to flavor veal, liver and sausage.

Salt *(Sale)* The salt generally used in Italy is sea salt, extracted from evaporated sea water. The fruity flavor improves the simplest dish. Sea salt can be obtained in many markets as well as in natural-food stores. Since so many people are sensitive to salt, I have listed quantities only in a few recipes where I think it is essential. Otherwise "salt to taste" is indicated and it means exactly that. When adding salt, keep in mind that some ingredients called for in a recipe can be salty. I like to use "pinches" rather than "spoonfuls" of salt, and then correct the seasoning as necessary. In many recipes, a small amount of lemon juice is the perfect substitute. When sauces and broths are to be reduced, salt to taste after you have reached the proper reduction.

Thyme *(Timo)* This easy-to-grow herb, with its mintlike aroma, is used in stuffings, soups, casseroles and beans.

Vanilla *(Vaniglia)* To flavor cakes, keep a vanilla bean (which is expensive) in ordinary sugar to give additional flavor to whatever sweet you are preparing.

Recipes

Recipes

Appetizers

Antipasto, like our appetizers or hors d'oeuvres, is eaten at the beginning of a meal. Served hot or cold, an antipasto can consist of sliced meats, with or without melon or figs, cheeses, fish, eggs, vegetables, or a combination.

A common sight just inside the entrance of many restaurants in Italy is the tempting antipasto table, laden with a colorful selection of foods.

BRESAOLA

Bresaola is cured beef; the lengthy curing process accounts for its high price. However, a small amount goes a long way. Have the beef sliced paper-thin where you buy it. It's best served with virgin olive oil. **Serves 12**

¼ pound *bresaola*, cut into 12 thin
    slices
Olive oil

Fresh lemon juice
Freshly ground pepper

1. Arrange beef on a platter in one layer.
2. Drizzle lightly with olive oil and lemon juice. Grind fresh black pepper over the beef.
3. Serve with crusty Italian bread.

To Prepare in Advance: Through #2.

Freezing Instructions: Do not freeze.

Variation: The dried beef may also be arranged over slices of melon or fresh figs, then drizzled with the olive oil and lemon juice and sprinkled with freshly ground pepper.

Suggested Wine:
Italian: TORGIANO BIANCO, a dry, white wine from Umbria
American: Jordan CHARDONNAY

CROSTINI WITH CHICKEN LIVERS
Crostini con Fegatini di Pollo

Crostini are part of the hot antipasti in Italy, *Crostini di Fegatini* a Tuscan specialty. The bread is usually fried or baked, but toasting simplifies the procedure and the result is just as delicious. **Serves 6**

6 tablespoons unsalted butter
½ medium onion, chopped fine
½ pound chicken livers
2 bay leaves
¾ cup dry Marsala
¼ cup Chicken Broth (see page 48)

1 tablespoon capers, drained
4 anchovy filets, drained
Salt
Freshly ground pepper
6 thick slices Italian bread

1. Melt 3 tablespoons butter in a sauté pan large enough to hold the livers in a single layer.
2. Over medium heat, sauté onion until golden, about 5 minutes. Add livers and bay leaves and cook 2 minutes longer, turning livers once.

3. Add Marsala and cook until almost all the wine evaporates, about 10 minutes.

4. Cook 5 minutes longer, adding stock as needed to keep livers slightly moist.

5. Remove bay leaves and transfer liver mixture to bowl or board. Add capers and anchovy filets and chop fine, using knife or mezzaluna.

6. In a clean pan, melt the remaining 3 tablespoons butter. Return the liver mixture to the pan and heat through, stirring occasionally. Season with salt and pepper to taste. (For added moisture and flavor, a bit more Marsala can be stirred into mixture.)

7. Toast bread. Spread with liver paste and serve warm or at room temperature.

To Prepare in Advance: Through #5 or #6.

Freezing Instructions: Through #5. Defrost in refrigerator and continue with recipe.

Note: For convenience in serving, the chicken liver can also be mounded in the center of a serving plate and surrounded by thin slices of toasted Italian bread.

Suggested Wine:
Italian: FRANCIACORTA ROSSO, a red wine from Lombardy. It can be served cool as well as at room temperature.
American: MERLOT

CROSTINI WITH MOZZARELLA AND ANCHOVY
Crostini con Mozzarella ed Acciughe

The buffalo was brought to Italy in the 7th century and buffalo milk mozzarella has been a delicacy ever since. The cheese is difficult to obtain in the United States, and when available it is very expensive. Fortunately, many Italian markets now carry fresh cow's milk mozzarella, plain and smoked, which can be used instead of the buffalo. The packaged kind found in supermarkets bears no resemblance to the fresh and should not be used for this dish. **Serves 6**

6 tablespoons unsalted butter
6 slices Italian or French bread, ½ inch thick
6 slices fresh mozzarella cheese (about ½ pound), cut to fit bread

2 tablespoons olive oil
1 2-ounce can anchovy filets

1. Preheat oven to 400°F.
2. Using 3 tablespoons butter, butter each slice of bread and cover with 1 slice of cheese.
3. Arrange bread slices on a baking sheet and bake 10 to 15 minutes, until cheese melts and is lightly golden.
4. While bread is baking, melt remaining 3 tablespoons butter with olive oil in a small skillet over low heat. Add the anchovies and mash until blended.
5. Remove bread from oven and drizzle an equal amount of anchovy mixture on each piece. Serve immediately.

To Prepare in Advance: Through #2.

Freezing Instructions: Do not freeze.

Variation: Substitute prosciutto, chopped fine, for anchovies. Heat prosciutto in 4 tablespoons unsalted butter and divide evenly over the melted cheese.

Suggested Wine:
Italian: PINOT NERO, a light red wine from the Veneto
American: Mount Eden PINOT NOIR

DEEP-FRIED SQUID Calamari Fritti

Squid can be stuffed, cooked in wine or simply deep-fried. They vary in size, shape, color and degree of toughness. Those found on the Genoese and Adriatic coasts are tender and flavorful.

To test whether oil is hot enough for deep-frying, place a small piece of green onion in the oil. When the onion turns brown, oil is ready.

Squid (¼ pound per person)	Sauce, optional
Flour for dusting	½ cup Tomato Sauce (see page 60)
Oil for deep-frying	1 teaspoon capers, drained
Salt to taste	

1. Cut squid into ¼-inch pieces and coat lightly with flour.
2. In a deep skillet, heat oil. Submerge squid in oil and cook until golden brown, about 2 minutes.
3. Drain fried squid on paper towels, season with salt and serve immediately as is or with tomato sauce spiked with capers.

To Prepare in Advance: Through #1, refrigerating until needed.

Freezing Instructions: Do not freeze.

Suggested Wine:
Italian: CORTESE DI GAVI, a light dry white wine
American: David Bruce CHARDONNAY

EGGPLANT APPETIZER Caponata

A Sicilian dish, *caponata* can be served as a vegetable or as part of an antipasto. **Serves 6 to 10**

2 pounds eggplant, trimmed and cut into 1-inch cubes
Salt
About 1 cup cooking oil
2 medium onions, thinly sliced
1 pound tomatoes, peeled, seeded and chopped
½ cup green olives, halved and pitted

3 tablespoons capers, drained
Freshly ground pepper
3 large celery stalks, strings removed, cut into 1-inch pieces and blanched
¼ cup red wine vinegar
2 tablespoons sugar
8 fresh basil leaves, cut into julienne

1. Salt eggplant cubes and let drain in colander for about 1 hour. Pat dry.
2. In a large skillet heat ¼ cup oil. Over medium heat, sauté onions until golden, about 10 minutes. Add the tomatoes, olives and capers, and season lightly with salt and pepper. Lower heat and cook about 30 minutes, stirring occasionally.
3. In a separate skillet, heat ¼ cup oil. Over medium heat, sauté eggplant cubes in batches until tender, adding more oil as necessary. Drain on paper towels. Add to tomato mixture with blanched celery, vinegar and sugar and simmer 3 to 4 minutes. Correct seasoning to taste. (Caponata should be seasoned well since it will be served cold.)
4. Transfer to a large bowl and refrigerate until needed.
5. To serve, arrange on a platter and garnish with julienned basil leaves.

To Prepare in Advance: Through #4.

Freezing Instructions: Do not freeze.

Variation: Green or red pepper, cut into julienne, cauliflower, cut into florets and blanched, and/or blanched asparagus, cut into 2-inch pieces, may be substituted for or added to vegetables. When basil is not in season, chopped parsley may be used.

CAPONATA TIMBALES Timballos di Caponata

Introductions from Piero of Valentino and Mauro of Rex, two well-known Los Angeles restaurateurs, opened many kitchens to me on my last trip to Italy. One of the more impressive meals was at Il Teatro, a small restaurant in Piacenza, just outside Milan. The chef prepared a menu which included this timbale, served as a first course. **Serves 8 to 10**

1 medium eggplant
1 medium zucchini
1 small red pepper, cored and seeded
6 to 8 medium mushrooms, stemmed
5 to 6 tablespoons olive oil
1 garlic clove, peeled, stuck on a toothpick

2 eggs
2 tablespoons heavy cream
Leaves from 1 large sprig fresh basil, minced
Salt
Freshly ground pepper
Red Pepper Sauce (see page 69)
Whole fresh basil leaves for garnish

1. Preheat oven to 325°F. Butter 8 or 10 ½-cup timbales or soufflé dishes.
2. Cut eggplant, zucchini, red pepper and mushrooms into very small dice.
3. In a 10-inch skillet, sauté each vegetable separately in olive oil until al dente, using about 1 tablespoon oil for each, a bit more for the eggplant.
4. As each vegetable is cooked, swirl the garlic through to flavor. Drain the vegetables in a colander to remove any excess oil and any liquid that may have accumulated.
5. In a large mixing bowl, whisk the eggs and cream together. Add the drained vegetables and minced basil and stir to combine. Season with salt and pepper to taste.
6. Divide the mixture among the prepared timbales. Arrange timbales in roasting pan and add enough boiling water to pan to come halfway up sides of timbales. Butter a piece of aluminum foil large enough to cover all the timbales and place over bain-marie, buttered side down. Bring water to a simmer and transfer to oven. Bake 15 to 20 minutes or until firm.
7. Serve immediately. To serve, gently run knife around timbales to loosen. Spoon a layer of red pepper sauce onto each plate. Unmold timbale in the center and garnish with whole basil leaves.

To Prepare in Advance: Through #4.

Freezing Instructions: Do not freeze.

EGGPLANT ROLLS Involtini di Melanzane

A specialty at Valentino, the Los Angeles restaurant, this is served as part of an antipasto. You'll need to prepare this a day ahead. **Serves 5 to 6 (10 to 12 slices)**

1 medium or 2 small eggplants	*Dressing*
Salt	1 tablespoon Dijon mustard
1 to 2 cups cooking oil	1 tablespoon red wine vinegar
3 to 4 ounces soft goat cheese	2 teaspoons Worcestershire sauce
5 or 6 radicchio leaves	1 small garlic clove, chopped fine, optional
3 to 4 tablespoons olive oil	Salt
	Freshly ground pepper

1. Cut eggplant lengthwise into ½-inch slices. Sprinkle with salt and let drain in colander 10 to 15 minutes. Pat dry.
2. Heat a 10-inch skillet. Pour in 1 cup cooking oil and cook eggplant over medium heat. Cook eggplant slices a few at a time until barely tender, about 1 minute, adding more oil as necessary; *do not overcook.* Drain eggplant on paper towels and cool.
3. Divide cheese and place a small piece of goat cheese in the center of each cooked slice of eggplant. Roll eggplant lengthwise, starting from long end, enclosing the cheese. Trim ends as necessary. Arrange on a large platter.
4. In a small bowl, whisk together mustard, vinegar, Worcestershire sauce, garlic, and salt and pepper to taste. Sprinkle over rolled eggplant slices and refrigerate for 24 hours.
5. To serve, place a leaf of radicchio on each plate. Arrange 2 eggplant rolls on each leaf and moisten with olive oil.

To Prepare in Advance: Through #4.

Freezing Instructions: Do not freeze.

Place a small piece of goat cheese in the center of each slice of eggplant. Roll lengthwise, starting from the long side, enclosing the cheese.

FONDUE Fonduta

Piedmont is cheese country, its fontina the base for this dish. *Fonduta* is similar to the French and Swiss fondue. However, the Italians combine their melted cheese with milk and eggs rather than with alcohol. Fondue is usually kept warm in small pots while chunks of bread are dipped in to coat; *fonduta* is served on individual plates and is sometimes poured over sliced polenta. While the truffles add a delicate touch, they are optional. You must begin this recipe a day ahead. **Serves 8**

1 pound Italian fontina cheese	Freshly ground pepper
1½ to 2 cups milk	8 slices toast, each slice cut into 4 triangles
2 tablespoons unsalted butter	
6 egg yolks, well beaten	Sliced white truffle, optional

1. Remove rind from cheese and cut cheese into 1-inch cubes. Place in a bowl, pour in enough milk to cover and steep overnight in the refrigerator.
2. Melt butter in top of a double boiler. Over low heat, add cheese and milk, stirring with a wooden spoon as necessary.
3. When cheese begins to melt, add egg yolks one at a time, continuing to stir until *fonduta* is smooth and creamy. Season with pepper.
4. To serve, arrange toast triangles in 8 ramekins. Divide *fonduta* and pour over toast. Sprinkle with sliced truffle, if desired.

To Prepare in Advance: Through #1 or #2.

Freezing Instructions: Do not freeze.

Suggested Wine:
Italian: DOLCETTO, a dry red wine from the Piedmont.
American: GAMAY BEAUJOLAIS

GARLIC AND ANCHOVY SAUCE Bagna Cauda

The *Bagna cauda* is a hot sauce in which to dip vegetables. The raw vegetables can be any you choose to serve, from sliced fennel to endive or carrot and celery sticks. They should be chilled so that there is a contrast between the vegetables and the hot oil, which improves the flavor. **Yield: About 2 cups**

½ cup cooking oil, preferably safflower or almond	6 anchovy filets, drained and coarsely chopped
½ cup (1 stick) unsalted butter	1 cup heavy cream
7 garlic cloves, mashed	Sliced raw vegetables

1. In a heavy saucepan, combine oil and butter and heat slowly until butter melts.
2. Sauté garlic until just golden.
3. Add anchovies and, over low heat, stir with wooden spoon until anchovies dissolve into a paste.
4. Stir in cream and heat through. Correct seasoning to taste.
5. Keep hot in chafing dish and serve with a variety of fresh vegetables cut into slices or bite-size pieces.

To Prepare in Advance: Through #4.

Freezing Instructions: Do not freeze.

Suggested Wine:
Italian: PINOT GRIGIO, a light white varietal from Friuli-Venezia Giulia and Trentino-Alto Adige
American: Dry FRENCH COLOMBARD

MASCARPONE AND GORGONZOLA PUFFS
Crema di Mascarpone e Gorgonzola

This is an original recipe from the kitchen of Valentino, the Los Angeles restaurant. It is meant to be part of an antipasto, something on which to nibble. **Filling for 60 small puffs**

¼ pound mascarpone cheese
¼ pound gorgonzola cheese
1 tablespoon heavy cream

1 recipe Cream Puff Paste (see page 187), baked

1. Preheat oven to 400°F.
2. In a small bowl, combine mascarpone, gorgonzola and cream and mix until smooth.
3. Cut each puff in half. Fill bottom half with ½ to ¾ teaspoon cheese mixture and cover with top half. (If desired, some of the cheese can be spooned on top of the puffs.)
4. Bake 3 to 4 minutes, until puffs are warm and cheese is heated through and melted.
5. Serve immediately.

To Prepare in Advance: Through #3. Refrigerate until needed.

Freezing Instructions: Through #2. Defrost overnight in refrigerator. Through #3. Bake in preheated 400°F oven 5 to 6 minutes.

Variation: 1. Drain 2 or 3 anchovies and mash. Add to cheese in step #2 above and continue with recipe.
2. Lightly brown 2 tablespoons pine nuts. Add to cheese mixture in step #2 above and continue with recipe.

MELTED MOZZARELLA, TOMATO AND BASIL
Sformato di Pomodoro, Mozzarella e Basilico

If fresh mozzarella, which melts quickly, is not available, try Bel Paese. In my travels through Italy, I have often lunched on this, accompanied by a glass of white wine. **Serves 4**

4 slices Italian or French bread, ¾ inch thick

½ pound fresh buffalo mozzarella cheese (or fresh cow's milk mozzarella), cut into 4 slices to fit bread

½ pound tomatoes, peeled, seeded and chopped

6 to 8 fresh basil leaves, coarsely chopped
Olive oil
Salt
Freshly ground pepper
Oregano

1. Lightly toast bread.
2. Cover each slice of bread with a slice of cheese. Divide tomatoes equally and arrange on top of cheese.
3. Divide chopped basil equally and arrange over tomato.
4. Drizzle a bit of oil over each and season with salt, pepper and oregano to taste.
5. Place under broiler for 1 or 2 minutes, until cheese melts slightly, or bake in preheated 450°F oven for about 5 minutes, until cheese melts.

To Prepare in Advance: Through #3. Refrigerate until needed. (If heated directly from refrigerator, cooking time will be slightly longer.)

Freezing Instructions: Do not freeze.

Suggested Wine:
Italian: Antinori ORVIETO, a dry white wine from Umbria
American: Mondavi FUMÉ BLANC

ONION TART Torta di Cipolle

From northern Italy, this is simple to prepare and is perfect as a first course or a light supper with a salad. Before freezing the finished tart, cut into portions, if desired. **Serves 8 to 10 as appetizer, 6 as main dish**

1 recipe One-Crust Pastry (see page 187) *or*	Salt
½ pound Puff Pastry (see page 188)	Freshly ground white pepper
	Freshly grated nutmeg
1½ pounds onions, thinly sliced	1 heaping teaspoon fresh rosemary leaves, chopped fine *or*
¼ cup (½ stick) unsalted butter	¼ teaspoon Italian Seasoning (see page 12)
4 eggs	
⅔ cup heavy cream	

1. On a lightly floured board, roll out pastry large enough to fit a 9- or 10-inch pie plate. Fit dough into plate and trim edges. Refrigerate until needed, at least 30 minutes.
2. Preheat oven to 350°F.
3. Prick bottom of pastry shell with tines of a fork and lay waxed or parchment paper on top. Fill with dried beans, rice or pie weights and bake 15 minutes. Remove beans and paper, return to oven and bake 5 minutes longer.
4. Meanwhile, place onions in mixing bowl and cover with boiling water. After 5 minutes, drain and chill with ice water. Drain and dry thoroughly. (This will sweeten the onions.)
5. In a 10-inch skillet, melt butter. Over medium heat, sauté onions until golden, about 10 minutes. Cool slightly. Arrange evenly in prepared pastry shell.
6. Whisk together eggs and cream. Season with salt, pepper and nutmeg to taste. Stir in rosemary leaves. Carefully pour over onions.
7. Bake 40 to 45 minutes, until filling is firm to the touch and golden brown.
8. Let rest 5 minutes and serve.

To Prepare in Advance: Through #3. Or through #5, reserving onions until ready to bake. Then arrange in pastry shell and continue with recipe.

Freezing Instructions: Through #1. Bake directly from freezer as in step #3 and continue with recipe. Through #7. Defrost overnight in refrigerator. Warm in preheated oven about 15 minutes. Or bake directly from freezer about 35 minutes or until heated through.

Variation: Brown 2 or 3 whole sausages. Cut into thin slices and arrange slices on top of sautéed onions in step #5. Continue with recipe.

Suggested Wine:
Italian: ARNEIS, a dry white wine from the Piedmont
American: Stag's Leap CHENIN BLANC

ROASTED PEPPERS Peperoni Arrostiti

Roasting brings out the best flavor in peppers. In Italy, peppers are roasted over a hot charcoal fire and served as an antipasto. Peppers can be red, green, yellow or a combination. **Serves 4 to 6**

4 medium green, red, *or* yellow
     bell peppers
½ cup olive oil
2 small garlic cloves, minced
1 shallot, minced
   Salt
   Freshly ground pepper
6 fresh basil leaves, minced

1. Roast peppers over an open flame or under a broiler until skin blisters and is charred on all sides and both ends.
2. Place in a covered pan or in a paper bag with top twisted closed. Let rest 15 to 20 minutes.
3. Peel away charred skin, rinsing peppers well. Dry thoroughly.
4. Cut peppers in half lengthwise and remove stems, seeds and ribs. Cut into 1-inch strips and place in a mixing bowl.
5. Stir in the olive oil, garlic, shallot, and salt and pepper to taste. Sprinkle with basil leaves.
6. Marinate, refrigerated, at least 2 hours, preferably overnight.
7. Use as needed.

To Prepare in Advance: Through #6. Peppers will keep, refrigerated, up to 1 week.

Freezing Instructions: Do not freeze.

Suggested Wine:
Italian: LACRIMA CHRISTI (TEAR OF CHRIST), a sweet, sparkling white wine from the Piedmont
American: Spring Mountain SAUVIGNON BLANC

SCALLOPS WRAPPED IN RADICCHIO
Capesante al Radicchio

The very large scallops from New Zealand come with the roe attached and are particularly delicious. Smaller scallops can be used with the baking time lessened, depending on the size. **Serves 8 as appetizer, 4 as main dish**

16	New Zealand scallops with roe, rinsed, *or* 1½ pounds sea scallops	16	radicchio leaves
	Salt	1½	tablespoons unsalted butter
	Freshly ground white pepper	2	shallots, chopped fine
	Juice of 2 medium lemons	2	cups dry white wine
		8	green lettuce leaves
			Lemon wedges

1. Place scallops in a bowl or flat dish. Season with salt and pepper to taste and pour lemon juice over. Let marinate 10 to 15 minutes, turning occasionally.
2. Preheat oven to 450°F.
3. Blanch radicchio leaves in boiling water just until wilted, about 1 minute. Immediately transfer to ice water to stop cooking process. Dry each leaf thoroughly and wrap one leaf around each scallop.
4. In an ovenproof skillet large enough to hold scallops, melt butter. Over medium heat, sauté shallots until translucent, 2 to 3 minutes. Add wine and reduce by half.
5. Arrange wrapped scallops in skillet and transfer to the oven. Bake 3 to 4 minutes, basting once or twice during cooking.
6. To serve, arrange green lettuce leaves on plates. Place 2 wrapped scallops on each leaf. Spoon sauce over and garnish with lemon wedges. Serve immediately.

To Prepare in Advance: Through #3.

Freezing Instructions: Do not freeze.

Suggested Wine:
Italian: GAVI LA BATISTINA, a dry white wine from the Piedmont
American: Durney DRY RIESLING

SLICED RAW BEEF WITH MUSTARD MAYONNAISE
Carpaccio

The first time I ate *carpaccio* was at the Hotel Cipriani in Venice. We arrived too late for hot food and the captain suggested this instead. It was perfect. **Serves 4**

½ pound filet mignon, trimmed of all fat

Lemon wedges
1 small can (3½ ounces) anchovy filets, optional

Mayonnaise
2 egg yolks
3 tablespoons Dijon mustard
Salt
Freshly ground white pepper
½ cup olive oil
½ cup safflower oil
1 teaspoon chopped fresh basil
Juice of ½ small lemon

1. Freeze beef just until firm, not hard, about 2 hours, to facilitate slicing.
2. *To prepare mayonnaise:* In a small bowl, combine egg yolks, mustard, a pinch of salt and pepper. Slowly whisk in olive and safflower oils until quite smooth. Fold in chopped basil and lemon juice, and refrigerate, covered, until needed.
3. Cut the filet into ¼-inch slices, using a meat slicer or a very sharp knife. Place each slice between 2 pieces of waxed paper or plastic wrap and gently pound with a heavy flat object, forming paper-thin round or rectangular slices.
4. To serve, mound mayonnaise in center of chilled plates. Arrange beef slices around mayonnaise and garnish with lemon wedges. Top each slice of beef with anchovy filets, if desired.

To Prepare in Advance: Through #3, stacking meat between waxed paper or plastic wrap and refrigerating until needed.

Freezing Instructions: Do not freeze.

Suggested Wine:
Italian: FRANCIACORTA ROSSO, a red wine from Lombardy that can be served cool or at room temperature
American: MERLOT

STUFFED ZUCCHINI FLOWERS Fiori di Zucchini Ripieni

This is an adaptation of a specialty of Marcello, a small restaurant in Rome. It is delicate, delicious and different. It is not difficult to prepare, but finding the zucchini flowers can be. They are attached to the very young zucchini and break off easily. Save the zucchini for another meal. **Serves 4 to 6**

Batter
½ cup beer
½ cup all-purpose flour
1 egg
   Pinch of salt
   Dash of Tabasco

Stuffing
2 ounces mozzarella cheese, cut into small pieces
1 ounce gorgonzola cheese, broken into small pieces
¼ cup (1 ounce) grated Parmesan cheese
1 tablespoon unsalted butter

12 zucchini flowers
1½ cups cooking oil
   Sauce, optional (see next page)

1. *To prepare batter:* In a small bowl, combine all ingredients and mix well. Let rest 30 minutes.
2. In a food processor fitted with a steel blade, combine mozzarella, gorgonzola and Parmesan cheeses and butter and process until mixture forms a paste (or chop fine with knife or mezzaluna).
3. Carefully open flowers (if you have difficulty, blow gently into the center; the petals will separate) and remove the stamen and pistils projecting from the center.

Carefully open the zucchini flower, separating the petals.

To enclose the filling, gently twist the ends of the petals to secure.

4. Spoon 1 teaspoon of the cheese mixture into the center of each flower. Enclose by gently twisting the ends of the petals to secure.
5. In a medium saucepan, heat oil. Dip each flower in the batter, shaking off excess. When oil is hot, carefully place (do not drop) flower in the oil with a slotted spoon. Cook until golden brown on all sides, about 2 minutes.
6. Remove with slotted spoon and drain on paper towels. Repeat procedure until all the flowers are cooked. Serve as is, sprinkled with salt, or with sauce.

Sauce for Stuffed Zucchini Flowers

2 tablespoons olive oil
2 medium tomatoes, peeled, seeded and chopped
2 baby zucchini (from recipe), chopped fine

4 fresh basil leaves *or* pinch of Italian Seasoning (see page 12)
Salt
Freshly ground pepper

1. In a small skillet, heat olive oil. Stir in tomatoes and, over medium heat, cook about 10 minutes. Add zucchini and cook 5 minutes longer, or until zucchini is tender.
2. Cut basil leaves into julienne. Stir into sauce and season to taste with salt and pepper.
3. Pour into bowl and serve surrounded with stuffed zucchini flowers.

To Prepare in Advance: Through #4.

Freezing Instructions: Do not freeze.

Suggested Wine:
Italian: CORVO COLOMBA PLATINO, a dry, platinum-colored wine from Sicily
American: Mondavi FUMÉ BLANC

Salads

Italians, like Americans, usually have their salads before the main dish, at times as part of the antipasto. And like Americans, they prefer a mixed salad rather than one of only greens. The Romans have their own theory about what it takes to make a proper salad—"a wise man to season it, a miser for the vinegar, a spendthrift to pour the oil, and a madman to mix it."

Salad is usually dressed at the table. The dressing is quite simple: the best quality olive oil, vinegar, salt, pepper and perhaps some fresh basil.

Salad greens need to be thoroughly washed to remove dirt. The best way to clean large heads is to hold them under a stream of running water, leaf by leaf; they must then be drained and the excess moisture completely shaken off. To keep salad crisp, it is best to store it in a moist cloth or covered container in the refrigerator.

Salad ingredients familiar in Italy are now becoming available in the United States. Arugula, radicchio and fennel can now be purchased in better markets.

BREAD SALAD Panzanella

Panzanella, considered a poor man's lunch, was brought to the fields by the peasants for a filling, flavorful meal. Since our bread is not as coarse or as dense as Italian bread, I have adapted this classic Roman recipe. I prefer using balsamic vinegar for my salads. The vinegar comes from Modena, a small city between Bologna and Parma. **Serves 6**

½ pound day-old Italian or French bread, cut into bite-size pieces	10 fresh basil leaves, cut into julienne
½ pound tomatoes, thinly sliced (see Note)	Salt
	Freshly ground pepper
½ medium onion, thinly sliced	¼ cup olive oil
½ medium cucumber, peeled, halved lengthwise, seeded and cut into ¼-inch slices	3 tablespoons red wine vinegar
	6 large lettuce leaves

1. Place bread in salad bowl.
2. Add tomatoes, onion, cucumber and basil.
3. Season with salt and pepper to taste. Pour over oil and vinegar, toss and let sit about 20 minutes.
4. Arrange the lettuce leaves on individual plates. Divide the salad and arrange on each leaf.

To Prepare in Advance: Through #2 or #3.

Freezing Instructions: Do not freeze.

Note: Plum tomatoes are perfect for this salad. However, if using larger tomatoes, cut in half and then slice thin.

MUSHROOM SALAD Insalata di Funghi

An adaptation from the Piedmont-Valle d'Aosta region, our cultivated mushrooms work very well in this salad. **Serves 4**

Dressing

2 teaspoons anchovy paste
Juice of 1 medium lemon
½ cup olive oil
Freshly ground pepper

½ pound small mushrooms
2 large fennel bulbs, cut into ¼-inch sticks *or*
2 large celery stalks, strings removed, cut into ⅛-inch slices
¼ cup (1 ounce) grated Parmesan cheese
4 butter lettuce leaves

1. To prepare dressing: whisk together anchovy paste and lemon juice in a small bowl. Gradually whisk in oil. Season to taste with pepper and reserve.
2. Clean or peel mushrooms, cut into quarters and place in salad bowl.
3. Add fennel or celery and sprinkle with cheese.
4. Toss with dressing. Place a lettuce leaf on each plate. Divide salad and heap on top of each leaf.

To Prepare in Advance: Through #3.

Freezing Instructions: Do not freeze.

Variation: In step #3, add thin slices of pepperoni or salami.

PEPPERS, TOMATOES AND ONION Peperonata

Peperonata can be served as a salad or heated and served with eggs. **Serves 6**

3 tablespoons olive oil
2 tablespoons unsalted butter
1 pound onions, thinly sliced
2 garlic cloves, minced
1 pound green peppers, cored, seeded and cut into julienne

1 pound red peppers, cored, seeded and cut into julienne
2 pounds tomatoes, peeled, seeded and chopped
2 teaspoons red wine vinegar
Salt
Freshly ground pepper

1. In a large skillet heat the oil and butter. Over medium heat, sauté onions until golden, about 10 minutes.
2. Add the garlic and julienned green and red peppers and lower heat. Cover the skillet and simmer 10 minutes longer, stirring occasionally.
3. Add the tomatoes and vinegar and season lightly with salt and pepper. Cover and cook 15 minutes. Remove cover, raise heat, and cook until most of the liquid has evaporated, 3 to 4 minutes, stirring occasionally to prevent sticking. Correct seasoning to taste.
4. Serve hot or cold. If serving cold, additional seasoning may be necessary.

To Prepare in Advance: Through #3. *Peperonata* can be stored in a container, olive oil poured over, and refrigerated up to 4 days.

Freezing Instructions: Do not freeze.

RADICCHIO AND ARUGULA WITH WARM GOAT CHEESE
Insalata di Radicchio, Ruchetta e Formaggio Caldo di Capra

Wolfgang Puck, chef and owner of Spago in Los Angeles, first introduced me to this lovely salad. Radicchio is a red, winter lettuce with a red and white veined leaf, and is traditionally served at Christmas in Treviso. This king of salad greens, as it is called, can be cooked as well as served raw. Radicchio and arugula have sharp flavors but complement each other. This salad must be started a day ahead. **Serves 4**

½ pound goat cheese, cut into 8
    1-ounce slices
6 tablespoons olive oil
    Pinch of thyme
6 fresh basil leaves, cut into juli-
    enne

2 heads radicchio (see Note)
½ pound arugula (see Note)
    Juice of ½ medium lemon
2 teaspoons red wine vinegar
    Salt
    Freshly ground pepper

1. Marinate the goat cheese overnight in olive oil, thyme and 3 basil leaves.
2. Separate the radicchio leaves and wash both radicchio and arugula. Dry thoroughly.
3. Combine the lemon juice, vinegar and 4 tablespoons olive oil from the marinade. Season lightly with salt and pepper. Toss with salad greens. Divide salad and arrange on 4 small plates.
4. In a small skillet, heat remaining 2 tablespoons oil from the marinade. Over low heat, sauté the slices of cheese 1 minute on each side.
5. Using a slotted spoon, remove cheese from skillet and arrange 2 slices on top of each salad. Garnish with remaining basil and serve immediately.

To Prepare in Advance: Through #2.

Freezing Instructions: Do not freeze.

Suggested Wine:
Italian: AMARONE, a dry, distinguished red wine from the Veneto
American: High-alcohol ZINFANDEL

    Note: Other greens may be substituted—curly endive, dandelion greens, and, if radicchio is not available, red cabbage for color.

SALAD VALENTINO Insalata di Valentino

The ingredients for this salad, which is from Valentino restaurant, can be chopped fine for a slightly different presentation. **Serves 6**

1 medium head romaine lettuce, washed and dried	½ green pepper, cored, seeded and cut into 1-inch strips
3 thin slices (2 ounces) provolone cheese	½ cup cooked or canned kidney beans
3 thin slices (2 ounces) mortadella sausage	Salt
	Freshly ground pepper
2 medium tomatoes	⅓ cup olive oil
1 small cucumber, peeled	2 tablespoons red wine vinegar
2 celery stalks, strings removed, cut into ½-inch strips	

1. Break romaine into small pieces and place in salad bowl.
2. For easier cutting, place provolone on top of mortadella and cut into ¼-inch julienne. Separate and add to salad bowl.
3. Core tomatoes and cut into quarters. Add to salad bowl.
4. Cut cucumber in half lengthwise and scoop out seeds using a teaspoon or melon baller. Cut cucumber into thin slices and add to salad bowl.
5. Add celery, green pepper and kidney beans. Season with salt and pepper to taste.
6. Prepare dressing by whisking together olive oil and vinegar. Pour over salad and toss. Serve immediately.

To Prepare in Advance: Through #5, without seasoning.

Freezing Instructions: Do not freeze.

GREEN BEAN SALAD Insalata di Fagiolini

The haricot bean was brought to Italy from the New World and was adopted very quickly. This is best when made with the small bean. If you can only find the larger bean, cut in half lengthwise. **Serves 6**

1½ pounds green beans, trimmed	1 medium-size red onion, thinly sliced
Salt	Freshly ground pepper
½ cup fresh lemon juice	2 to 3 tablespoons grated Parmesan cheese
2 tablespoons red wine vinegar	
1 garlic clove, minced	
½ cup olive oil	Julienned pimento for garnish

1. Cook green beans in boiling salted water until al dente (if using long green beans, 12 to 15 minutes; if using small beans, 8 to 10 minutes). Refresh in ice water and dry thoroughly. Refrigerate until needed.
2. *To prepare dressing:* In a small bowl combine lemon juice, vinegar and garlic. Slowly whisk in olive oil. Reserve.
3. To assemble salad, place green beans and onion in a salad bowl. Season with salt and pepper to taste and toss with salad dressing as needed. Let sit for 10 or 15 minutes.
4. To serve, divide salad and arrange on 6 plates. Sprinkle with grated cheese and garnish with julienned pimento.

To Prepare in Advance: Through #3.

Freezing Instructions: Do not freeze.

Variation: Mash 1 or 2 anchovy filets and add to dressing. Garnish with sieved hard-cooked egg.

Note: Dressing will keep refrigerated for one week.

STUFFED TOMATOES Pomodori Ripieni

Tomatoes can be filled with meat, pasta and breadcrumbs and then baked, or they can be filled with tuna and served cold. **Serves 12**

6 medium tomatoes, ripe but firm	*Mayonnaise*
1 7-ounce can of tuna in oil, well drained	3 egg yolks
	1 tablespoon Dijon mustard
	1 tablespoon red wine vinegar
1 teaspoon capers, drained	1 garlic clove, minced
Chopped parsley for garnish	½ cup olive oil
	1 cup salad oil
	Salt
	Freshly ground pepper
	Fresh lemon juice

1. Cut the tomatoes in half. Carefully remove the seeds and ribs to make a cup. Invert on paper towels and drain.
2. Flake the tuna and reserve in medium bowl.
3. *To prepare mayonnaise:* Combine egg yolks, mustard, vinegar and garlic in a mixing bowl or a food processor. Gradually whisk in the oils until the mayonnaise is very thick. Season with salt, pepper and lemon juice to taste.

4. Fold the mayonnaise into the tuna. Stir in the capers and correct seasoning to taste.

5. Divide the tuna and spoon into the tomato cups. Garnish each with chopped parsley. Arrange on a platter and chill. Serve cold.

To Prepare in Advance: Through #5.

Freezing Instructions: Do not freeze.

Stocks
and Soups

Soups are a conspicuous f ature of Italian cuisine, each region having its own specialties. The soups are categorized as *brodo* or broth, made from chicken, meat or vegetables; *minestrone* or thick vegetable soups, thickened further with pasta or rice; and *minestra in brodo*, pasta or rice cooked and served in a broth. Grated cheese is often stirred in to flavor and to thicken.

CHICKEN BROTH Brodo di Pollo

Chicken broth is used as the base for many soups and as the liquid for risotto. Broth will keep in freezer up to 4 months. **Yield: About 2 quarts**

1 whole chicken, 3½ to 4 pounds
2 pounds chicken wings and backs
2 medium carrots, peeled and cut into 2-inch pieces
1 medium onion, quartered
1 leek, white part only, cut into 2-inch pieces
2 celery stalks, cut into 2-inch pieces
   Tops from 2 celery stalks
4 sprigs parsley
1 bay leaf
10 whole peppercorns
½ teaspoon salt
10 cups cold water

1. In a 6-quart saucepan, combine all ingredients. Bring to a rolling boil and skim off the impurities and fat that rise to the top. Reduce heat and let simmer about 1 hour, or until chicken is very tender. Continue to skim off fat. Correct seasoning to taste.
2. Remove chicken and allow it to cool. Skin chicken and use as desired. Strain broth into a clean bowl and cool.
3. Refrigerate broth up to 3 days and use as needed, discarding hardened layer of fat before reheating.

To Prepare in Advance: Through #3.

Freezing Instructions: Through #2. Broth will keep in freezer up to 4 months. Warm over low heat.

BEEF BROTH Brodo di Manzo

A basic broth that is used in many soups and sauces, this freezes well. Freeze in 1-pint containers for easy use. **Yield: About 2 quarts**

4 pounds lean beef, cut into 4 or 5 pieces
1 or 2 beef bones, optional
2 medium carrots, peeled and cut into 2-inch pieces
1 medium onion, quartered
2 celery stalks, cut into 2-inch pieces
8 to 10 whole peppercorns
4 quarts cold water
   Salt

1. In a 10- or 12-quart stockpot, combine all ingredients except salt. Bring to a rolling boil and with a ladle skim off the impurities and fat that rise to the top.
2. Lower heat and let soup simmer slowly for 4 to 5 hours. Continue to skim impurities and fat as they accumulate. Season broth with salt to taste.

3. Strain into a bowl and set in larger bowl or pot filled with ice cubes to cool. Refrigerate. Remove layer of hardened fat that forms.
4. Use as needed. Broth will keep, refrigerated, up to 3 days.

To Prepare in Advance: Through #3.

Freezing Instructions: Through #3. Broth will keep in freezer up to 4 months. Warm over low heat.

BROWN STOCK Salsa Bruna

In Italy, France and the United States, this is a much-used stock for sauces. Browning the bones and then deglazing the pan produces the good flavor of the stock. When cooking with veal or beef, reserve the bones and freeze. When you have accumulated enough bones, you can prepare this stock, thus reducing the cost considerably. **Yield: 2 quarts**

10 pounds veal or veal and beef bones, cut into 2-inch pieces	2 fresh tomatoes, quartered
2 large onions, quartered	1 teaspoon tomato paste
1 large carrot, coarsely cut	1 bouquet garni (1 bay leaf, 8
1 large celery stalk, coarsely cut	whole peppercorns, 3 sprigs
1 leek, white part only, coarsely cut	parsley, pinch of thyme wrapped in cheesecloth)
	About 4 quarts water

1. Preheat oven to 450°F.
2. Arrange the bones in a large uncovered roasting pan and brown on all sides in oven, turning as necessary, about 1 hour.
3. Transfer bones to a 12-quart stockpot. Add the vegetables, tomato paste and bouquet garni.
4. Discard fat from roasting pan. On stove top, deglaze pan with 1 cup of water, scraping up any particles that stick to the bottom of the pan. Pour into stockpot with enough additional water to cover ingredients by 2 inches.
5. Bring to a boil and then reduce heat, skimming foam as it accumulates.
6. Simmer 4 to 6 hours, skimming as necessary, and adding water as needed to keep bones and vegetables covered at all times.
7. Strain into a clean pot and skim if necessary. Reduce, over medium heat, until 2 quarts remain.
8. Cool and refrigerate in covered containers up to 3 days, discarding hardened layer of fat before reheating.

To Prepare in Advance: Through #8.

Freezing Instructions: Through #8. Stock can be frozen up to 4 months. Warm over low heat.

FISH BROTH Brodo di Pesce

For flavor, fish broth is preferable to water for fish soups and for poaching fish. **Yield: 1 to 1½ quarts**

2	tablespoons cooking oil	2	pounds fish bones and heads
1	large onion, sliced		from white flat fish
1	medium carrot, peeled and sliced	4	or 5 whole white peppercorns
			Pinch of thyme
1	celery stalk, sliced	2	garlic cloves, mashed
¼	pound mushroom stems, optional	1	cup dry white wine
		6	cups cold water

1. In a 6-quart saucepan, heat oil. Over medium heat, sauté onion, carrot, celery, mushrooms and fish bones and heads just until onion colors slightly, 10 to 12 minutes.
2. Add remaining ingredients and bring to a boil. Skim and reduce heat to a simmer for 20 to 25 minutes, continuing to skim as necessary.
3. Strain and refrigerate up to 2 days.

To Prepare in Advance: Through #3.

Freezing Instructions: Through #3. Stock can be frozen up to 4 months. Warm over low heat.

ASPARAGUS RICE SOUP Zuppa d'Asparagi

Substantial soups are typical of mountainous regions of Italy. Using 1 cup of rice will result in a very thick soup. If you prefer a less dense soup, decrease the amount of rice to ½ cup. **Serves 6 to 8**

2	quarts Beef Broth (see page 48) or 4 beef bouillon cubes dissolved in 2 quarts boiling water	3	tablespoons unsalted butter
		1	medium onion, thinly sliced
		¼	cup (1 ounce) grated Parmesan cheese
½	to 1 cup rice		Salt
1½	pounds asparagus		Freshly ground pepper

1. In a 6-quart saucepan, bring broth to a boil.
2. Pour rice into the boiling broth and cook over medium heat for 10 minutes.
3. Cut away rough bottoms of asparagus and peel stalks with vegetable peeler. Cut into 1-inch pieces.
4. Melt butter in a 10-inch skillet. Over medium heat, sauté onion until

golden, about 5 minutes. Add asparagus and sauté 10 minutes longer, stirring occasionally.

5. Add onion and asparagus to broth and cook 10 to 12 minutes longer, or until rice and asparagus are tender. Stir in grated cheese and season with salt and pepper to taste.

6. Serve hot with additional grated cheese passed in a separate bowl.

To Prepare in Advance: Through #5, cooking 5 minutes.

Freezing Instructions: Through #5. Defrost overnight in refrigerator. Warm over low heat.

Suggested Wine:
Italian: PINOT BIANCO, a white wine from Lombardy
American: FRENCH COLOMBARD

BEAN AND BARLEY SOUP Zuppa di Fagioli ed Orzo

A thick, filling soup that is perfect for a chilly day. The soup thickens as it stands; if too thick, thin with chicken broth as necessary. **Serves 8 to 10**

1½	cups dried white beans		Freshly ground pepper
¾	cup barley	¾	pound new potatoes, peeled and cut into 2-inch pieces
¼	pound pancetta, cut into small pieces (see Note)	2	sweet Italian sausages, skinned and sliced
2	garlic cloves, diced		Grated Parmesan cheese, optional
	Leaves of 1 large parsley sprig		
8	cups cold water		
	Salt		

1. Soak beans and barley separately in cold water to cover for 2 to 3 hours. Drain.

2. In a heavy 6- to 8-quart saucepan, combine drained beans, pancetta, garlic, parsley, water and salt and pepper to taste. Bring to a boil, lower heat and simmer 1 hour.

3. Add the barley, potatoes, and sausage and continue to cook over low heat about 1 hour longer or until beans are tender. Correct seasoning to taste.

4. Serve hot with grated Parmesan cheese, if desired.

To Prepare in Advance: Through #3.

Freezing Instructions: Through #3. Defrost overnight in refrigerator. Warm over low heat.

BEAN AND BARLEY SOUP, continued

Suggested Wine:
Italian: MERLOT, a smooth red wine
American: Clos du Val MERLOT

Note: Additional sausage or blanched thick-sliced bacon can be substituted for the pancetta.

EGG AND CHEESE DUMPLING SOUP
Passatini in Brodo

A traditional peasant dish from Emilia-Romagna, this soup consists of tiny strands of egg, cheese and crumb mixture cooked in broth. **Serves 6**

¾ cup (3 ounces) grated Parmesan
    cheese
⅔ cup fresh breadcrumbs
4 eggs
3 tablespoons unsalted butter,
    softened

Pinch of freshly grated nutmeg
Salt
Freshly ground pepper
7 cups Chicken or Beef Broth (see
    page 48)
Grated Parmesan cheese

1. In a bowl, combine Parmesan cheese, crumbs, eggs, butter and nutmeg. Season to taste with salt and pepper.
2. In a 4-quart saucepan, over medium heat, bring the broth to a boil. Reduce heat. Using a potato ricer, press cheese mixture into simmering soup. Cook until ribbons of dough rise to the surface, about 2 to 3 minutes.
3. Serve immediately. Pass additional cheese in a separate bowl.

To Prepare in Advance: Through #1.

Freezing Instructions: Through #2. Warm over low heat.

Suggested Wine:
Italian: TOCAI, a white wine from Friuli-Venezia Giulia
American: FRENCH COLOMBARD

FISH SOUP Zuppa di Pesce

The Italians make a variety of fish soups depending upon the region and the availability of the fish. Around Genoa it could be a *burrida*, along the Adriatic a *brodetto*, or simply *zuppa di pesce*, with local fish. It is not uncommon to serve the soup with *bruschetta*, toasted or baked bread slices rubbed with garlic and drizzled with olive oil. **Serves 8 to 10**

3	pounds fish bones, cut into small pieces	1	tablespoon tomato paste
3	or 4 fish heads, gills removed, cut into small pieces	2	bay leaves
		8	whole peppercorns
6	tablespoons olive oil	12	langostinos *or* large prawns
1	medium onion, sliced		Salt
1	medium carrot, peeled and sliced		Freshly ground pepper
		1	shallot, diced
1	medium celery stalk, sliced	2	dozen mussels, cleaned and bearded
3	cups dry white wine		
2½	quarts Fish Broth (see page 50) or water	2	to 3 ounces long pasta, cut into 2-inch pieces *or* rigatoni
12	ripe plum tomatoes, cut in half and seeded	1	pound red snapper, cut into 2-inch pieces
2	or 3 garlic cloves, mashed	1	pound turbot, cut into 2-inch pieces
1	bunch Italian parsley		Toasted Italian or French bread slices

1. Clean fish bones and heads under cold running water until water runs clear.

2. Heat a heavy 6-quart saucepan. Add 4 tablespoons oil, fish bones and heads. Cover and steam, over medium heat, 8 to 10 minutes, until the fish on the bones becomes opaque.

3. Add the sliced onion, carrot and celery and cook 10 minutes, stirring occasionally.

4. Pour in 1 cup white wine and 1 cup fish broth or water. Add tomatoes, garlic, parsley stems, tomato paste, bay leaves and peppercorns and bring to a boil. Skim as necessary.

5. Meanwhile, heat a 12-inch skillet. Pour in remaining 2 tablespoons olive oil and sauté the langostinos or prawns over high heat 2 to 3 minutes, turning as necessary. Remove from pan and cool.

6. Pour out oil and deglaze pan with 1 cup wine. Add to saucepan.

7. Separate heads from tails of langostinos (or peel prawns and reserve meat). Remove meat from tails and reserve. Add shells and heads to saucepan.

8. Over medium-high heat, cook soup at a rolling boil for 1 hour. Strain into a clean pot and season with salt and pepper to taste. Lower heat and continue to simmer soup.

9. In a medium saucepan, heat shallots and remaining 1 cup wine. Add the mussels, cover pan and steam over medium heat until mussels open, about 5 minutes, discarding any unopened mussels. Remove mussels and add strained broth to soup. Shell mussels and reserve.

10. Add pasta and cook 3 to 4 minutes. Add snapper and cook 1 minute; add

FISH SOUP, continued

turbot, reserved langostinos and mussels and cook 2 to 3 minutes longer, or until fish is tender. Correct seasoning to taste.
11. Serve immediately, garnishing soup with a few parsley leaves. Serve with thick slices of toasted bread.

To Prepare in Advance: Through #9.

Freezing Instructions: Through #8. Reheat over low heat and continue with recipe.

Suggested Wine:
Italian: VERDICCHIO, a dry white wine from the Marche
American: Biander SAUVIGNON BLANC

LEEK SOUP Zuppa di Porro

This hearty soup can be prepared in less than an hour. The cheese gives the soup additional texture and flavor. **Serves 6 to 8**

¼ cup (½ stick) unsalted butter
1 medium onion, diced
3 tablespoons chopped parsley
¾ pound leeks, white part only, cut into ½-inch slices
2 medium potatoes, peeled and cut into ½-inch slices

6 cups Beef Broth (see page 48) *or* 3 beef bouillon cubes dissolved in 6 cups boiling water
½ cup Arborio rice
Salt
Freshly ground pepper
¼ cup (1 ounce) grated Parmesan cheese

1. In a 4-quart saucepan, melt butter over medium heat. Sauté onion and parsley until onion is golden, about 10 minutes.
2. Stir in leeks and potatoes, pour in broth and bring to a boil. Let simmer 25 minutes.
3. Add rice, season with salt and pepper to taste, and cook about 15 minutes, or until rice is tender.
4. Stir in cheese and correct seasoning to taste.
5. Serve hot. Pass additional cheese in a separate bowl.

To Prepare in Advance: Through #3 or #4.

Freezing Instructions: Through #3 or #4. Warm over low heat.

Suggested Wine:
Italian: CABERNET FRANC, a fruity red wine
American: Chalone PINOT NOIR

MUSHROOM SOUP Zuppa di Funghi

In early fall, varieties of fresh mushrooms are brought in from the country to the cities and sold from huge baskets. There are some markets where nothing but mushrooms are sold. Wild mushrooms, becoming more available in this country, can be combined with cultivated white mushrooms for more interesting flavor. **Serves 6 to 8**

1 pound fresh mushrooms, sliced or coarsely chopped	Freshly ground pepper
Juice of 1 medium lemon	½ cup dry white wine
3 tablespoons unsalted butter	6 cups Chicken Broth (see page 48)
1 small onion, chopped fine	½ cup heavy cream
2 tablespoons all-purpose flour	2 egg yolks
½ teaspoon salt	Chopped parsley

1. In a bowl, sprinkle mushrooms with lemon juice. Reserve.
2. In a 4-quart saucepan, over medium heat, melt butter. Sauté onion until translucent, about 5 minutes.
3. Stir in flour and cook 1 or 2 minutes. Add mushrooms, stir to coat well and season with salt and pepper to taste. Pour in wine and cook until it is absorbed.
4. Pour in chicken broth, bring to a boil, and then simmer about 20 minutes.
5. In a medium bowl, combine cream and egg yolks, blending well. Gradually whisk in 2 cups of hot soup. Return mixture to saucepan and heat through; do not boil.
6. Serve hot, sprinkled with chopped parsley.

To Prepare in Advance: Through #4.

Freezing Instructions: Through #4. Defrost and warm in saucepan over low heat, then continue with recipe.

Suggested Wine:
Italian: SAUVIGNON, a white wine from Friuli-Venezia Giulia
American: SAUVIGNON BLANC

ONION SOUP Zuppa di Cipolle

The French are not the only ones boasting onion soup. There is a recipe for onion soup dating back to the early 1600's at which time it was a popular Florentine dish. **Serves 6**

¼ cup cooking oil	Freshly grated nutmeg
1 pound onions, thinly sliced	6 slices day-old Italian bread or
6 cups hot Beef Broth (see page 48)	Country Bread (see page 176)
Salt	1 pound fontina cheese, thinly
Freshly ground pepper	sliced

1. In a 4-quart, ovenproof sauté pan or casserole, heat oil. Over low heat, sauté onions until golden, 25 to 30 minutes.
2. Pour in hot beef broth, raise heat, and cook 20 minutes, stirring occasionally. Season to taste with salt, pepper and nutmeg.
3. Preheat oven to 450°F.
4. Arrange bread slices in soup. (If you wish, you may divide soup among 6 ovenproof bowls and place a bread slice in each.) Cover with slices of cheese and transfer to oven. Bake 10 to 15 minutes, or until cheese melts and turns golden.
5. Serve immediately.

To Prepare in Advance: Through #2.

Freezing Instructions: Through #2. Warm over low heat and continue with recipe.

SPINACH SOUP Zuppa di Spinaci

From Emilia-Romagna. **Serves 6**

1½ pounds fresh spinach, stemmed and washed	⅓ cup (1½ ounces) grated Parmesan cheese
5 tablespoons unsalted butter	2 quarts Chicken Broth (see page 48)
Salt	
Freshly ground pepper	Grated Parmesan cheese, optional
Freshly grated nutmeg	
4 eggs	

1. In a covered saucepan, over medium heat, cook spinach in water that clings to leaves until wilted, about 5 minutes. Drain, squeeze dry and chop coarsely. Reserve.
2. In the same saucepan, melt butter. Stir in spinach and coat with butter. Season with salt, pepper and nutmeg to taste.

3. In a medium bowl, whisk together eggs and cheese. Stir in the spinach.
4. In a 4-quart saucepan, bring the chicken broth to a rolling boil. Whisk 2 cups broth into the spinach mixture and then return to the saucepan, whisking to combine thoroughly.
5. Heat but do not boil.
6. Serve immediately. Pass additional grated cheese, if desired.

To Prepare in Advance: Through #2.

Freezing Instructions: Do not freeze.

SPRING SOUP Zuppa di Primavera

This is a minestrone from the Piedmont. **Serves 6 to 8**

¼ cup (½ stick) unsalted butter
1 medium onion, chopped fine
1 garlic clove, chopped fine
3 slices day-old Italian or French bread
½ pound shelled green peas *or* 1 10-ounce package frozen peas
½ pound zucchini, trimmed and sliced

½ pound fontina cheese, sliced
½ cup Arborio rice
2 medium tomatoes, peeled, seeded and chopped
2 quarts warmed Beef Broth (see page 48)
Salt
Freshly ground pepper
Grated Parmesan cheese

1. In a heavy 4-quart saucepan melt butter. Over medium heat, sauté onion and garlic until golden, about 5 minutes.
2. Stir in bread, green peas, zucchini, fontina cheese, rice and tomatoes. Pour in broth and season lightly with salt and pepper. Cover and cook 15 to 20 minutes, or until rice is tender, stirring occasionally. Correct seasoning to taste.
3. To serve, ladle soup into heated bowls. Pass Parmesan cheese in a separate bowl.

To Prepare in Advance: Through #2, warming over low heat. Thin with additional broth or water if necessary.

Freezing Instructions: Same as above.

VEGETABLE SOUP WITH PESTO Minestrone al Pesto

The addition of the pesto and the pasta identifies this as a Genoese dish. The Milanese version would substitute rice for pasta and, of course, there would be no pesto. But no matter the region, an Italian housewife will usually include any vegetable she may have in her larder in an end-of-the-week soup. One or two veal bones will give the soup additional flavor. **Serves 10 to 12**

1	cup dried white beans	3	large tomatoes, peeled and seeded
1	bunch fresh spinach, stemmed and washed	2½	quarts Chicken or Beef Broth (see page 48)
1	leek, white part only	1	tablespoon salt
1	medium onion	6	ounces pasta
3	medium potatoes, peeled	4	to 6 tablespoons Pesto (see page 64)
2	celery stalks, strings removed		Freshly ground pepper
½	head (½ pound) cabbage		Grated Parmesan cheese
2	medium zucchini, trimmed		

1. Soak beans in water to cover for 2 to 3 hours. Drain and transfer to an 8-quart saucepan.
2. Coarsely cut all the vegetables into approximately 1- to 1½-inch pieces.
3. Add broth to beans in saucepan. Add the vegetables and salt and bring to a boil. Simmer for 1½ hours over low heat, stirring occasionally.
4. Add the pasta during the last 10 minutes of cooking. (If using long pasta strands, you may want to break into smaller pieces.)
5. Dissolve the pesto in 1 or 2 cups of broth and stir through the soup. Correct seasoning to taste with salt and pepper. Or pass the pesto in a separate bowl, each person stirring in the desired amount.
6. Serve immediately. Pass grated Parmesan cheese in a separate bowl.

To Prepare in Advance: Through #4.

Freezing Instructions: Through #3 or #4. Warm over low heat and continue with recipe.

Sauces

The French are commonly thought of as the great sauce makers of the world, but it was the Italians who first developed sauces, and these were brought to France by Catherine de Medici.

In Italy, the sauce is part of the dish, a necessary ingredient. It is not used to mask the food, but rather to enhance it. And though used sparingly, there is a great variety of sauces, with tomato only one of the many sauces for pasta, meat, poultry, fish and even some vegetables.

SIMPLE TOMATO SAUCE
Salsa di Pomodoro

This is an excellent all-purpose tomato sauce which is quite simple to prepare. **Yield: About 2 cups**

¼ cup olive oil
½ medium onion, chopped fine
2 garlic cloves
1 tablespoon chopped parsley
1 pound tomatoes, peeled, seeded and chopped *or* 1 1-pound can tomatoes, with juice, chopped

1 bay leaf
½ teaspoon salt
Freshly ground pepper
5 or 6 fresh basil leaves

1. In a heavy skillet or saucepan, heat oil. Over medium heat, sauté onion, garlic and parsley until garlic colors slightly, 10 to 12 minutes. Discard garlic.
2. Add tomatoes with juice, bay leaf, salt and pepper and cook until sauce thickens, 20 to 30 minutes, stirring occasionally. Discard bay leaf and correct seasoning to taste.
3. When ready to serve, cut basil leaves into julienne and stir into sauce.

To Prepare in Advance: Through #2.

Freezing Instructions: Through #2. Warm over low heat.

SPICY TOMATO SAUCE
Salsa di Pomodoro Piccante

This spicy Neapolitan sauce can be served over spaghetti or with a sautéed veal chop. It is more flavorful than the marinara. **Yield: About 2 cups**

¼ cup olive oil
1 small red chili pepper (fresh or dried), chopped fine
2 garlic cloves, chopped fine
½ cup dry white wine

1½ pounds tomatoes, peeled, seeded and chopped
2 tablespoons chopped parsley
Pinch of oregano
Salt

1. In a 2½-quart saucepan, heat oil. Over medium heat, sauté chili pepper and garlic until garlic begins to color slightly, about 10 minutes.
2. Pour in wine and cook until most of the liquid evaporates.
3. Add tomatoes and parsley and cook over low heat about 20 minutes, until sauce thickens slightly.
4. Add oregano and season with salt to taste.

To Prepare in Advance: Through #4.

Freezing Instructions: Through #4. Warm over low heat.

Variation: After step #4, transfer sauce to a food processor fitted with steel blade and process until puréed. Sauce will be thicker and smoother.

UNCOOKED TOMATO SAUCE
Salsa di Pomodoro Crudo

From northern Italy, this sauce can be served with meat, fish or shellfish. **Yield: About 2 cups**

2 medium tomatoes (1 pound), peeled, seeded and diced
½ small onion, diced
1 garlic clove
3 tablespoons chopped parsley
2 anchovy filets, chopped fine, optional

6 pitted olives, black or green, chopped
½ cup olive oil
Salt
Freshly ground pepper

1. In a medium bowl, combine tomatoes, onion, garlic, parsley, anchovy filets, and olives and blend well.
2. Stir in olive oil and season to taste with salt and pepper. Refrigerate overnight.
3. Correct seasoning to taste and remove garlic clove.
4. Use as needed. Serve at room temperature.

To Prepare in Advance: Through #2.

Freezing Instructions: Do not freeze.

MARINARA SAUCE Salsa Marinara

For this familiar Neapolitan sauce, dried basil and rosemary are never as flavorful as fresh. If you cannot get the fresh herbs, use a pinch of Italian Seasoning, which is a combination of 4 or 5 herbs (see page 12). This too is a good all-purpose sauce. **Yield: About 5 cups**

½ cup olive oil
2 large onions, coarsely chopped
3 large garlic cloves, minced

2 small carrots, peeled and coarsely chopped
2 cans (1 pound 12 ounces each) Italian plum tomatoes, with juice

Salt
Freshly ground pepper
8   fresh basil leaves, cut into juli-
    enne

1   teaspoon fresh rosemary leaves,
    chopped fine
¼   cup (½ stick) unsalted butter

1. In a 4-quart saucepan, heat olive oil. Add onions, garlic and carrots and cook over medium heat, stirring occasionally, until onions are golden, 15 to 20 minutes.
2. Coarsely chop the tomatoes and add to vegetables. Season lightly with salt and pepper to taste. Bring to a boil, lower heat and simmer 15 minutes.
3. Strain sauce, returning liquid to saucepan.
4. Place all the vegetables in a food processor fitted with the steel blade or in a blender, and purée. Transfer to saucepan, add remaining ingredients and stir to combine thoroughly. Cook over low heat 20 minutes. Correct seasoning to taste. (If sauce is too thick, thin with either chicken or beef broth.)

To Prepare in Advance: Through #4.

Freezing Instructions: Through #4. Warm over low heat.

RAGÙ BOLOGNESE
Sugo di Carne alla Bolognese

Ragù comes from the French *ragoût,* which in turn is from *ragoûter—* meaning to arouse or enhance taste. In Bologna, cream is added to the sauce, enriching it further. **Yield: About 2½ cups**

2   tablespoons unsalted butter
2   tablespoons olive oil
1   small onion, chopped fine
1   small carrot, peeled and
    chopped fine
1   celery stalk, strings removed,
    chopped fine
½   pound ground pork

½   pound ground beef
2   teaspoons tomato paste
1   cup Brown Stock (see page 49)
½   cup dry red wine
    Salt
    Freshly ground pepper
1   cup heavy cream
6   fresh basil leaves, chopped

1. In a heavy sauté pan, heat butter and olive oil.
2. Stir in the vegetables and cook over medium heat until vegetables are lightly colored but not brown, 6 to 8 minutes.
3. Add the pork and the beef and stir until meat loses its pink color, about 5 minutes.

4. Dissolve tomato paste in ½ cup brown stock and pour into pan with wine. Season lightly with salt and pepper.

5. Cover and simmer gently over low heat 1 hour, adding remaining stock as sauce thickens. Stir occasionally. Most of the liquid will be absorbed at end of the hour.

6. Add cream and cook about 5 minutes. Add basil and stir through. Correct seasoning to taste and serve. This is a thick sauce.

To Prepare in Advance: Through #5 or #6.

Freezing Instructions: Through #5 or #6. Defrost in refrigerator overnight. Warm over low heat.

MEAT SAUCE Sugo di Carne

Another version of *ragù*, this is a more classic recipe, with no cream or vegetables, just tomatoes. It is served over pasta, especially ravioli, as well as with chicken and lamb. **Yield: About 2 cups**

3	tablespoons olive oil		Salt
1	onion, chopped fine		Freshly ground pepper
2	ounces bacon, chopped	1	cup warm Chicken Broth (see
½	pound ground veal		page 48) or Brown Stock (see
2½	cups fresh or canned tomatoes,		page 49)
	peeled, seeded and chopped	6	fresh basil leaves, chopped
1	tablespoon chopped parsley		

1. In a heavy 10- or 12-inch skillet, heat olive oil. Add onion and bacon and cook, over medium heat, until onion is translucent, about 5 minutes.

2. Add ground veal and cook 10 minutes longer, stirring to color the meat evenly.

3. Add tomatoes, parsley and salt and pepper to taste. Simmer for about 1 hour, thinning with warm broth or stock if sauce becomes too thick. Add chopped basil and stir through.

To Prepare in Advance: Through #3.

Freezing Instructions: Through #3. Defrost overnight in refrigerator. Warm over low heat.

PESTO Pesto alla Genovese

Pesto is a sharp basil sauce that goes into Genoese minestrone and is served over pasta and spinach gnocchi. The Italians feel strongly that only a mortar and pestle will do for preparing a good pesto. However, the food processor simplifies the job and makes a fine sauce (see Note). If the sauce is too strong for your taste, a little heavy cream can be added to smooth the flavor. I like to serve pesto stirred into cooked julienned zucchini. **Yield: About 2 cups**

3 ounces Parmesan cheese, at room temperature	½ cup chopped walnuts
1 ounce pecorino or Romano cheese, at room temperature	3 or 4 garlic cloves
	½ teaspoon salt
	Freshly ground pepper
3 cups tightly packed fresh basil leaves	1 cup olive oil

1. Cut cheese into 1-inch pieces and, using steel blade of food processor, grate fine. Set aside.
2. Combine basil, walnuts, garlic, salt and pepper in processor and process to a fine paste.
3. With machine running, pour oil through feed tube in a steady stream. Add reserved cheeses and process until well combined.

To Prepare in Advance: Through #3. Pour a small amount of oil over the sauce and store in a covered jar in the refrigerator for up to 1 week. Bring to room temperature before serving; do not heat or pesto will separate.

Freezing Instructions: Through #3. Defrost in refrigerator. (I recommend freezing in ice cube trays. When cubes harden, unmold and place in plastic bags in freezer so you can use as much or little as you need.) Bring to room temperature; do not heat.

Note: To prepare with mortar and pestle, combine chopped basil leaves, walnuts and garlic in a mortar. Mash with the pestle to a coarse paste. Transfer to a bowl and stir in some of the cheese, adding oil drop by drop as the mixture thickens. Continue this procedure until all the cheese and oil is added. Correct seasoning to taste.

GREEN SAUCE Salsa Verde

Another version of pesto, Green Sauce is a combination of parsley and basil with toasted pine nuts. **Yield: About 2 cups**

½ cup packed Italian parsley leaves	2 tablespoons toasted pine nuts (see Note)
2 cups packed fresh basil leaves	4 or 5 garlic cloves, peeled

½ teaspoon salt	1½ cups olive oil
½ teaspoon freshly ground pepper	½ cup (2 ounces) grated Parmesan cheese

1. Chop parsley leaves very fine or purée in a food processor fitted with the steel blade. Squeeze the juice through a double thickness of cheesecloth or an old linen napkin. Reserve the juice. Discard parsley leaves.
2. Combine the basil leaves, pine nuts, garlic, salt and pepper in a food processor fitted with the steel blade. Process to a fine paste. With machine running, pour oil through feed tube in a steady stream.
3. Transfer to a mixing bowl and stir in the cheese and reserved parsley juice.

To Prepare in Advance: Through #3. Pour a small amount of oil over the sauce and store in a covered jar in the refrigerator for up to 1 week. Bring to room temperature before serving.

Freezing Instructions: Through #3. Defrost in refrigerator. Bring to room temperature.

Note: To toast pine nuts, heat a small skillet. Over medium heat, add nuts and toast until golden, stirring all the while. This will take about 3 to 4 minutes.

BECHAMEL SAUCE I Salsa Besciamella

Béchamel is from northern Italy. Below are two versions, one richer than the other. The sauce is not difficult to prepare, but there are a few tips that will insure a smooth texture. Add the milk gradually to prevent lumps from forming, and use a wooden spoon rather than a whisk so that the flour can be stirred from around the edges of the pot. **Yield: About 2¼ cups**

2 cups milk	½ teaspoon salt
2 tablespoons unsalted butter	¼ teaspoon white pepper
2 tablespoons all-purpose flour	Freshly grated nutmeg

1. In a small saucepan, bring milk to a simmer.
2. Meanwhile, in a heavy saucepan, over low heat, melt butter. Gradually whisk in flour and cook 1 to 2 minutes, or until smooth; do not brown.
3. Gradually whisk in heated milk. Raise heat to medium and cook, stirring occasionally with a wooden spoon, until sauce thickens (sauce should coat the spoon heavily).

BÉCHAMEL SAUCE I, continued

4. Remove from heat and add salt, pepper and nutmeg to taste. If there are lumps in your sauce, strain through a fine sieve. If sauce is too thick, thin with a few drops of warm milk.
5. Use as needed, keeping warm in a water bath or the top of a double boiler. If sauce is not to be used immediately, pour a bit of melted butter over top so that film does not form.

To Prepare in Advance: Through #5.

Freezing Instructions: Through #4. Defrost in refrigerator. Warm over low heat.

Variation: To enhance flavor of sauce, sauté in a separate pan in ¼ cup unsalted butter ½ small onion, a garlic clove, ½ small carrot (peeled), and ½ small celery stalk (strings removed), all coarsely chopped. Gradually whisk in flour and continue with recipe as above. Strain before using.

Note: In step #3, sauce can be transferred to preheated 350°F oven to cook. Place buttered waxed paper, buttered side down, directly on sauce and cook about 30 minutes. Sauce will thicken with no need to stir.

BÉCHAMEL SAUCE II Salsa Besciamella

This is a richer béchamel sauce. **Yield: About 2 cups**

1¼ cups heavy cream	Salt
1 cup milk	Freshly ground white pepper
¼ cup (½ stick) unsalted butter	Freshly grated nutmeg
¼ cup all-purpose flour	

1. In a small saucepan, over medium heat, bring cream and milk to a simmer.
2. Meanwhile, in a heavy saucepan, over low heat, melt butter. Gradually whisk in flour and let cook 1 to 2 minutes, stirring constantly; do not brown.
3. Gradually whisk in heated cream mixture. Raise heat to medium and cook, stirring occasionally with a wooden spoon, until sauce thickens (sauce should coat the spoon heavily).
4. Remove from heat and season with salt, pepper and nutmeg to taste.
5. Use as needed (see Béchamel Sauce I, page 65).

To Prepare in Advance: Through #4.

Freezing Instructions: Through #4. Defrost in refrigerator. Warm over low heat.

CHICKEN LIVER SAUCE Salsa di Fegatini

Chicken Liver Sauce is usually served over spinach gnocchi, but also try tossing it with fettuccine. **Yield: About 1½ cups**

2 tablespoons unsalted butter	½ pound chicken livers, cut into small pieces
1 tablespoon olive oil	
½ cup finely chopped onion	½ cup dry red wine
1 teaspoon finely chopped fresh sage *or* a pinch of dried leaf sage	¾ cup Brown Stock (see page 49)
	Salt
	Freshly ground pepper

1. In a 10-inch skillet heat butter and oil.
2. Over medium heat, sauté onion and sage until onion is translucent, about 5 minutes.
3. Add chicken livers and sauté 1 minute, stirring to coat.
4. Add red wine and brown stock and reduce until sauce thickens slightly, about 5 minutes.

To Prepare in Advance: Through #4.

Freezing Instructions: Through #4. Defrost overnight in refrigerator. Warm over low heat.

CURRY CORN SAUCE Grano ed Indiano

A friend gave me this unusual recipe, which he discovered while living in Rome. The combination of corn and pasta is lighter than you might expect. I prefer fresh corn, but canned or frozen will do. **Yield: About 2½ cups**

2 ears fresh corn, cooked *or* 1½ cups frozen or canned corn kernels	2 tablespoons water
	2 tablespoons unsalted butter
	2 cups heavy cream
1½ teaspoons curry powder	Salt, if needed

1. If using fresh corn, cut corn kernels off cob. Separate and reserve.
2. In a 10-inch skillet, dissolve curry powder in water and heat for 1 minute.
3. Immediately stir in butter. When butter has melted, add cream and reduce over medium heat until sauce thickens, 5 to 8 minutes.
4. Add corn kernels to sauce, stirring until corn is heated through and tender. Correct seasoning, adding salt if necessary.
5. Combine with pasta of your choice and serve immediately.

CURRY CORN SAUCE, continued

To Prepare in Advance: Through #4.

Freezing Instructions: Through #4. Defrost overnight in refrigerator. Warm over low heat.

HORSERADISH SAUCE Salsa al Rafano

From the Veneto, this pungent sauce is excellent with boiled meat or poultry or with cold ham. **Yield: About ⅔ cup**

½ cup peeled, finely grated horse-
    radish root
¼ cup fresh breadcrumbs

6 to 8 tablespoons heavy cream
1 teaspoon white wine vinegar
  Salt

1. In a small bowl, combine grated horseradish and breadcrumbs.
2. Stir in enough cream to make a very thick sauce. Flavor with vinegar and season to taste with salt.
3. Refrigerate, covered, until needed, at least 30 minutes.

To Prepare in Advance: Through #3.

Freezing Instructions: Do not freeze.

MUSHROOM SAUCE Salsa di Funghi

This delicious Veronese sauce is more like stewed mushrooms. It can be served with meat or poultry, pasta or rice. **Yield: About 2 cups**

½ cup dried porcini mushrooms
3 tablespoons olive oil
2 tablespoons unsalted butter
1 small onion, diced
2 tablespoons chopped parsley
1 garlic clove, chopped fine

½ pound fresh mushrooms, thinly
    sliced
2 ounces prosciutto, thinly sliced
½ cup Brown Stock (see page 49)
  Salt
  Freshly ground pepper

1. In a bowl large enough to let them double in size, cover dried mushrooms with warm water and let soak for 25 to 30 minutes. Drain thoroughly and cut into slices. Reserve.
2. In a 10-inch skillet, heat olive oil and butter. Over medium heat, sauté onion, parsley and garlic until onion is translucent, about 5 minutes.

3. Stir in all the mushrooms and sauté until tender, 12 to 15 minutes, stirring occasionally. Add the prosciutto after 10 minutes.

4. Stir in the brown stock and cook 2 to 3 minutes longer.

5. Season with salt and pepper to taste.

To Prepare in Advance: Through #5.

Freezing Instructions: Through #5. Defrost in refrigerator. Warm over low heat.

Variation: In step #4, stir in ½ cup heavy cream with stock. Cook until sauce thickens slightly.

RED PEPPER SAUCE Salsa al Peperoncino

Red Pepper Sauce will liven up steamed cauliflower. Pour sauce over and garnish with strips of whole roasted red peppers (for roasting method, see page 34). **Yield: About 1½ cups**

½ pound red bell peppers, coarsely chopped
¾ to 1 cup Chicken Broth (see page 48)
1 cup heavy cream

Salt
Freshly ground pepper
Juice of ½ medium lemon or to taste

1. Place peppers in a small saucepan. Pour in enough chicken broth to cover and bring to a boil. Reduce heat and simmer until tender, about 15 minutes.

2. Pour contents of saucepan into a blender or food processor and purée.

3. In a clean saucepan, reduce cream by half. Stir red pepper purée into cream and reduce slightly. Season with salt, pepper and lemon juice to taste.

4. Use as needed.

To Prepare in Advance: Through #3, reheating as necessary.

Freezing Instructions: Through #3. Reheat over very low flame.

SWEET AND SOUR SAUCE Salsa Agrodolce

In Milan, this sauce is served over boiled onions; in other regions, with rabbit or roasted duck. **Yield: About ¾ cup**

2 tablespoons raisins
½ cup plus 1 tablespoon dry white wine
2 tablespoons sugar
2 tablespoons red wine vinegar

1 medium shallot, minced
½ cup Brown Stock (see page 49)
1 tablespoon toasted pine nuts (see page 65)

1. In a small bowl, plump raisins in 1 tablespoon white wine.
2. In a small saucepan, combine sugar and vinegar. Cook over medium heat until thick, 4 to 5 minutes.
3. Add shallot and ½ cup wine and reduce almost to a glaze, about 10 minutes.
4. Pour in brown stock and bring to a boil. Strain.
5. Return sauce to pan and stir in raisins and pine nuts. Heat through and serve.

To Prepare in Advance: Through #5, reheating when ready to serve.

Freezing Instructions: Through #4. Warm over low flame and continue with recipe.

WALNUT SAUCE Salsa di Noci

This unique sauce from northern Italy is served over ravioli stuffed with spinach and ricotta. It is also excellent with grilled fish. **Yield: About 1½ cups**

2 ounces chopped walnuts	½ cup olive oil
3 tablespoons unsalted butter	¼ cup heavy cream, whipped
2 tablespoons grated Parmesan cheese	Salt
1 garlic clove	Freshly ground pepper
	Chicken Broth (see page 48)

1. In a food processor or blender, combine walnuts, butter, grated cheese and garlic. Process until mixture becomes pasty.
2. With machine running, slowly pour oil through feed tube and process until smooth.
3. Transfer to a mixing bowl and fold in whipped cream. Season with salt and pepper to taste. Refrigerate until needed.
4. For each serving, stir 1 or 2 tablespoons walnut mixture into ¼ cup broth. Cook over medium heat until sauce thickens slightly. Pour over pasta and serve immediately.

To Prepare in Advance: Through #3.

Freezing Instructions: Through #3. Defrost in refrigerator.

ZUCCHINI SAUCE Salsa di Zucchini

From the Marche, this delicious sauce can be prepared early in the day. Zucchini should be al dente. **Yield: About 3 cups**

¾ pound zucchini
½ pound tomatoes, seeded but unpeeled
2 tablespoons unsalted butter
2 cups heavy cream
½ teaspoon salt
Freshly ground pepper
¼ cup (1 ounce) grated Parmesan cheese

1. Wash and trim zucchini. Cut into 2-inch-long julienne. Cook in boiling salted water until al dente, about 2 minutes. Drain and reserve.
2. Cut tomatoes into 2-inch-long julienne.
3. In a medium saucepan, melt butter over medium heat. Add tomatoes and cook until very soft, 2 to 3 minutes, stirring occasionally.
4. Add cream and reduce until sauce thickens, 5 to 8 minutes.
5. Stir in reserved zucchini and heat through. Season with salt and pepper. Sprinkle with cheese and correct seasoning to taste.
6. Serve hot over pasta.

To Prepare in Advance: Through #4.

Freezing Instructions: Through #4. Warm over low heat.

Pastas, Polenta and Rice

Marco Polo has been credited with bringing pasta back to Italy from China. However, historians have noted the introduction of pasta to Italy in the 5th century B.C., probably by the Etruscans. Whatever its beginnings, all regions of Italy embrace pasta. Pasta is the generic term for the product resulting from a basic combination of flour and water which is then cooked in boiling water. In the north, it is more often flat and soft, made with eggs; in the south, the pasta is generally the tubular variety—more brittle, with no eggs, and factory-produced rather than homemade. Not only does pasta come in a variety of sizes and shapes, but it can be served with any number of sauces, or simply with butter or olive oil and grated cheese.

Pasta is served as a separate course, after the antipasto and before the main dish.

Rice is almost as widely cooked in Italy as pasta, which is natural for a country that boasts the largest rice-producing areas in Europe. Rice is combined with vegetables, fish, chicken or meat, is added to soups and prepared as a dessert. The Italians never serve rice as an accompaniment to a main dish except in the form of *Risotto alla Milanese* which is traditionally served with *Ossobuco*.

Polenta is one of the staples of northern Italy. Yellow cornmeal is generally used, but in the Trentino-Alto Adige region, the polenta is made from buckwheat or mixed with potato flour, giving unusual texture and color. Polenta can be served plain or combined with meat, fish or game. When truffles are fresh, they can be grated over the polenta. Many Italian cooks shape leftover polenta into a loaf, slice it and sauté the slices in butter for another meal.

For perfect pasta there are just a few basic rules to follow. For every pound of pasta, use 4 quarts of water. Bring water to a boil over high heat, add salt and a little oil, if desired, to help keep pasta from sticking together. When water comes back to a rolling boil, add pasta, stirring it gently into the water. Again bring water to a boil and cook until pasta is ready. Pasta can be drained in a colander or plucked out of the water with tongs. Serve on heated plates.

To cook packaged pasta, follow directions on the package, tasting to determine the degree of doneness. It will take anywhere from 6 to 15 minutes, depending upon the size and thickness.

For homemade pasta, the smaller pasta shapes can cook in 2 to 5 minutes and the larger may take as much as 6 to 7 minutes. To test for doneness, taste small bits. Pasta should be cooked al dente (to the tooth), tender but still firm.

I find all-purpose flour most satisfactory in making pasta. However, if you want to combine it with semolina (durum wheat) flour, I recommend a combination of 80% all-purpose and 20% semolina flours for best results.

The ease of making dough in the food processor allows even a beginner the satisfaction of making his or her own pasta. But for the purist who insists that pasta dough can be made only by hand, I have also included a recipe for that. Dough rolled out by hand should be softer than that rolled through a machine.

I do not feel that an expensive pasta machine is necessary. In my classes I recommend two small machines, the Atlas and the Imperia, both hand-cranked machines that are simple to operate and easy to clean.

YELLOW EGG PASTA DOUGH Pasta all'Uovo

This is a basic pasta dough, which can be prepared by hand or machine.
Yield: 1½ pounds, serves 6 to 8

3 cups all-purpose flour
  Large pinch of salt
4 extra large eggs

2 tablespoons olive oil
  Additional flour for dusting

1. In a food processor fitted with steel blade, combine flour, salt, eggs and olive oil. Process for 1 minute. When mixture pinches together when pressed, dough is ready.
2. Turn dough out on very lightly floured board and knead, forming a ball. Wrap in plastic wrap and let rest 30 minutes. (If refrigerated at this point, remove from refrigerator 30 minutes before rolling.)
3. When ready to roll, cut into 3 pieces. Roll out 1 piece at a time, keeping other pieces wrapped. If using a pasta machine, set rollers at widest opening. Flatten first ball of dough into a thick strip no wider than machine, to enable it to pass through rollers. If necessary, dust lightly with flour and run through machine. Fold in thirds crosswise and run through machine again. Repeat this procedure 2 more times, dusting with flour as necessary.
4. Set machine to next smaller opening and run dough through rollers. Continue rolling and stretching dough, using smaller opening each time, until next to smallest or smallest opening is reached, dusting lightly with flour only as necessary. (Dough strip will be long, so have enough work table space. If not, cut dough in half halfway through the rolling process and continue with each half separately.)
5. Adjust cutting mechanism to desired width and cut strips of dough. A convenient way to dry pasta as dough is cut is to arrange pasta on pastry tray sprinkled lightly with flour. As one layer is completed, cover with parchment paper and continue layering with noodles and sprinkling with flour. Dry 15 to 20 minutes. Repeat with remaining balls of dough.

To Prepare in Advance: Through #2 or #5.

Freezing Instructions: Through #2, defrosting overnight in refrigerator, or #5, freezing in single-serving bundles on a tray and then packaging in a plastic bag and refreezing. Bundles can be cooked directly from freezer, but cooking time will be 1 to 2 minutes longer than for fresh pasta.

To make pasta by hand, heap flour in a mound on the work table, making a well in the center. Break the eggs into the well, add the salt, olive oil, and 1 tablespoon water and gently whisk with a fork. Gradually stir the flour into the eggs until almost all the flour is incorporated. Then knead for about 10

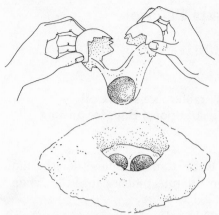

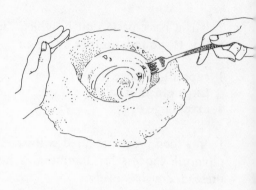

To make pasta by hand, heap flour in a mound, making a well in the center. Break the eggs into the well.

Gently whisk the eggs with a fork, gradually stirring the flour into the eggs.

YELLOW EGG PASTA DOUGH, continued

minutes, using fingers and heel of your hand, until dough is smooth and elastic.

Divide dough into 3 pieces, wrap each piece in plastic wrap and let rest 30 minutes.

To roll out dough by hand, sprinkle work table lightly with flour. With rolling pin, roll out first piece of dough in one direction, then turn dough and roll in the other direction until dough stretches and gets larger. Roll dough around rolling pin; unroll so that side of dough formerly at bottom is now on top. Try to keep the thickness of the dough as even as possible. Roll out the dough to a rectangle as thin as possible, cutting edges so that lengths and widths are even.

Bring long ends together to meet at the center. Sprinkle lightly with flour and repeat 2 more times. Using a sharp chef's knife, cut dough into noodles

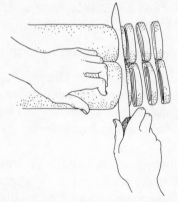

Bring the long ends of the dough together to meet at the center. Repeat 2 more times.

Using a sharp chef's knife, cut the dough into noodles.

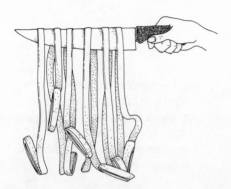

Slip the dull edge of the knife under the center of the dough (where the ends met) and let the noodles unravel.

⅛, ¼, or ½ inch wide, as desired. Slip the dull edge of the knife under the center of the dough and let the noodles unravel.

See page 75 for drying procedure.

GREEN SPINACH PASTA Pasta Verde

Pasta is colored for eye appeal rather than flavor. The combination of green spinach pasta and red beet pasta makes an attractive presentation on your table and is worth the extra effort. **Yield: 1½ pounds, serves 6 to 8**

½ pound fresh spinach, washed *or*
    2 tablespoons puréed cooked
      spinach, drained well
3 cups all-purpose flour

Large pinch of salt
3 extra large eggs
1 tablespoon olive oil

1. In a food processor fitted with steel blade, process spinach to a purée.
2. Transfer spinach to a clean napkin, squeeze out ¼ cup spinach juice and reserve. Clean bowl and blade.
3. In the processor, combine flour, salt, eggs, olive oil and spinach juice (or puréed spinach). Process until a mass begins to form on the blade.
4. Continue as for Yellow Egg Pasta Dough (see page 75), proceeding from step #2.

Note: Using the puréed vegetable will give the dough a speckled color.

RED BEET PASTA Pasta Rossa

Yield: 1½ pounds, serves 6 to 8

3 cups all-purpose flour
Large pinch of salt
3 extra large eggs
1 tablespoon olive oil

¼ cup beet juice, canned or squeezed from 2 puréed cooked beets *or* ¼ cup liquid from cooked beets *or* 2 tablespoons puréed cooked beets, drained well

1. In a food processor fitted with steel blade, combine all ingredients and process. When dough pinches together when pressed, dough is ready.
2. Continue as for Yellow Egg Pasta Dough (see page 75), proceeding from step #2.

Note: Using the puréed vegetable will give the dough a speckled color. I was told by one chef that his customers prefer the speckling because they know it is vegetable purée and not food coloring.

MUSHROOM PASTA Pasta di Fungo

The mushrooms add a delicate flavor to this pasta. To further enhance the flavor, serve with Mushroom Sauce (see page 68). Season with salt and pepper and toss with the pasta. **Yield: 1½ pounds, serves 6 to 8**

1 ounce dried porcini mushrooms
3 cups all-purpose flour
Large pinch of salt

3 extra large eggs
2 tablespoons olive oil

1. Soak mushrooms in warm water for 25 to 30 minutes. Drain and dry thoroughly. Cut into strips.
2. In a food processor fitted with steel blade, process mushrooms until coarsely chopped.
3. Add remaining ingredients and process for 1 minute. When dough pinches together when pressed, dough is ready.
4. Continue as for Yellow Egg Pasta Dough (see page 75), proceeding from step #2.

BAKED NOODLES Taglierini al Forno

A very simple preparation in which cooked macaroni or rigatoni may be substituted for the thin noodles. **Serves 4 to 6**

¼ cup olive oil
½ medium onion, chopped fine
1 pound tomatoes, peeled, seeded and chopped
2 tablespoons chopped fresh basil leaves or ½ teaspoon Italian Seasoning (see page 12)
Salt
Freshly ground pepper

½ pound thin noodles (taglierini) (see Note)
½ cup fresh breadcrumbs
6 tablespoons unsalted butter
¾ cup (3 ounces) grated Parmesan or pecorino cheese
2 cups Chicken Broth, heated (see page 48)
Grated Parmesan or pecorino cheese, optional

1. Preheat oven to 350°F.
2. Butter a 6-cup ovenproof dish or a 9-inch-square baking dish. Sprinkle lightly with breadcrumbs and shake out excess.
3. In a 10-inch skillet, heat olive oil. Over medium heat, sauté onion until golden, about 5 minutes. Add tomatoes, stir and cook until most of the moisture evaporates, about 20 minutes. Sprinkle with basil and season with salt and pepper to taste. Let cool 5 to 10 minutes.
4. Arrange half the noodles in the prepared dish. Layer with half the tomato mixture, cover with half the breadcrumbs, dot with 3 tablespoons butter, and sprinkle with half the grated cheese.
5. Repeat layers, starting with remaining noodles.
6. Season broth with salt and pepper to taste. Ladle over noodles and place in oven. Bake 40 to 45 minutes, or until noodles are golden brown and broth is absorbed.
7. Serve hot, with additional cheese, if desired.

To Prepare in Advance: Through #5. Or through #6, baking 20 minutes.

Freezing Instructions: Through #6. Defrost overnight in refrigerator. Place in preheated oven 10 to 15 minutes.

Suggested Wine:
Italian: CABERNET FRANC, a red wine from the Veneto
American: CHARIGNANET

Note: If using homemade noodles, there is no need to cook them first. If using packaged noodles, cook in boiling salted water for 5 minutes, drain, and continue with recipe.

CREPES WITH RICOTTA-SPINACH FILLING
Crespelle di Ricotta e Spinaci

In the northern regions of Italy, crepes are wrapped around a filling and baked. Southern Italians stuff large tubular pasta instead. Ask any Italian and he or she will tell you that the crepe originated in Italy and was adopted by the French. On my last trip to Rome, I dined at Mastrostefani in the Piazza Navona. This is an adaptation of their superb dish. **Serves 4 to 8**

½	pound fresh spinach, washed, stemmed, cooked and squeezed dry		Salt
			Freshly ground pepper
¾	pound ricotta cheese		Freshly grated nutmeg
¼	cup (1 ounce) grated Parmesan cheese	½	cup heavy cream, whipped
		1	cup Béchamel Sauce I (see page 65)
2	eggs	8	Crepes (½ recipe) (see page 186)

1. Preheat oven to 350°F. Butter a 9 × 5 × 3-inch loaf pan.
2. In a food processor fitted with steel blade, chop spinach.
3. Add ricotta, grated Parmesan and eggs and process until well combined, scraping down sides of bowl as necessary (or chop fine with knife or mezzaluna). Season with salt, pepper and nutmeg to taste.
4. Pour mixture into prepared pan. Bake 30 to 35 minutes, until puffed and firm to the touch. Remove from oven and let cool.
5. Fold whipped cream into cooled bechamel. Reserve.
6. Raise oven heat to 400°F. Butter a 13 × 9 × 2-inch baking dish or 4 to 8 individual dishes.
7. Divide ricotta-spinach mixture among the 8 crepes, folding over to enclose. Arrange in baking dish in one layer, seam side down, and spoon bechamel sauce over. Sprinkle lightly with nutmeg.
8. Place baking dish in oven and bake 8 to 10 minutes. Transfer to broiler until golden brown, 1 to 2 minutes.
9. Serve immediately.

To Prepare in Advance: Through #4.

Freezing Instructions: Do not freeze.

Suggested Wine:
Italian: TRAMINER COLLIO, a white wine from Friuli-Venezia Giulia
American: Joseph Phelps GEWURZTRAMINER

CREPES WITH CHEESE Crespelle con Ricotta

This is a variation of the Crepes with Ricotta-Spinach Filling from my friend Frank Tudisco. It can be served as a main dish or a first course. **Serves 6 to 8**

1½ recipes Crepes (see page 186)
1½ pounds ricotta cheese
½   pound mozzarella cheese, coarsely grated
½   cup (2 ounces) plus 2 tablespoons grated Parmesan cheese
1   10-ounce package frozen spinach, cooked, drained and chopped or 1 bunch parsley, chopped

Freshly grated nutmeg
Salt
Freshly ground pepper
1   recipe Red Pepper Sauce (see page 69) or tomato sauce of your choice
Grated Parmesan cheese, optional

1. Prepare crepes and reserve.
2. In a large bowl, combine ricotta, mozzarella and ½ cup Parmesan cheeses. Stir in the chopped spinach and season with nutmeg, salt and pepper to taste.
3. Preheat oven to 350°F. Butter an 8½ × 11½ × 3½-inch baking dish.
4. Place 2 to 3 tablespoons filling in the center of each crepe. Fold crepe over filling, letter style, enclosing filling completely. Gently press the last fold to adhere.

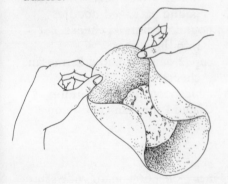  

Place 2 or 3 tablespoons of filling in the center of each crepe.

Fold the crepe over the filling, letter style, enclosing the filling completely.

5. Spoon a thin layer of sauce into the prepared baking dish. Arrange the stuffed crepes seam side down on the sauce. Pour 1 cup of sauce in a wide ribbon over centers of crepes and sprinkle with remaining 2 tablespoons grated Parmesan. Cover dish tightly with aluminum foil.
6. Bake 20 minutes, remove foil and bake 15 minutes longer.

CREPES WITH CHEESE, continued

7. Serve immediately, passing remaining sauce in a separate bowl. Pass additional grated Parmesan cheese, if desired.

To Prepare in Advance: Through #5.

Freezing Instructions: Do not freeze.

Suggested Wine:
Italian: FRASCATI, a dry white wine from the hills around Rome
American: Heitz CHABLIS

LASAGNE

Bologna claims this dish, perfect for a luncheon or brunch. Store-bought or homemade noodles, green, white, or a combination of the two, can be used. Noodles can be cooked early in the day and placed on a platter with a little oil poured over to keep them pliable and prevent them from sticking together. **Serves 8 to 10**

2 pounds sweet Italian sausage, casing removed *or* 1 pound sweet Italian sausage and 1 pound ground beef	2 tablespoons chopped parsley
1 tablespoon olive oil	½ recipe Yellow Egg Pasta Dough (cut into lasagne-style broad noodles) (see page 75) or ¾ pound packaged noodles
2 garlic cloves, diced	½ pound mozzarella cheese, cut into thin slices
Salt	
Freshly ground pepper	½ cup (2 ounces) grated Parmesan cheese
½ pound mushrooms, sliced	
5 cups Marinara Sauce (see page 61)	6 tablespoons unsalted butter
1 recipe Béchamel Sauce II (see page 66)	Grated Parmesan cheese, optional

1. Crumble or slice sausage meat. In a 14-inch skillet or 4-quart, wide saucepan, heat oil. Over medium heat, stir in the sausage, breaking apart if necessary. Add the garlic and cook, stirring frequently, until meat browns, about 10 minutes. Discard grease and season meat with salt and pepper to taste.

2. Add the mushrooms and marinara sauce. Loosely cover pan and simmer over low heat about 30 minutes, stirring occasionally. Stir in the bechamel sauce and the chopped parsley. Correct seasoning to taste.

3. Preheat oven to 375° F. Lightly butter a 13 × 9 × 2-inch baking dish.

4. Cook lasagne noodles in boiling salted water until al dente. (I like to cook noodles one at a time, remove with large strainer and place in ice water.) Drain and pat dry.

5. To assemble: spoon a layer of sauce over bottom of baking dish, add a layer of noodles, another layer of sauce and a layer of mozzarella. Sprinkle with one third of the grated Parmesan and dot with 2 tablespoons butter. Repeat the entire procedure two more times, ending with the butter. (There should be 6 layers of sauce, 3 layers of noodles, 3 layers of mozzarella, 3 layers of Parmesan cheese and 3 layers of butter.)

6. Bake 25 to 30 minutes, or until piping hot and cheese has melted.

7. Serve directly from pan, with additional Parmesan cheese, if desired.

To Prepare in Advance: Through #2, #5, or #6. If through #2 or #5, baking time may be 10 or 15 minutes longer to heat through.

Freezing Instructions: Through #6. Defrost overnight in refrigerator. Place in preheated oven about 15 minutes. If using a glass baking dish, remove from refrigerator 1 hour before baking time so glass will not crack going from cold to hot. You can also cut lasagne into individual portions so that you can take out as much as needed and reheat.

Variations: 1. Two pounds of shredded cooked chicken may be substituted for the sausage. Stir in with the bechamel sauce in step #2, and continue with recipe.

2. Combine 1 pound ricotta cheese, 1 cup grated Parmesan cheese, 3 tablespoons chopped parsley and 3 eggs. Season lightly with salt and pepper. Add layers of ricotta mixture between each layer of pasta. Or alternate meat and ricotta layers for a marvelous, *very* rich lasagne that may well feed twice as many people.

3. For vegetarian lasagne, substitute 1 to 2 cans (1 pound each) artichoke hearts for sausage. Slice hearts and stir into sauce in step #2.

Suggested Wine:
Italian: PINOT NERO, a light red wine from the Veneto
American: Mount Eden PINOT NOIR

DUCK LASAGNE Pasticcio d'Anatra

Making lasagne is time-consuming but well worth the effort since it is always a crowd pleaser. I like to make big batches and freeze so it will be ready when I need it. **Serves 8**

¼ pound dried porcini mushrooms
2 duck legs (about 1 pound) (see Note)
2 teaspoons all-purpose flour
Salt
Freshly ground pepper
2 tablespoons olive oil
1 tablespoon unsalted butter
1 celery stalk, strings removed, chopped fine
½ medium onion, chopped fine
2 small carrots, peeled and chopped fine
½ cup dry red wine

1 teaspoon tomato paste
½ teaspoon chopped fresh rosemary *or* a pinch of dried rosemary
1 bay leaf
1 cup Brown Stock (see page 49)
1 recipe Béchamel Sauce II (see page 66)
½ recipe Yellow Egg Pasta Dough (cut into lasagne-style broad noodles) (see page 75) or ¾ pound packaged noodles
½ cup (2 ounces) grated Parmesan cheese

1. Soak porcini mushrooms in warm water for 25 to 30 minutes. Drain and cut into thin slices.
2. Bone duck legs and cut meat into ¾-inch pieces. Reserve bones. Dust meat with flour and season with salt and pepper.
3. Preheat oven to 350°F.
4. In a medium skillet, heat 1 tablespoon oil. Over high heat, add duck pieces and brown on all sides. Drain grease and reserve meat.
5. Meanwhile, in a small ovenproof casserole, heat remaining 1 tablespoon oil and butter. Sauté celery, onion and carrots until onion is translucent, 8 to 10 minutes. Stir in duck meat, reserved bones, sliced mushrooms, wine, tomato paste, rosemary, bay leaf and brown stock. Transfer to oven and bake 30 to 40 minutes, or until duck is tender.
6. Remove from oven and let cool. Discard bones and bay leaf. Remove skin from duck. Stir in bechamel sauce and combine well. Correct seasoning to taste.
7. Cook lasagne in boiling salted water until al dente. Drain and dry.
8. Butter a 13 × 9 × 2-inch baking dish. Spoon a layer of sauce over bottom of baking dish, add a layer of lasagne and sprinkle with a layer of Parmesan cheese. Continue layering until all the ingredients are used, ending with a layer of sauce. There should be 4 or 5 layers.
9. Bake 20 to 25 minutes, until hot and bubbly. Serve directly from pan.

To Prepare in Advance: Through #6, #8 or #9. Through #8, baking time may be a bit longer.

Freezing Instructions: Through #9. Defrost overnight in refrigerator. Place in preheated oven about 15 minutes.

Suggested Wine:
Italian: CHIANTI, a light red wine from Tuscany
American: CARIGNANE

Note: Reserve duck breasts and grill or sauté for another meal. Duck breasts are much more tender than the legs and thus more of a delicacy.

FETTUCCINE WITH TOMATO AND CREAM SAUCE
Fettuccine Villa Medici

This is a speciality of the Hotel Hassler in Rome. **Serves 6 to 8**

7 tablespoons unsalted butter	Salt
¼ pound prosciutto, cut into julienne	Freshly ground pepper
	1 cup heavy cream
¼ pound sweet sausage, sliced	1½ pounds fettuccine
½ pound mushrooms, sliced	¼ cup (1 ounce) grated Parmesan cheese
½ cup dry white wine	
1 pound fresh tomatoes, peeled, seeded and chopped	

1. In a large skillet, melt 4 tablespoons butter. Over high heat, sauté prosciutto and sausage for 2 to 3 minutes. Stir in mushrooms and cook 2 to 3 minutes longer. Discard grease.
2. Deglaze pan with wine and cook over high heat, until wine evaporates. Lower heat, add tomatoes, salt and pepper to taste and cook 10 to 15 minutes, stirring occasionally. Pour in cream and cook just until sauce thickens, about 5 minutes.
3. Meanwhile, cook fettuccine until al dente. Drain. Add to skillet, tossing to combine with sauce. Stir in remaining 3 tablespoons butter and the Parmesan cheese. Correct seasoning to taste.
4. Serve immediately.

To Prepare in Advance: Through #2, without reducing cream.

Freezing Instructions: Do not freeze.

Suggested Wine:
Italian: PINOT NOIR, a light red wine from the Veneto
American: SYRAH

PASTA ROLL Rotolo di Pasta

Pasta Roll, from Emilia-Romagna, is generally served as a first course. The pasta is rolled out into a large rectangle, the filling is spread on the dough, and then the dough is rolled to enclose the filling. Don't let the number of steps in this recipe discourage you; the roll can be prepared the day before. This is a very stiff dough; you may want to roll it through your pasta machine to begin to stretch the dough and then continue by hand. **Yield: 16 ¾-inch slices**

Filling
3 pounds fresh spinach, washed and stemmed

5 tablespoons unsalted butter, softened

2 tablespoons grated Parmesan cheese

Pinch of freshly grated nutmeg

Salt

Freshly ground pepper

3 tablespoons cooking oil

½ pound mushrooms, thinly sliced

¼ pound chicken livers

¼ cup minced cooked ham

Dough
1½ cups all-purpose flour

Salt

2 extra large eggs

1 tablespoon cooking oil

1 tablespoon water

¼ cup (½ stick) unsalted butter, melted

½ cup (2 ounces) grated Parmesan cheese

1. *To prepare filling:* In a large, covered saucepan, over medium heat, cook spinach in moisture that clings to leaves until just wilted, about 5 minutes. Drain thoroughly and chop fine. Transfer to a medium bowl.

2. Add 4 tablespoons butter, grated Parmesan cheese, nutmeg and salt and pepper to taste. Reserve.

3. In a 10-inch skillet, heat oil. Over medium heat, sauté mushrooms, stirring occasionally, 8 to 10 minutes. Drain and add to spinach.

4. In a small skillet, heat remaining 1 tablespoon butter. Over medium heat, sauté chicken livers about 2 minutes on each side. Remove from skillet, chop into small pieces and add to spinach mixture along with ham. Combine well. Let cool while preparing dough.

5. *To prepare dough:* In a food processor fitted with steel blade, combine flour, a large pinch of salt and eggs. Process until texture is somewhat mealy. Add the oil and water and process until a solid mass begins to form on the blade. (Or to prepare by hand, heap flour in a mound on the work table, making a well in the center. Break the eggs into the well, add the salt, oil and water and whisk with a fork. Gradually work the flour into the eggs until al-

most incorporated. Then knead with your hand about 10 minutes, or until dough is smooth and elastic.)

6. Turn the dough out onto a lightly floured board and knead into a ball. Wrap in plastic wrap and let rest at room temperature 30 minutes.

7. On a lightly floured board, roll out dough to a rectangle 14 × 18 inches. Cut off 1 inch from all sides, leaving a 12 × 16-inch rectangle.

8. *To assemble:* Spread the filling evenly over the surface of the dough, leaving a 1-inch border. Starting with the 16-inch side, roll up to enclose filling, jelly roll fashion. Completely wrap roll in cheesecloth and tightly secure both ends with string.

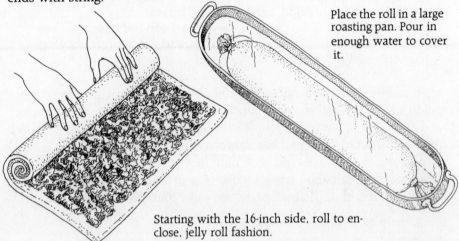

Place the roll in a large roasting pan. Pour in enough water to cover it.

Starting with the 16-inch side, roll to enclose, jelly roll fashion.

9. Place roll in large roasting pan. Pour in enough salted water to cover roll and bring to a boil. Lower heat and simmer 30 minutes.

10. Preheat oven to 350°F.

11. Remove roll from water and carefully unwrap the cheesecloth. Cut a small piece from both ends and discard. Cut the roll into 16 ¾-inch slices.

12. Arrange slices in a buttered oven-to-table pan. Pour melted butter over and sprinkle with grated Parmesan cheese. Cover with aluminum foil and bake 15 minutes.

13. Remove foil and continue to bake 10 to 15 minutes longer, or until cheese is melted and slices are hot. Serve immediately.

To Prepare in Advance: Through #9 or #11.

Freezing Instructions: Through #9. Defrost overnight in refrigerator and continue with recipe.

PASTA WITH TOMATOES AND BLACK OLIVES
Pasta al Pomodoro ed Olive

Rome has more restaurants than any other city in Italy, and I have enjoyed this pasta often in the small *trattorie.* The olives of Rome are coal black and quite small. **Serves 4 to 6**

2 tablespoons olive oil
1 small onion, chopped fine
2 garlic cloves, chopped fine
1 pound tomatoes, peeled, seeded
   and chopped
1 cup heavy cream
½ cup chopped black olives

Salt
Freshly ground pepper
1 tablespoon chopped fresh basil
   leaves
½ teaspoon red pepper flakes
1 pound pasta, preferably penne

1. Heat a heavy 10-inch skillet and add olive oil. Over medium heat, sauté onion and garlic until onion is translucent, about 5 minutes. Add tomatoes and cook about 30 minutes longer, stirring occasionally, until sauce is quite thick and most of the liquid has evaporated.
2. Add cream and olives and cook until sauce thickens slightly.
3. Season with salt and pepper to taste. Stir in basil and red pepper.
4. Toss with cooked, drained pasta and serve immediately.

To Prepare in Advance: Through #2.

Freezing Instructions: Through #2. Warm over low heat and continue with recipe.

PASTA WITH FOUR CHEESES
Pasta ai Quattro Formaggi

The Italians are always experimenting with their cuisine. This is one of the newer recipes that has become popular in restaurants and homes alike. The choice of cheeses may vary, but I find this combination excellent. If you cannot get mascarpone in your local market, substitute cream cheese. **Serves 4 to 6**

¼ pound Italian fontina cheese, cut
   into small pieces
2 ounces gorgonzola cheese, cut
   into small pieces
¼ pound mascarpone cheese, cut
   into small pieces
1 cup heavy cream

1 pound pasta, preferably
   fettuccine
¼ cup (½ stick) unsalted butter, cut
   into small pieces
2 tablespoons Cognac, optional
¼ cup (1 ounce) grated Parmesan
   cheese

Freshly ground pepper   Salt, if needed

1. In a medium saucepan, over low heat, melt fontina, gorgonzola, and mascarpone cheeses in heavy cream stirring occasionally.
2. Cook pasta in boiling salted water until al dente. Drain. Return to pot in which it was cooked.
3. Over low heat, toss pasta with butter.
4. Add cheese mixture to pasta and toss until well coated.
5. Heat Cognac and pour over pasta. Sprinkle with grated Parmesan cheese and pepper. Correct seasoning to taste, adding salt if necessary.
6. Serve immediately.

To Prepare in Advance: Through #1.

Freezing Instructions: Do not freeze.

Suggested Wine:
Italian: BARBERA D'ALBA, a full-bodied red wine from the Piedmont
American: Stag's Leap MERLOT

PASTA WITH PECORINO AND ASPARAGUS
Pasta con Pecorino ed Asparagi

The Italians enjoy the combination of asparagus and cheese. The asparagus are picked young and require very little cooking. In this recipe, only the tips are used. The remaining asparagus stalks can be used for soup (see page 50). Pecorino, a hard sheep's cheese, has the same consistency as Parmesan.
Serves 6 to 8

¼	pound bacon, cut into ½-inch pieces	1½	pounds pasta, preferably fettuccine
½	pound asparagus, tips only	1	medium tomato, peeled, seeded and diced
3	garlic cloves, blanched twice and minced (see Note)	1	tablespoon minced fresh chives
1	cup heavy cream		Salt
½	cup (2 ounces) grated pecorino cheese		Freshly ground pepper

1. In a 12-inch saucepan over medium heat, sauté bacon until golden brown. Remove from pan and drain on paper towels. Reserve.
2. Over medium heat, sauté asparagus tips in the bacon drippings until al

dente, 6 to 8 minutes. Remove the tips from the pan, pat dry and reserve.
3. Discard the grease from the pan. Add the garlic, cream and pecorino cheese. Stir until incorporated and heated.
4. Cook pasta in boiling salted water until al dente. Drain and return to pot.
5. Add cream sauce to pasta and toss. Stir in reserved bacon and asparagus tips as well as the tomato, chives, and salt and pepper to taste. Heat through.
6. Serve immediately.

To Prepare in Advance: Through #2.

Freezing Instructions: Through #3. Defrost in refrigerator. Warm over low heat and continue with recipe.

Note: To blanch garlic twice, cook in boiling water for 30 seconds, drain, and repeat procedure.

PASTA WITH SAUSAGE Pasta e Salsiccie

Calabria is famous for its wide variety of sausages. Though this is usually prepared with ricotta cheese, it takes on an even lighter texture when cream is used. The tubular rigatoni absorbs the sauce more readily than a flat pasta. **Serves 4 to 6**

¼ cup (½ stick) unsalted butter
2 pounds sweet Italian sausage, casing removed, cut into small pieces
Salt

Red pepper flakes to taste
4 cups heavy cream
1 pound rigatoni, cooked
Grated pecorino cheese

1. In a heavy 10-inch skillet, melt butter. Over medium heat, add sausage and cook, stirring occasionally, until meat has lost its pink color, 5 to 6 minutes. Discard grease from pan. Season with salt and red pepper to taste.
2. In a medium saucepan, bring cream to a simmer. Pour over sausage and, over medium heat, reduce liquid until slightly thickened.
3. Add rigatoni and heat thoroughly, stirring to coat all the pieces. Correct seasoning to taste.
4. Serve immediately. Pass grated cheese in a separate bowl.

To Prepare in Advance: Through #2.

Freezing Instructions: Through #2. Warm over low heat.

Suggested Wine:
Italian: CAREMA, a medium-bodied red wine from the Piedmont
American: Acacia PINOT NOIR

RIGATONI WITH ONION
Rigatoni con Cipolle

Macaroni is associated with Naples, where food is served simply and with a minimum of fuss. This is a perfect example of the Neapolitan philosophy.
Serves 4 to 6

½ cup olive oil
3 pounds onions, thinly sliced
½ cup water
  Salt
  Freshly ground pepper

1 pound rigatoni or penne
½ cup (2 ounces) grated Parmesan cheese
  Grated Parmesan cheese

1. In a 10-inch skillet, heat oil. Add onions and water and season lightly with salt and pepper. Cover and cook over low heat for 30 minutes.
2. Remove cover, raise heat to medium, and cook until the liquid has evaporated, 15 to 20 minutes longer.
3. Cook the pasta until al dente and stir into onions, combining well. Stir in the grated cheese and correct seasoning to taste.
4. Serve immediately. Pass additional cheese in a separate bowl.

To Prepare in Advance: Through #1.

Freezing Instructions: Do not freeze.

Suggested Wine:
Italian: GRECO DI TUFO, a dry, delicate white wine from Campania
American: Vichon CHARDONNAY

SPAGHETTI ALL'AMATRICIANA

Legend has it that this recipe was brought to Rome from the small village of Amatrice, in the mountainous region of Abruzzo. No matter its origin, it has since become one of Rome's most famous pasta dishes. **Serves 4 to 6**

2 to 3 tablespoons olive oil
1 medium onion, minced
1 can (1 pound 12 ounces) Italian plum tomatoes, drained and mashed
  Red pepper flakes

¼ pound thick bacon slices, cut into small chunks
  Salt
1 pound spaghetti
  Grated Parmesan cheese

1. In a 10-inch skillet, heat oil. Add onion and bacon and cook over medium heat, stirring occasionally, until onion is wilted, about 5 minutes.
2. Lower heat, add tomatoes and let simmer, partially covered, until sauce thickens, 20 to 30 minutes.
3. Season to taste with red pepper flakes and salt.
4. Cook spaghetti in boiling salted water until al dente. Drain and place in serving bowl. Pour sauce over, toss, and sprinkle with grated cheese.
5. Serve immediately. Pass additional grated cheese in a separate bowl.

To Prepare in Advance: Through #3, reheating as necessary.

Freezing Instructions: Through #3. Warm over low heat.

Suggested Wine:
Italian: FRASCATI, a dry white wine from the hills around Rome
American: Heitz CHABLIS

SPAGHETTI WITH PANCETTA AND RAW EGG
Spaghetti alla Carbonara

A Tuscan specialty, this can be prepared with or without pancetta, with or without cream. I have included two recipes so that you can decide which you prefer. **Serves 4 to 6**

3 tablespoons olive oil
½ pound pancetta, diced
3 eggs
½ cup (2 ounces) grated pecorino
    cheese

1 pound spaghetti
Salt
Freshly ground pepper

1. In a small skillet over medium heat, heat olive oil. Lightly sauté pancetta but do not brown.
2. In a small bowl, whisk together the eggs and ¼ cup grated cheese.
3. Cook the spaghetti in boiling salted water until al dente. Drain thoroughly.
4. Place spaghetti in a heated serving bowl. Toss well with the pancetta and a little oil from pan. (Fresh pasta absorbs liquid more quickly than packaged pasta; with fresh pasta you may need to add a bit more oil.) Quickly add the whisked eggs, salt and lots of pepper. Again, toss well to coat spaghetti with sauce.

5. Serve immediately. Pass the remaining grated cheese in a separate bowl.

To Prepare in Advance: Do not prepare in advance.

Freezing Instructions: Do not freeze.

Suggested Wine:
Italian: FIORANO, a red wine, similar to French Bordeaux
American: Mondavi CABERNET SAUVIGNON

SPAGHETTI WITH BACON AND RAW EGG
Spaghetti alla Carbonara

Serves 4 to 6

½ pound bacon	1 pound spaghetti
6 tablespoons heavy cream	1 tablespoon unsalted butter
2 egg yolks	Salt
1 whole egg	Freshly ground pepper
½ cup (2 ounces) grated Parmesan cheese	

1. Blanch bacon by placing in simmering water for 1 to 2 minutes (this removes the smoked flavor and saltiness). Drain and dry.
2. Cut blanched bacon into small dice. In a small skillet, over medium heat, sauté until crisp. Drain. Add cream and keep warm.
3. In a small bowl, whisk together the egg yolks, whole egg and 5 tablespoons grated cheese.
4. Cook spaghetti in boiling salted water until al dente. Drain well.
5. Pour spaghetti into a heated large serving bowl. Toss with egg mixture, bacon mixture and butter until well coated. Season with salt and pepper to taste.
6. Serve immediately. Pass the remaining grated cheese in a separate bowl.

To Prepare in Advance: Do not prepare in advance.

Freezing Instructions: Do not freeze.

Suggested Wine:
Italian: FIORANO, a red wine similar to French Bordeaux
American: Mondavi CABERNET SAUVIGNON

STRAW AND HAY WITH FRESH VEGETABLES
Paglia e Fieno alla Primavera

Straw and hay refers to the colorful combination of green and yellow noodles. They are usually combined with prosciutto and peas in a cream sauce. This is a variation, using fresh vegetables. **Serves 4 to 6**

¾ cup (1½ sticks) unsalted butter
¼ cup plus 2 tablespoons olive oil
1 small onion, diced
1 medium carrot, peeled and diced
1½ to 2 cups small broccoli florets
1 medium zucchini, trimmed and diced
6 medium mushrooms, diced

1 garlic clove, minced
½ pound Green Spinach Pasta (see page 77)
½ pound Yellow Egg Pasta (see page 75)
1 cup heavy cream
Freshly ground pepper
Grated Parmesan cheese

1. In a large sauté pan, melt 6 tablespoons butter with ¼ cup olive oil. Over medium heat, sauté the onion and carrot for 3 to 4 minutes.
2. Add the broccoli, zucchini and mushrooms and sauté until just tender, 3 to 4 minutes longer. Add garlic and stir.
3. In a large pot, bring 4 quarts salted water to a boil with remaining 2 tablespoons olive oil. Stir in green and yellow pasta and cook until al dente.
4. Drain pasta and return to pot. Add vegetables and stir in remaining 6 tablespoons butter and heavy cream. Season with pepper to taste. Cook and toss until heated through.
5. Serve immediately. Pass grated cheese in a separate bowl.

To Prepare in Advance: Through #2.

Freezing Instructions: Do not freeze.

Suggested Wine:
Italian: TOCAI FRIULANO, a white wine from Friuli-Venezia Giulia
American: Parducci CHARDONNAY

SPINACH DUMPLINGS Gnocchi di Spinaci

This peasant dish is from Trentino-Alto Adige and reflects its Austrian neighbor's influence. The dumplings can be prepared the day before and baked with sauce when ready to serve. **Serves 6 (18 dumplings)**

1 pound fresh spinach, washed and stemmed *or* 1 10-ounce package frozen spinach

4 slices (1½ ounces) Italian or French bread
1 tablespoon olive oil

1	small onion, chopped fine	Freshly ground pepper
1	garlic clove	1½ cups Tomato Sauce (see pages
½	cup fresh breadcrumbs	60 or 61)
¾	cup (3 ounces) grated Parmesan	2 tablespoons unsalted butter
	cheese	Freshly ground pepper
2	eggs, lightly beaten	1½ cups Tomato Sauce (see pages
¼	cup chopped parsley	60 or 61)
6	fresh basil leaves, chopped fine	2 tablespoons unsalted butter
	Salt	

1. In a covered saucepan, cook spinach in water that clings to the leaves just until wilted, about 5 minutes. Drain, squeezing out as much water as possible. Reserve.

2. Soak the bread in warm water. Squeeze dry. Reserve.

3. In a small skillet, heat oil. Over medium heat, sauté onion and garlic until golden, about 5 minutes.

4. In a food processor fitted with steel blade, combine reserved spinach, bread, sautéed onion and garlic. Process with on/off turns until chopped fine (or chop with heavy knife or mezzaluna). Transfer to a medium mixing bowl and cool slightly.

5. Stir in the breadcrumbs, ½ cup grated cheese, eggs, chopped parsley and chopped basil, mixing with your hands to combine thoroughly. Season with salt and pepper to taste.

6. With moistened hands, shape the spinach mixture into 18 round or oval dumplings, about 1½ inches in diameter.

7. Preheat oven to 350°F. Grease an 8 × 11-inch baking dish.

8. In a large saucepan, bring 3 quarts salted water to a boil. Add the dumplings, a few at a time, and lower heat so that water simmers gently. When dumplings rise to the surface, about 2 minutes, they are cooked. Remove with a slotted spoon and drain on paper towels.

9. Arrange dumplings in prepared baking dish. Heat tomato sauce and pour over dumplings. Sprinkle with remaining ¼ cup grated cheese and dot with butter.

10. Bake 15 to 20 minutes. Serve immediately.

To Prepare in Advance: Through #8.

Freezing Instructions: Through #8. Defrost in refrigerator.

SEMOLINA GNOCCHI Gnocchi di Semolina

Gnocchi date back to the 12th century. During the Renaissance, gnocchi were made from bread, water and flour; in some parts of Italy they are still prepared that way. They can be made with a mixture of mashed potatoes and flour or with only flour. They can be served with cream, melted butter and grated cheese; with butter, cinnamon and sugar; or with butter, sage and grated cheese. This is my favorite. **Serves 6 to 8**

4½ cups milk	¾ cup (1½ sticks), unsalted butter,
¼ teaspoon salt	cut into small pieces
Freshly ground white pepper	1 cup (4 ounces) grated Parmesan
Pinch of freshly grated nutmeg	cheese
1½ cups imported semolina (not	2 egg yolks
quick-cooking farina)	1 cup heavy cream

1. In a 4-quart saucepan, over medium heat, bring milk to boil with salt, pepper and nutmeg. Pour in semolina in a slow, steady stream, stirring constantly with a wooden spoon to prevent lumps from forming.

2. Over low heat, cook 6 to 8 minutes, stirring occasionally, until very thick and smooth.

3. Remove from heat. Stir in 10 tablespoons butter (1 stick plus 2 tablespoons), then ¾ cup grated cheese and finally the egg yolks. Combine thoroughly.

4. Butter a jelly roll pan or baking sheet, approximately 11 × 13 inches, and sprinkle with water, pouring off the excess. Turn out semolina mixture onto the pan, spreading with a moistened spatula to a thickness of about ½ inch. Let cool. (Or mixture can be turned out onto a flat Formica surface; proceed as above.)

5. Preheat oven to 375°F. Butter a 13 × 9 × 2-inch baking dish (or use individual casseroles if desired).

6. With a cookie cutter moistened in cold water, cut semolina mixture into 1½- to 1¾-inch circles and arrange in prepared baking dish in overlapping layers.

7. As circles are cut out, reshape remaining dough into a ½-inch-thick rectangle and continue above procedure until all the dough has been used.

8. Dot each layer with remaining butter and sprinkle with remaining ¼ cup grated cheese.

9. Bake 25 to 30 minutes, until lightly golden.

10. In a small saucepan, reduce cream until slightly thickened. Pour over gnocchi and serve immediately.

To Prepare in Advance: Through #8.

Freezing Instructions: Do not freeze.

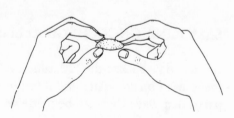

Variation: Cut the cylinders into 1½-inch pieces and pinch the ends together.

Variation: After step #3, let semolina mixture cool slightly. Roll out into cylinders ½ inch in diameter. Cut into 1½-inch pieces and pinch the ends together. Cook in boiling salted water until the gnocchi rise to the surface, 3 to 5 minutes. Drain and arrange in buttered baking dish. Dot with butter and sprinkle with grated Parmesan cheese. Bake until cheese melts and the gnocchi are hot. Or pour tomato sauce of your choice over and bake until hot. Serve with grated cheese passed in a separate bowl.

Suggested Wine:
Italian: GAVI, a dry white wine from the Piedmont
American: SAUVIGNON BLANC

POTATO AND SPINACH GNOCCHI WITH GORGONZOLA BUTTER
Gnocchi alla Gorgonzola

The sharpness of gorgonzola cheese makes the sauce for these gnocchi particularly interesting. In Liguria, potato and spinach gnocchi are served with a pesto sauce. **Serves 6 to 8**

2	pounds baking potatoes, peeled and cubed	2	eggs, lightly beaten
1½	cups all-purpose flour		Salt
½	package (5 ounces) frozen spinach, cooked, drained and chopped fine *or* ⅔ cup cooked fresh spinach, chopped fine		Freshly ground pepper
		2	tablespoons unsalted butter
		½	pound gorgonzola cheese, cut into small pieces
			About ½ cup heavy cream

1. In a 4-quart saucepan, cook potatoes in boiling salted water to cover until tender. Drain, cool and mash potatoes.
2. On a lightly floured board, combine mashed potatoes, flour, chopped spinach, eggs and salt and pepper to taste. Mix well.
3. To make the gnocchi, shape dough into cylinders ½ inch in diameter. Cut into 1½-inch lengths and pinch each end together.
4. Preheat oven to 350°F. Butter a 13 × 9 × 2-inch baking dish (or use individual casseroles, if desired).
5. Bring 2 quarts of salted water to a boil. Add a handful of gnocchi at a time. When the gnocchi rise to the surface, they are cooked. Remove with slotted spoon.

6. In a small skillet or saucepan, over medium heat, melt butter. Stir in gorgonzola cheese until combined. Add just enough cream to make a smooth sauce. Keep warm.
7. Arrange gnocchi in baking dish and cover with sauce. Bake 10 to 15 minutes, or until heated through.
8. Serve immediately.

To Prepare in Advance: Through #6.

Freezing Instructions: Through #3, adding a bit more flour for a firmer dough. Or, through #5. Defrost in refrigerator and continue with recipe.

Suggested Wine:
Italian: FIROANO BIANCO, a dry white wine from the Latium
American: BONE DRY RIESLING

POLENTA

Polenta can be served with cheese or with a meat sauce. When accompanying roasted meat, the pan juices can be poured over the polenta. **Serves 6 to 8**

6 cups water *or* 3 cups water and 3 cups milk	½ cup (2 ounces) grated fontina cheese
2 tablespoons olive oil	Salt
1 teaspoon salt	Freshly ground pepper
2 cups yellow cornmeal	Freshly grated nutmeg
10 tablespoons (1 stick plus 2 tablespoons) unsalted butter, softened	Grated Parmesan cheese, optional

1. In a 4-quart saucepan, bring water, olive oil and salt to a boil. Slowly pour in cornmeal, stirring occasionally to prevent lumps from forming.
2. Turn heat to very low and cook about 20 minutes, stirring often. If polenta is cooking too quickly, place saucepan on flameproof pad.
3. Combine butter and fontina cheese, mashing well (a food processor can be used, if desired). Stir into cooked polenta until completely absorbed. Season with salt, pepper and nutmeg to taste.
4. Serve hot in soup bowls, passing grated Parmesan cheese, if desired.

To Prepare in Advance: Through #2, 30 minutes before ready to serve. Keep saucepan on flameproof pad over low heat, stirring occasionally.

Freezing Instructions: Through #3. See variation, freezing in slices.

Variation: Prepare polenta through #3. Pour into a buttered 9 × 5 × 2-inch loaf pan and let cool. Refrigerate until firm. Turn out on flat surface and cut into 8 slices. Sauté slices in butter until golden on both sides. Sprinkle with grated Parmesan cheese and serve. Or serve with a favorite tomato sauce spooned over the slices.

POLENTA WITH RICOTTA Polenta con Ricotta

This is a delicious sauce to serve over sliced polenta. **Serves 8**

1 recipe Polenta (see page 98)	Salt
3 tablespoons unsalted butter	Freshly ground pepper
1 medium onion, chopped fine	¾ pound ricotta cheese
1 pound tomatoes, peeled, seeded and chopped	¼ cup (1 ounce) grated Parmesan cheese

1. Prepare polenta. Pour into loaf pan, cool and then slice.
2. Preheat oven to 375°F. Butter a 13 × 9 × 2-inch baking dish.
3. In a 10-inch skillet, melt butter. Over medium heat, sauté onion for 5 minutes. Stir in tomatoes and continue to cook about 5 minutes longer, or until sauce thickens slightly. Season with salt and pepper to taste.
4. In a small bowl, combine ricotta and Parmesan cheeses. Season lightly with salt and pepper.
5. Pour a small amount of tomato sauce onto the bottom of the prepared baking dish. Arrange 4 slices of polenta in dish, spoon half the remaining sauce over the slices and top with half the ricotta cheese mixture. Continue with remaining 4 slices of polenta, sauce and finally the ricotta mixture.
6. Bake until heated through, 25 to 30 minutes. Serve immediately.

To Prepare in Advance: Through #5.

Freezing Instructions: Through #3. Warm sauce over low heat and continue with recipe.

RISOTTO MILANESE Risotto alla Milanese

Risotto should be creamy and slightly al dente, and in Italy it is eaten with a spoon. Though saffron is an expensive spice, it is used sparingly and a few threads go a long way. If you do not want to use saffron, try a pinch or two of red pepper flakes for color and taste. **Serves 4 to 6**

¼ cup (½ stick) unsalted butter
1 tablespoon olive oil
¼ cup minced onion
¼ cup dry white wine
1 cup Arborio rice
3½ cups heated Chicken Broth (see page 48)

⅛ teaspoon saffron
¼ cup (1 ounce) grated Parmesan cheese
Salt
Freshly ground pepper

1. In a 4-quart saucepan, melt 2 tablespoons butter with the olive oil. Sauté onion over medium heat until translucent, about 5 minutes. Add wine and cook over low heat until all moisture is evaporated.
2. Add rice gradually and stir over low heat for 2 or 3 minutes to coat. Pour in the broth one third at a time, allowing broth to absorb into the rice after each addition. Stir occasionally. Dissolve the saffron in the last addition of broth.
3. After all the broth has been absorbed, taste to see that the rice is creamy yet slightly firm. Stir in the remaining 2 tablespoons butter and the grated cheese. Season with salt and pepper to taste.
4. Serve immediately.

To Prepare in Advance: Through #2, cooking half the amount of time.

Freezing Instructions: Do not freeze.

Suggested Wine:
Italian: Old BARBARESCO, a fruity red wine from the Piedmont
American: Old Louis Martini CABERNET

RISOTTO WITH ASPARAGUS Risotto con Asparagi

From Lombardy. **Serves 8 to 10**

6 tablespoons unsalted butter
3 tablespoons cooking oil
½ medium onion, chopped fine
2 pounds asparagus, peeled and cut into ½-inch pieces (discard hard bottoms)
2 cups (1¼ pounds) Arborio rice

Salt
Freshly ground pepper
6 cups heated Chicken Broth (see page 48)
¼ cup (1 ounce) grated Parmesan or Romano cheese

1. In a 4-quart saucepan, melt 3 tablespoons butter with oil. Over medium heat, sauté onion until golden, about 5 minutes.
2. Add asparagus and cook, stirring, for 2 to 3 minutes.

3. Gradually stir in rice, coating well with butter. Season lightly with salt and pepper.

4. Lower heat and pour in 2 cups broth. Stir occasionally. When broth has been absorbed, stir in 2 more cups. Repeat procedure with remaining 2 cups of broth.

5. After all the broth has been absorbed, taste to see that rice is creamy yet slightly firm. Stir in remaining 3 tablespoons butter and grated cheese. Correct seasoning to taste.

6. Serve immediately.

To Prepare in Advance: Through #2 or #3.

Freezing Instructions: Do not freeze.

Suggested Wine:
Italian: PINOT BIANCO, a dry white wine from Lombardy
American: FRENCH COLOMBARD

RISOTTO WITH MUSHROOMS Risotto con Funghi

From the Tuscan region. Wild mushrooms can be used to enhance the flavor of the rice. **Serves 8 to 10**

½	cup (1 stick) unsalted butter	2	garlic cloves, minced
½	medium onion, chopped fine	½	pound mushrooms, sliced
2	cups (1¼ pounds) Arborio rice	3	tablespoons chopped parsley
	Salt	¼	cup (1 ounce) grated Parmesan
	Freshly ground white pepper		or Romano cheese
5	to 6 cups heated Chicken Broth (see page 48)		

1. In a 4-quart heavy saucepan, melt 4 tablespoons butter. Over medium heat, sauté onion until golden, about 5 minutes. Stir in rice, coating well with butter. Season lightly with salt and pepper.

2. Lower heat and stir in 2 cups of broth. Stir occasionally. When broth has been absorbed, stir in 2 more cups. Repeat procedure with remaining 1 to 2 cups of broth until rice is creamy yet slightly firm.

3. In a 10-inch skillet, melt 2 tablespoons butter. Over medium heat, sauté garlic for 1 to 2 minutes. Add sliced mushrooms and continue to sauté 10 to 15 minutes longer, or until most of the moisture has evaporated. Season lightly with salt and pepper.

4. When rice is tender, stir in sautéed mushrooms, remaining 2 tablespoons butter and grated cheese. Correct seasoning to taste.

RISOTTO WITH MUSHROOMS, continued

5. Serve immediately.

To Prepare in Advance: Through #2, keeping rice warm.

Freezing Instructions: Do not freeze.

Suggested Wine:
Italian: DOLCETTO D'ALBA, a dry red wine from the Piedmont
American: ACACIA PINOT NOIR

Seafood

Fish, almost as popular as veal, is even more available in Italy since no town is very far from the sea, a river or a lake. Fish markets display the catches of the day in overflowing baskets, tempting passersby.

There is no substitute for fresh fish. Look for bright eyes, red rather than dark-colored gills, and firm scales. There should never be a strong fishy odor.

Ideally, fish should be eaten the day of purchase, but when that is not possible, it is important to store it properly. To store, place fish on a dish and cover with ice cubes and a damp cloth. Then refrigerate.

Shellfish, such as clams, crabs and lobsters, should be live when cooked.

BAKED SWORDFISH Pesce Spada al Forno

Swordfish is a Mediterranean staple. The texture is firm, the flesh fat and white and the meat tasty. If swordfish is not available, fresh light tuna can be used. **Serves 4**

2 pounds baking potatoes, peeled	2 garlic cloves, mashed
¾ pound onions	2 tablespoons chopped parsley
Salt	½ pound tomatoes, peeled, seeded
Freshly ground pepper	and chopped
½ teaspoon Italian Seasoning (see page 12)	1 cup dry white wine
	¼ cup olive oil
2 pounds swordfish, cut into 4 8-ounce portions	¼ cup cooking oil

1. Preheat oven to 375°F.
2. Cut potatoes and onions into very thin slices using a sharp knife or mandoline.
3. Butter a 13 × 9 × 2-inch baking dish. Arrange half the sliced potatoes in a layer in the prepared dish. Top with a layer of half the onions. Sprinkle with salt, pepper and ¼ teaspoon Italian Seasoning.
4. Arrange the fish on the onions and sprinkle with salt, pepper, garlic and parsley. Top with tomatoes.
5. Add a layer of the remaining onion slices and finish with the remaining potatoes. Pour wine, olive oil and cooking oil over. Again, season with salt, pepper and remaining ¼ teaspoon Italian Seasoning.
6. Bake 50 to 60 minutes, or until potatoes are tender and lightly browned.
7. To serve, divide onions and potatoes among 4 plates, top with a slice of fish and pour sauce over.

To Prepare in Advance: Through #5.

Freezing Instructions: Do not freeze.

Suggested Wine:
Italian: RAPITALÀ, a dry white wine from Sicily
American: Sterling SAUVIGNON BLANC

GRILLED SWORDFISH STEAKS
Pesce Spada alla Griglia

A simple and delicious fish preparation. The sauce can be spooned over most any grilled fish. **Serves 4**

1½ pounds swordfish, cut into 4 ½-inch-thick steaks	2 tablespoons olive oil
Salt	Juice of 1 medium lemon
Freshly ground pepper	2 tablespoons chopped parsley
2 tablespoons unsalted butter	1 teaspoon capers, drained

1. Preheat grill.
2. Season swordfish steaks with salt and pepper to taste.
3. Grill swordfish until firm to the touch, about 3 minutes on each side.
4. Meanwhile, combine remaining ingredients in a small saucepan and heat through.
5. To serve, place 1 steak on each plate and pour sauce over. Serve immediately.

To Prepare in Advance: Do not prepare in advance.

Freezing Instructions: Do not freeze.

Variation: For a vinegar sauce, heat 2 tablespoons unsalted butter, 2 tablespoons vinegar and ¼ cup Brown Stock (see page 49).

Suggested Wine:
Italian: RAPITALÀ, a dry white wine from Sicily
American: Sterling SAUVIGNON BLANC

PAN-FRIED TROUT Trota in Padella

Trout is plentiful in the lakes and rivers of northern Italy. Trout can be fried, grilled or poached. **Serves 4**

2 tablespoons olive oil	Freshly ground pepper
1 garlic clove, minced	4 whole trout, 6 ounces each, boned
3 tablespoons chopped parsley	
1 pound tomatoes, peeled, seeded and chopped	6 tablespoons cooking oil
Salt	Chopped parsley, optional

PAN-FRIED TROUT, continued

1. In a medium skillet, heat olive oil. Over medium heat, sauté garlic and parsley 2 to 3 minutes.
2. Stir in tomatoes and cook 15 minutes. Season with salt and pepper to taste. Keep warm.
3. Season trout lightly with salt and pepper. In a 12-inch skillet, heat the cooking oil. Arrange trout in pan and, over high heat, cook 5 minutes on one side. Turn and cook 4 minutes longer.
4. To serve, place trout on plate and spoon sauce over. Sprinkle with additional chopped parsley, if desired.

To Prepare in Advance: Through #2.

Freezing Instructions: Through #2. Warm over low heat and continue with recipe.

Suggested Wine:
Italian: BARDOLINO, a light-bodied red wine from Verona
American: Light PINOT NOIR

TROUT WITH BASIL SAUCE Trota in Basilico

Here trout is poached in the oven and served with a basil sauce. This is a useful technique when you want to poach slices of fish for a large group.
Serves 6

½ cup parsley leaves
1 small bunch fresh basil, leaves only
1 cup (2 sticks) unsalted butter, cut into small pieces
6 trout, 6 ounces each, boned, skinned and halved
Salt

Freshly ground pepper
¼ cup Fish Broth (see page 50)
¾ cup dry white wine or white vermouth
1 shallot, chopped
¼ cup heavy cream
Juice of ½ medium lemon
Fresh basil leaves for garnish

1. Preheat oven to 375°F. Butter a 12 × 16-inch baking pan.
2. In a food processor fitted with steel blade, or in blender, purée parsley and basil. Add the butter and process until herbs and butter are well blended. Reserve.
3. Arrange the fish filets, skinned side down, in the prepared baking pan. Season with salt and pepper. Heat fish broth and ¼ cup wine. Pour over trout and bake 5 to 6 minutes. Transfer fish to a platter and keep warm.
4. Meanwhile, in a small saucepan, combine the chopped shallot, the re-

maining ½ cup wine and cream. Over high heat reduce until ¼ cup remains. Over very low heat, whisk in the basil butter, a small amount at a time. Strain and season to taste with salt, pepper and lemon juice.

5. To serve, arrange 2 filets on each plate. Ladle sauce over filets and garnish with basil leaves.

To Prepare in Advance: Through #2.

Freezing Instructions: Through #2. Defrost in refrigerator.

Suggested Wine:
Italian: TOCAI FRIULANO, a white wine from Friuli-Venezia Giulia
American: Parducci CHARDONNAY

STRIPED BASS WITH FENNEL SEED
Spigola Arrosta con "Finocchiella"

An elegant company dish from the kitchens of the Hotel Hassler in Rome. The managing director was kind enough to give me the recipe after I had dined there the evening before. *Spigola*, one of the most flavorful fish in the Mediterranean, is best roasted or grilled. The potatoes need not be peeled, but do scrub them well. **Serves 6**

1	whole striped bass, 6 to 7 pounds	1	teaspoon fresh rosemary leaves, chopped
	Salt	4	tablespoons chopped parsley
	Freshly ground pepper	¼	cup cooking oil
¼	small onion	¼	cup dry white wine or white vermouth
2	garlic cloves		
1	small celery stalk, strings removed	4	medium lemons
½	small carrot, peeled	6	tablespoons unsalted butter, cut into small pieces
2	tablespoons fennel seed	12	small whole new potatoes, steamed
1	bay leaf		

1. Preheat oven to 375°F.
2. Rinse bass and dry thoroughly. With a sharp knife, make a small slit down the side of the fish, opening the fish slightly. Season lightly with salt and pepper.
3. Finely chop onion, 1 garlic clove, celery and carrot. Combine with 1 tablespoon fennel seed, bay leaf, rosemary and 2 tablespoons chopped parsley. Season with salt and pepper and stuff mixture inside fish.
4. In a shallow roasting pan large enough to hold fish, heat oil. Carefully lay fish in pan and brown over high heat, about 2 minutes per side.

5. Transfer to oven, pour wine over and cover pan with aluminum foil. Roast 15 to 20 minutes, basting occasionally, until fish flakes when lightly pressed with fork. Transfer fish to a warm serving platter. Strain fish liquid and juice of 2 lemons into small saucepan.

6. Over medium heat, stir in remaining garlic clove, chopped fine, 1 tablespoon fennel seed and 2 tablespoons chopped parsley. Whisk in the butter. Correct seasoning to taste.

7. Pour sauce over fish and surround with steamed potatoes. Cut remaining 2 lemons into quarters and arrange on platter. Serve immediately.

To Prepare in Advance: Through #3.

Freezing Instructions: Do not freeze.

Suggested Wine:
Italian: GAVI, a dry white wine from the Piedmont
American: CHABLIS

SEA BASS OR TURBOT WITH BUTTER AND PARSLEY
Branzino in Burro e Prezzemolo

Sea bass is at its best sautéed and then served with a simple sauce. This is from Emilia-Romagna. **Serves 4**

2 eggs, beaten	3 tablespoons cooking oil
¼ cup all-purpose flour	Salt
1½ pounds sea bass or turbot filets, cut into 4 ½-inch-thick portions	Freshly ground pepper
	3 tablespoons unsalted butter
	2 tablespoons chopped parsley

1. Place eggs and flour in separate bowls. Dip each piece of fish into the beaten eggs first and then lightly dredge with flour. Refrigerate for 20 minutes (this helps coating to adhere better).

2. In a 10-inch skillet, heat the oil. Arrange fish in pan, skin side up. Over medium heat, sauté 2 minutes, turn and sauté the other side; fish will be golden brown.

3. Transfer fish to warm platter. Season with salt and pepper to taste. Keep warm.

4. Discard grease and wipe skillet. Melt butter and stir in the chopped parsley. Pour over fish and serve immediately.

To Prepare in Advance: Through #1.

Freezing Instructions: Do not freeze.

Suggested Wine:
Italian: SOAVE, a dry white wine from Verona
American: Mirassou WHITE BURGUNDY

SOLE FILETS WITH VINEGAR SAUCE
Sfogi in Saor

A Venetian specialty. The sauce can be served over any grilled fish. **Serves 6**

½	cup cooking oil		Pinch of salt
1½	pounds onions, chopped fine		Freshly ground white pepper
2	cups dry white wine	1	bay leaf
1	cup white wine vinegar	2¼	pounds sole filets, cut into 12
¼	cup white raisins		filets
3	tablespoons pine nuts		Flour

1. In a medium saucepan, heat ¼ cup oil. Over medium heat, sauté onions until golden, 8 to 10 minutes. Add the remaining ingredients except the sole filets and flour and cook for 15 minutes. Correct seasoning to taste. Remove bay leaf. Keep warm.
2. Dust fish filets with flour. Season lightly with salt and pepper.
3. In one or two skillets large enough to hold fish in a single layer, heat remaining ¼ cup oil. Over medium heat, sauté fish until golden, about 2 minutes per side. Let rest 2 to 3 minutes.
4. To serve, place 2 filets on each plate and spoon sauce over.

To Prepare in Advance: Through #2, reheating sauce when needed.

Freezing Instructions: Do not freeze.

Suggested Wine:
Italian: CORVO PRIMA GOCCIA, a straw-colored wine from Sicily
American: SAUVIGNON BLANC

STEAMED MUSSELS Cozze a Vapore

This Tuscan specialty consists of steamed mussels with their broth. Clams can be substituted for the mussels. **Serves 6**

4 pounds mussels	½ teaspoon red pepper flakes
½ cup olive oil	Salt
½ small onion, minced	1 cup dry white wine
2 garlic cloves, minced	Bread for dipping
3 tablespoons chopped parsley	

1. Scrub each mussel well, discarding shells that are broken or that do not close when tapped. Remove beards and soak in cold water to cover 2 to 3 hours. Drain.
2. In a pan large enough to hold the mussels, heat oil. Over medium heat, sauté onion and garlic until golden, about 5 minutes. Stir in the parsley, pepper and season lightly with salt.
3. Add the drained mussels and the wine. Bring liquid to a boil, cover pan, and cook over low heat until mussels open, about 5 minutes.
4. Serve immediately in warm bowls. Pour liquid over and serve with slices of bread that can be dipped into the sauce.

To Prepare in Advance: Do not prepare in advance.

Freezing Instructions: Do not freeze.

Suggested Wine:
Italian: PINOT BIANCO, a dry white wine from Lombardy
American: PINOT BLANC

SCAMPI ALLA CARLINA

This recipe comes from the kitchen of the Hotel Hassler in Rome. Shrimp, as well as other shellfish, must be cooked quickly. If overcooked, they will be tough and stringy. Have all other ingredients ready for use. Perfect for this dish is the Santa Barbara shrimp, or you can use any large shrimp. **Serves 4**

2 pounds large shrimp, shelled and deveined	3 tablespoons capers, drained
All-purpose flour	½ medium tomato, peeled, seeded and chopped fine
Salt	¼ cup clarified unsalted butter, melted and kept warm
⅓ cup cooking oil	

1. Dust shrimp lightly with flour, shaking off any excess. Season with salt to taste.

2. In 2 12-inch skillets, heat oil. Carefully arrange shrimp in skillets in one layer (do not crowd). Over high heat, sauté shrimp until golden, about 3 minutes per side. Drain on paper towels.

3. To serve, arrange shrimp on plate, sprinkle with capers and tomatoes and pour the warm melted butter over. Serve immediately.

To Prepare in Advance: Through #1.

Freezing Instructions: Do not freeze.

Suggested Wine:
Italian: VERDICCHIO, a dry white wine from the Marche
American: Biander SAUVIGNON BLANC

STEAMED SHRIMP WITH ZABAGLIONE SAUCE
Gamberi Gratinati allo Zabaione

Steaming and a zabaglione sauce, both common in Italian cooking, are combined to make a unique dish. The sauce, made without the shrimp shells, is excellent on grilled or broiled chicken breasts. **Serves 6**

36 large unshelled shrimp with heads	4 whole cloves
¼ cup (½ stick) unsalted butter	6 whole peppercorns
1 medium carrot, peeled and diced	2 cups dry white wine
1 medium onion, diced	½ cup brandy
3 celery stalks, strings removed, diced	Salt
1 garlic clove, diced	2 teaspoons tomato paste
2 sprigs each fresh thyme, tarragon, parsley and chervil, tied together	2 cups cold water
	4 egg yolks
	½ cup dry red wine
	6 sprigs fresh thyme for garnish

1. Preheat oven to 450°F.

2. Shell and devein shrimp and remove heads. Reserve shrimp.

3. In a large ovenproof pan, melt the butter. Stir in shrimp shells and heads and place in oven until they begin to turn pink, 4 to 5 minutes.

4. Remove to stove top. Stir in vegetables, garlic, herbs, cloves and peppercorns. Pour in white wine and brandy and cook over high heat until almost

all the liquid is evaporated, 22 to 25 minutes. Season to taste with salt.

5. Dissolve tomato paste in the cold water and pour into pan. Bring to a boil and cook over medium-high heat until 1 cup liquid remains, 15 to 20 minutes. Strain and reserve.

6. To make the zabaglione, in a large stainless steel or copper mixing bowl, combine egg yolks and red wine, using a wire whisk. Set the bowl over hot but *not* boiling water and whisk until mixture begins to thicken, about 10 minutes. Slowly whisk reserved sauce into zabaglione and whisk until mixture thickens again.

7. Steam the shrimp over boiling water for 4 minutes.

8. Arrange 6 shrimp on each of 6 ovenproof dishes. Spoon sauce evenly over shrimp.

9. Place under broiler to glaze, 2 to 3 minutes; watch carefully so that sauce does not burn.

10. Garnish each dish with 1 sprig of thyme and serve immediately.

To Prepare in Advance: Through #5.

Freezing Instructions: Do not freeze.

Suggested Wine:
Italian: LA CRIMA CRISTIA, a sweet sparkling wine from the Piedmont
American: CHABLIS

Meat

Because the quality of the meat in most of Italy is good, the preparation is usually very simple. Roasting, grilling and sautéing are the most popular methods of cooking meat. The seasoning is usually very simple as well—herbs, butter, a trace of garlic, a light sauce.

BRAISED LAMB Stufato d'Agnello

This peasant dish is surprisingly elegant and a wonderfully different way to serve lamb. The chops must be at least ½ pound each for best results; if too thin, the cooked chop will be dry and have little flavor. **Serves 4**

2	tablespoons cooking oil		Freshly ground pepper
4	shoulder lamb chops, about ½ pound each (see Note)	2	eggs
1	cup dry white wine		Juice of ½ medium lemon
1½	cups Brown Stock (see page 49)	⅔	cup (about 3 ounces) grated Parmesan cheese
	Salt		Chopped parsley

1. Heat oil in a 12- or 14-inch skillet. Over high heat, brown the chops on each side, about 5 minutes. Remove chops from skillet and discard grease.

2. Pour in wine and cook until reduced to a glaze. Return chops to skillet.

3. Lower heat, add stock and season with salt and pepper to taste. Partly cover skillet and cook 40 to 45 minutes, or until chops are tender; if sauce reduces too much, add small amounts of water as necessary.

4. In a small bowl, whisk together eggs and lemon juice. Have grated cheese in a separate small bowl.

5. Remove chops from skillet and dry on paper towels. Immediately dip both sides in egg mixture and then coat with cheese. (The heat from the warm chops will cook the egg.)

6. Sprinkle with parsley and serve immediately.

To Prepare in Advance: Through #3, cooking 20 minutes. When continuing, cooking time may be reduced 5 to 10 minutes.

Freezing Instructions: Through #3. Defrost overnight in refrigerator. Reheat in preheated 350°F oven about 15 minutes.

Suggested Wine:
Italian: BARBERA, a dry red wine
American: Monteviña BARBERA

Note: Loin lamb chops may be grilled or sautéed, dried on paper towels and then coated with the egg and cheese.

ROAST LEG OF LAMB
Cosciotto d'Agnello Arrosto

Rosemary is a preferred seasoning for the Italians, especially on roasted lamb. It is a very pungent herb and must be used sparingly. Spring lamb is always a treat and young lamb the most delicate. Cooking lamb to medium rare (pink) will give you tender, juicy meat. **Serves 8**

1 leg of lamb, with bone, 6 to 7 pounds	Leaves from 1 sprig fresh rosemary, chopped
Salt	Leaves from 1 sprig fresh mint
Freshly ground pepper	1 to 2 cups dry white wine
¼ cup olive oil	2 baking potatoes, about 1½ pounds total
2 garlic cloves, mashed	Mint leaves for garnish

1. Preheat oven to 450°F.
2. Season lamb with salt and pepper to taste and rub surface of meat with 2 tablespoons olive oil. Sprinkle with garlic, rosemary and mint.
3. Set lamb on rack in roasting pan and roast 20 minutes, turning to brown all sides.
4. Lower heat to 350°F and baste lamb with 1 cup wine. Pour in additional wine as liquid evaporates and baste lamb every 15 minutes. Total cooking time is 1 hour for medium rare, or until meat thermometer registers 130°F.
5. Meanwhile, scrub potatoes, but do not peel. Cut into ⅛-inch slices and coat very lightly with remaining 2 tablespoons oil. Season with salt and pepper to taste. Arrange on baking sheets in one layer.
6. About 15 minutes before roast is done, place potatoes in oven. Bake until golden brown on one side, about 15 minutes, then turn and brown on other side.
7. Remove meat from oven and let rest 15 minutes before slicing.
8. To serve, arrange slices of meat on platter, garnish with mint leaves and surround with the potato slices.

To Prepare in Advance: Through #3. You can also prepare potatoes in #5.

Freezing Instructions: Through #4. Defrost overnight in refrigerator, slice meat and serve at room temperature.

Suggested Wine:
Italian: CAREMA, a medium-bodied red wine from the Piedmont
American: Acacia PINOT NOIR

CALVES' LIVER VENETIAN STYLE
Fegato alla Veneziana

Though found all through Italy, this is notably a Venetian dish. To be enjoyed, liver must be perfectly cooked and should be served pink. Because the liver is cut into thin strips, it is cooked about 2 minutes, no longer. **Serves 2 or 3**

3 tablespoons olive oil
2 tablespoons unsalted butter
2 large onions, thinly sliced
1 pound calves' liver, membranes removed

Salt (see Note)
Freshly ground pepper
1 to 2 tablespoons chopped parsley

1. In a 10- or 12-inch skillet, heat oil and butter. Over medium heat, sauté onions until golden, 8 to 10 minutes.
2. Meanwhile, cut liver into ¼-inch strips. Add to onions, turn heat to high and cook about 2 minutes, stirring so that liver cooks evenly; do not overcook. Season with salt and pepper to taste and sprinkle with parsley. Serve immediately.

To Prepare in Advance: Through #1.

Freezing Instructions: Do not freeze.

Suggested Wine:
Italian: CARMIGNANO, a red wine, similar to Chianti, from Tuscany
American: Iron Horse PINOT NOIR

Note: If you prefer using less salt, season with fresh lemon juice to taste in step #2.

LIVER WITH SAGE
Fegato con Infusione di Salvia

On my last night in Milan, I had dinner at Da Franco, a *trattoria* on Via Fiori. It was memorable for many reasons, especially this rather simply prepared specialty. It was served with fresh sage, but dried leaf sage is one of the few herbs that retains its good flavor and can be used. **Serves 2**

1 pound calves' liver, cut into 2 portions
All-purpose flour
Salt
Freshly ground pepper

Large pinch of dried sage leaves
2 tablespoons unsalted butter
1 tablespoon olive oil
2 fresh sage leaves

1. Dust liver lightly with flour. Season with salt, pepper and dried sage.
2. In a heavy skillet, heat butter and oil. Over medium heat, sauté liver about 3 minutes on each side for medium rare.
3. Transfer liver to warm serving plate. Pour drippings over and top each piece with a fresh sage leaf. Serve immediately.

To Prepare in Advance: Through #1, refrigerating until needed.

Freezing Instructions: Do not freeze.

Suggested Wine:
Italian: CARMIGNANO, a red wine, similar to Chianti, from Tuscany
American: Iron Horse PINOT NOIR

GRILLED STEAK WITH PORCINI MUSHROOMS
Bistecca con Funghi Porcini

A recipe from Lombardy, the sauce can also be served over chicken or pasta. **Serves 4**

¼ cup (½ stick) unsalted butter
¾ pound porcini mushrooms, cut into ¼-inch-thick slices (see Note)
Salt
Freshly ground pepper
⅓ cup dry Marsala

½ cup Brown Stock (see page 49)
2 large red peppers, roasted (see page 34) and cut into ¼-inch strips
4 New York steaks, ½ pound each, about ½ inch thick
1 to 2 tablespoons cooking oil

1. Preheat grill or broiler.
2. In a heavy 10-inch skillet, melt 2 tablespoons butter. Over high heat, sauté the mushrooms until lightly browned, about 5 minutes. Season with salt and pepper to taste.
3. Deglaze pan with Marsala, pour in stock and cook over high heat until sauce thickens slightly, 4 to 5 minutes. Whisk in the remaining 2 tablespoons butter and stir in the roasted pepper strips. Correct seasoning to taste and keep warm.
4. Brush steaks with oil and season on both sides with salt and pepper to taste. Grill about 2 to 3 minutes per side for medium rare, or broil to desired degree of doneness.
5. Place 1 steak on each of 4 heated plates. Ladle sauce over, dividing mushrooms and peppers equally. Serve immediately.

GRILLED STEAK WITH PORCINI MUSHROOMS, continued

To Prepare in Advance: Through #2.

Freezing Instructions: Do not freeze.

Suggested Wine:
Italian: BARBARESCO, a red wine from the Piedmont
American: Stag's Leap CABERNET

Note: Three ounces dried porcini mushrooms can be substituted for fresh. Let soak in warm water to cover for 25 to 30 minutes. Drain thoroughly, cut into slices and continue with recipe.

STEAK FLORENTINE STYLE
Bistecca alla Fiorentina

The Chianina steer, raised in the province of Arezzo, provides the meat for Florentine steaks. This is *the* steak of Italy. It is basically a T-bone steak, weighing about one pound, and is served rare. However, any good cut of steak may be used. For a dinner party, a large entrecôte is most acceptable. **Serves 4 to 6**

1 entrecôte, about 2 pounds and 1½ inches thick Salt Freshly ground pepper ½ cup extra virgin olive oil	1 to 2 teaspoons fresh lemon juice 1 teaspoon minced fresh oregano leaves *or* a pinch of dried oregano

1. Preheat grill or broiler.
2. Season both sides of the steak with salt and pepper and brush with olive oil.
3. Cook 5 to 6 minutes per side for medium rare, or to desired degree of doneness.
4. Transfer meat to a carving board. Brush both sides generously with olive oil and drizzle with lemon juice to taste. Sprinkle steak lightly with oregano.
5. Cut meat diagonally into ⅜-inch slices. Serve immediately, spooning any collected juices over the top.

To Prepare in Advance: Through #2.

Freezing Instructions: Through #5, if you like cold steak. Defrost overnight in refrigerator.

Variations: 1. Use a flank steak, scored lightly on both sides. Cook 2 to 3 minutes per side. Cut diagonally into ½-inch slices to serve.
2. Roast a 2½- to 3-pound tenderloin of beef in a 425°F oven for 35 to 40 min-

utes or until medium rare. Allow the tenderloin to rest for 15 minutes before slicing and dressing with the olive oil, lemon juice and oregano. This will serve 6 to 8.

Suggested Wine:
Italian: CHIANTI, a light red wine from Tuscany
American: CARIGNANE

MEATBALLS Polpette

A very basic recipe. The meat can be shaped into large or small balls, as desired. **Serves 4 to 6**

½ pound ground beef, round or chuck	1 garlic clove, chopped fine
¼ pound ground veal	Salt
¼ pound ground pork	Freshly ground pepper
¼ cup fresh breadcrumbs	2 tablespoons cooking oil
3 tablespoons chopped parsley	½ medium onion, chopped
2 tablespoons grated Parmesan or Romano cheese	1 pound tomatoes, peeled, seeded and chopped
	½ cup Chicken Broth (see page 48)

1. In a mixing bowl, combine meat, breadcrumbs, parsley, cheese, garlic, salt and pepper. Mix well and with moistened hands form into small meatballs.
2. In a medium saucepan heat oil. Over medium heat, sauté onion for 3 to 4 minutes. Stir in tomatoes and cook a few minutes longer.
3. Pour in broth and season lightly with salt and pepper.
4. Add meatballs to pan, lower heat and cook 30 to 40 minutes, occasionally spooning sauce over the meatballs.
5. Serve immediately.

To Prepare in Advance: Through #4.

Freezing Instructions: Through #4. Defrost in refrigerator and warm over low heat.

Suggested Wine:
Italian: CHIANTI, a light red wine from Tuscany
American: CARIGNANE

PORK CHOPS WITH HORSERADISH SAUCE
Cotolette di Maiale al Rafano

From Alto Adige, this rib-sticking dish reflects the influence of its neighbor, Austria. **Serves 4**

4 pork chops, ½ pound each	½ cup (1 stick) unsalted butter
Salt	1 tablespoon red wine vinegar
Freshly ground pepper	1 cup Brown Stock (see page 49)
Flour	3 ounces peeled horseradish root,
2 eggs, lightly beaten	grated (¾ cup)
1 cup fresh breadcrumbs	Chopped parsley

1. Gently pound each pork chop with the flat side of a mallet to flatten slightly. Season with salt and pepper to taste.
2. Place flour, beaten eggs and breadcrumbs in separate dishes. Dust each chop with flour, shaking off any excess, dip in egg and then coat lightly with breadcrumbs. Refrigerate for 30 minutes so that mixture will adhere to chops.
3. In one skillet large enough to hold chops in a single layer, melt 5 tablespoons of the butter. Over medium heat, cook chops about 4 minutes on each side. Remove chops from skillet and keep warm while preparing sauce.
4. Discard grease from skillet. Deglaze pan with vinegar. Add stock and scrape up particles that stick to bottom of pan. Cook over high heat until sauce reduces and begins to thicken, about 5 to 7 minutes.
5. Stir in grated horseradish. Whisk in remaining 3 tablespoons butter. Correct seasoning to taste.
6. To serve, place 1 chop on each heated plate. Spoon sauce over chops and sprinkle with parsley.

To Prepare in Advance: Through #2.

Freezing Instructions: Do not freeze.

Suggested Wine:
Italian: BARBERA, a full-bodied red wine from various regions
American: Monteviña BARBERA

ROAST PORK WITH ORANGE SAUCE
Arista con Salsa d'Arancia

This is one version of Florentine roast pork with a delicate orange sauce.
Serves 6 to 8

1	3½-pound pork loin with bones detached (reserve bones)	1	tablespoon olive oil
			Salt
1½	teaspoons peppercorns, crushed	½	cup dry red wine
		1	cup Brown Stock (see page 49)
1	to 2 teaspoons minced fresh rosemary or thyme leaves		Grated rind and juice of 1 large orange
4	small garlic cloves, minced (see Note)	2	tablespoons unsalted butter

1. Preheat oven to 450°F.
2. Make 8 to 10 evenly spaced, narrow slits, not too deep, over the entire roast.
3. Combine the peppercorns, rosemary and garlic. Divide and stuff into the slits in the meat. Brush the roast with oil and season with salt to taste.
4. Place the pork bones in a shallow roasting pan. Set roast on top of the bones. Roast 1 hour and 30 minutes, or until meat thermometer inserted into center of roast registers 165° to 170°F.
5. Remove roast to cutting board, tent loosely with aluminum foil and let rest for 20 minutes.
6. Discard grease and deglaze pan with wine, scraping up particles on the bottom of the pan with a wooden spoon. Cook over high heat until 2 tablespoons liquid remains. Add the stock, orange rind and juice and continue to cook until the sauce thickens slightly, about 5 minutes. Lower heat and whisk in butter. Correct seasoning to taste. Strain into a clean saucepan and keep warm.
7. Slice roast and arrange on heated serving plates. Spoon sauce over and serve immediately.

To Prepare in Advance: Through #3, wrapping well and refrigerating. Roast directly from refrigerator, increasing cooking time by 15 to 20 minutes.

Freezing Instructions: Through #5. Defrost in refrigerator and serve cold or at room temperature.

Suggested Wine:
Italian: TAURASI, a full-bodied wine from Campania
American: Ridge ZINFANDEL

Note: If a milder garlic flavor is desired, blanch whole garlic in boiling water for 1 minute. Dry, mince and continue with recipe.

ROAST SUCKLING PIG Porchetta

A whole suckling pig arrayed on a platter of greens is an impressive culinary achievement, usually saved for special occasions. In Rome, the pig is fragrant with rosemary; in other regions it might be flavored with fennel. The Italians prefer their pig well cooked, but with the meat still juicy. Due to modern methods of raising pigs, the 20-pounder is just as tender and juicy as one weighing 10 to 12 pounds, and is particularly tasty if corn-fed. **Serves 12**

1	whole baby pig, about 15 pounds		Freshly ground pepper
2½	pounds fatback	1	medium onion, sliced
1	tablespoon chopped fresh rosemary leaves	1	medium carrot, peeled and diced
5	garlic cloves, diced	4	celery stalks, strings removed and diced
2	teaspoons cumin seed	4	cups dry white wine
2	bay leaves	2	cups white wine vinegar
	Salt		Parsley

1. Have butcher remove side bones of pig, from the head to the lower ribs. Reserve bones.
2. Preheat oven to 400°F.
3. Grind fatback. In a medium bowl, combine the fat with rosemary, garlic, cumin seed, bay leaves and salt and pepper to taste. Stuff three quarters of the mixture inside the pig and rub the remainder over the surface.
4. Truss the pig with string and cover the ears and tail with aluminum foil to prevent burning. Arrange the bones in a pan large enough to hold the pig and place it, feet first, on top of the bones. Sprinkle with onion, carrot and celery and pour in wine and vinegar.
5. Cover the pig loosely with foil and roast 50 minutes. Remove the foil and roast 30 minutes longer, or until the pig is golden brown and the skin crisp. Skim fat as necessary. During the last 30 minutes, baste the pig with the juices every 10 minutes, turning as necessary for even browning.
6. Remove pig from pan and let rest 15 to 20 minutes before slicing.
7. Meanwhile, place pan on stove and cook over high heat until sauce thickens slightly, 10 to 15 minutes. Strain and correct seasoning to taste.
8. To serve, arrange a bed of parsley on a platter large enough to hold the whole pig. Set the pig on the parsley, feet first, and spoon some of the sauce over.
9. Return pig to kitchen and carve. Pass sauce in a separate bowl.

To Prepare in Advance: Through #4.

Freezing Instructions: Through #8, freezing slices of meat. Defrost in refrigerator and serve cold or at room temperature.

Suggested Wine:
Italian: NEBBIOLO, a red wine from the Piedmont
American: Diamond Creek CABERNET SAUVIGNON

SPICY ITALIAN SAUSAGE Salsicce alla Napoletano

There is hardly a province in Italy which does not have its own special sausage. Sausages may be highly spiced with chili peppers or mild, made only with pork and pancetta, the meat stuffed into casing or formed into patties. Casing can be purchased from a butcher who specializes in pork products.

This is a Neapolitan sausage. The seasoning can be adjusted to your own taste. This must be prepared a day ahead. **Yield: About 12 6-inch links**

3½ pounds pork shoulder or loin, cut into 1-inch cubes
2 tablespoons coarse salt
2 tablespoons chopped parsley
1 tablespoon fennel seed, crushed
1 tablespoon coarsely ground pepper
1 teaspoon red pepper flakes
2 garlic cloves, chopped fine
2 yards pork casing

1. Coarsely grind pork. Transfer to large mixing bowl.
2. Add remaining ingredients except pork casing and combine well. Cover and refrigerate overnight so that spices blend into meat.
3. Before filling casing, check flavor by sautéing a small amount of meat in a dry skillet; correct seasoning to taste.
4. Rinse casing thoroughly in cold water. Blow through one end, inflating casing and insuring that it has no holes. Soak in cold water until needed.
5. To fill casing, slip the moistened casing over the funnel attachment of your

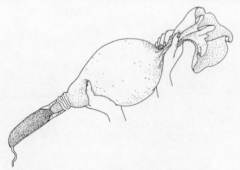

Using a pastry tube and bag, fit the tube into the bag, slipping the moistened casing over the tube. Fill the bag with meat and squeeze the meat into the casing, shaping the links as they are filled.

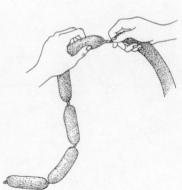

Twist and secure the links as filled.

grinder, working as much of the casing as possible onto the funnel. Gently push the seasoned meat through into the casing, shaping the meat into the desired number of links; do not overstuff the links. Links may be tied with kitchen string or twisted and securely closed (see illustrations). (Or, if using a pastry tube and bag, fit the tube into the bag. Slip as much of the moistened casing as possible over the tube. Fill the bag with the seasoned meat and squeeze into the casing, carefully shaping the meat into links. Proceed as above.)

6. Wrap links in plastic wrap and refrigerate until needed, no longer than 2 days.

7. To cook sausage, place in pan with just enough water to cover the bottom of the pan. Cover and poach over low heat about 5 minutes. Remove cover, raise heat to medium and cook 15 to 20 minutes longer, turning sausage to brown all sides (water will evaporate and sausage will brown).

8. Drain on paper towels and serve immediately.

To Prepare in Advance: Through #6.

Freezing Instructions: Through #6. Defrost in refrigerator and continue with recipe.

Suggested Wine:
Italian: CAREMA, a medium-bodied red wine from the Piedmont
American: Acacia PINOT NOIR

The Italians are experts at cooking veal and have an infinite number of ways to prepare it.

Italy's "white" veal, really a very pale pink, comes from milk-fed calves between eight and twelve weeks old. The slightly darker veal comes from grain-fed calves between four and five months old.

BREADED VEAL CUTLETS Cotolette alla Milanese

Milanese veal cutlets are served on the bone, the meat flattened slightly before cooking. Sometimes the cutlet is soaked in milk, drained, dusted with flour, dipped in egg and finally coated with crumbs. **Serves 4**

1 egg, beaten
1 teaspoon salt
  Freshly ground pepper
¼ cup fresh breadcrumbs
¼ cup (1 ounce) grated Parmesan cheese
4 veal chops, 1 inch thick

¼ cup all-purpose flour
3 tablespoons unsalted butter
1 tablespoon olive oil
  Tomato Sauce of your choice *or* lemon wedges and chopped parsley

1. Season beaten egg with salt and pepper.
2. Combine breadcrumbs and cheese.
3. With a mallet, gently pound chops. Dust lightly with flour, shaking off any excess.
4. Dip each cutlet first in egg and then in crumb and cheese mixture. Refrigerate for 30 minutes to help crumbs adhere.
5. In a skillet large enough to hold the chops in one layer, melt butter with oil. Over medium heat, sauté chops until golden brown and tender, 6 to 8 minutes on each side.
6. Serve immediately, passing tomato sauce in separate bowl, if desired. Or garnish with lemon wedges and chopped parsley.

To Prepare in Advance: Through #4.

Freezing Instructions: Do not freeze.

Suggested Wine:
Italian: TAURASI, a full-bodied red wine from Campania
American: Diamond Creek CABERNET SAUVIGNON

BRAISED VEAL SHANKS Ossobuco alla Milanese

Ossobuco is traditionally served with risotto in Italy. To the Italians, digging the marrow out of the bone is an important part of the meal. The marrow is spread on bread and eaten along with the meat. **Serves 4 to 6**

5 pounds veal shank, cut into 6 pieces	1 cup dry white wine
All-purpose flour	1 large tomato, peeled, seeded and chopped
Salt	1 teaspoon grated lemon rind
Freshly ground pepper	1½ cups heated Chicken Broth (see page 48)
3 tablespoons olive oil	
1 medium onion, coarsely chopped	Chopped parsley

1. Preheat oven to 350°F.

2. Lightly dust veal shanks with flour, shaking off any excess. Season both sides with salt and generous amount of pepper.

3. In a heavy-bottomed, ovenproof saucepan (6-quart Dutch oven), heat 2 tablespoons oil. Arrange shanks in pan and brown over high heat, about 5 minutes on each side. Remove shanks and discard grease.

4. Heat remaining 1 tablespoon oil in pan and lightly wilt onion, about 3 to 4 minutes.

5. Deglaze pan with white wine, scraping up particles on bottom of pan. Add chopped tomato and lemon rind and return shanks to pan.

6. Pour in chicken broth and bring to a boil.

7. Cover pan and transfer to oven. Roast 1½ to 2 hours, or until meat is tender.

8. Remove meat and set aside. Set pan on stove and, over high heat, cook sauce until slightly thickened. Strain sauce, mashing vegetables through strainer or food mill. Correct seasoning to taste.

9. Return meat to pan and heat through.

10. To serve, arrange meat on platter, pour sauce over and sprinkle with parsley.

To Prepare in Advance: Through #7.

Freezing Instructions: Through #7. Defrost overnight in refrigerator. Warm in preheated 350°F oven for 25 minutes.

Suggested Wine:
Italian: BARBARESCO, a hearty red wine from the Piedmont
American: Stag's Leap CABERNET

SAUTEED VEAL MEDALLIONS Rosette di Vitello

Medallions are cut from the veal loin. Do not confuse them with the thin scallops; these are rather thick. **Serves 4**

4 medallions of veal, 6 ounces each *or* 8 medallions of veal, 3 ounces each
All-purpose flour
2 tablespoons cooking oil
¼ cup (½ stick) unsalted butter, cut into small pieces

1 shallot, chopped fine
Salt
Freshly ground white pepper
2 tablespoons brandy
¼ cup Brown Stock (see page 49)
¼ cup heavy cream

1. Using the palm of your hand, press veal medallions to flatten slightly. Dust lightly with flour, shaking off any excess.
2. In a pan large enough to hold veal in a single layer, heat oil. Over very high heat, brown medallions about 30 seconds on each side.
3. Discard oil and lower heat. Add butter and shallot to pan. Season with salt and pepper to taste and cook about 1 minute.
4. Pour in brandy and ignite it; flame will go out within a few seconds. Add stock and cream and continue cooking until medallions are medium rare, about 5 minutes for 6-ounce medallions, 3 minutes for 3-ounce. Correct seasoning to taste.
5. To serve, place veal on heated plates and pour sauce over. Serve immediately.

To Prepare in Advance: Through #1.

Freezing Instructions: Do not freeze.

Suggested Wine:
Italian: BAROLO, a robust red wine from the Piedmont
American: Heitz CABERNET

STUFFED BREAST OF VEAL Cima alla Genovese

A Genoese specialty, this peasant dish is found in the *trattorie* of Genoa rather than in the expensive restaurants. Remember that any food served cold requires additional seasoning; season accordingly. **Serves 6**

1 completely boned breast of veal, about 2 pounds	Salt
¼ cup (½) stick unsalted butter	Freshly ground pepper
3 tablespoons cooking oil	Pinch of marjoram
½ medium onion, diced	Pinch of thyme
1 sweetbread, about ¼ pound, cooked (see Note)	*Stock for cooking veal*
½ pound cooked ham, diced	Boiling water
¾ cup cooked peas, frozen or fresh	1 large carrot, cut into large pieces
2 eggs	1 celery stalk, cut into large pieces
1 ounce dried porcini mushrooms, soaked in warm water for 30 minutes	½ medium onion, quartered
	Pinch of marjoram
	Pinch of thyme
	Salt
	Freshly ground pepper

1. Carefully sew up 3 sides of the veal with heavy thread, leaving a large enough opening for stuffing.

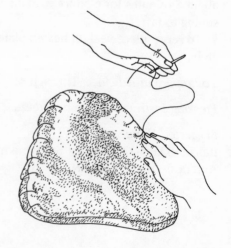

2. In a medium skillet melt butter with 2 tablespoons oil. Over medium heat, sauté onion until golden, about 5 minutes.

3. Remove skin from sweetbread and chop into small dice. Add to skillet. Add ham and peas, stir through and remove from heat.

4. Heat remaining 1 tablespoon oil in small skillet. Scramble eggs until quite firm. Add to ham and pea mixture.

5. Drain mushrooms and cut into thin slices. Add to mixture.

6. Season with salt, pepper, marjoram and thyme to taste. Cool.

7. Season veal with salt, pepper and marjoram. Fill veal with stuffing, occasionally pressing down so that the stuffing is evenly distributed inside. Sew up the opening.

8. Wrap veal securely in cheesecloth and tie both ends tightly with string; make sure you tie the cloth close to the veal ends.

9. Place veal in a large pot and pour in boiling water to cover. Add remaining stock ingredients, seasoning with salt and pepper to taste. Over medium heat, simmer about 1½ hours. Let cool in the stock.

10. Drain and transfer veal to a pan, cover with aluminum foil and weight down evenly to distribute filling for about 1 hour. Remove weight and chill.

11. Remove cheesecloth and thread. Slice and serve.

To Prepare in Advance: Through #10.

Freezing Instructions: Through #10 (slices can be frozen, too). Defrost overnight in refrigerator.

Suggested Wine:
Italian: RUBESCO, a red wine from Umbria
American: Matanzas Creek PINOT NOIR

Note: The best way to prepare the sweetbread is first to rinse it in cold running water until the water runs clear. Place the sweetbread in cold water to cover and season with salt, a bay leaf and a pinch of thyme. Bring to a boil and cook 5 minutes. Let cool in the cooking water. Peel away the membrane on the outside of the sweetbread and use as needed. Reserve the cooking water and add to the veal stock.

VEAL ROLLS Saltimbocca

The names of Italian dishes vary from region to region. Rolled slices of veal may be called *saltimbocca, braciolette, involtini* or *bocconcini gropetti,* depending upon the area. They may be rolled or flattened, sautéed or baked, and the stuffings vary. Thin slices of beef can also be used, but the cooking time will be longer. **Serves 6**

2	ounces dried porcini mushrooms	½	cup heavy cream
			Salt
1½	pounds veal, from leg or loin, cut into 12 scallops		Freshly ground white pepper
		¼	pound prosciutto, cut into 12 slices
1	tablespoon cooking oil		
7	tablespoons unsalted butter	½	pound mozzarella cheese, cut into 12 slices
1	small onion, chopped fine		
3	shallots, minced	12	fresh sage leaves *or* 1 teaspoon dried sage
1	garlic clove, minced		
¼	cup all-purpose flour	¼	cup (1 ounce) grated Parmesan cheese
½	cup dry Marsala		

1. Soak mushrooms in warm water for 25 to 30 minutes. Drain well, dry and chop.
2. Preheat oven to 375°F.
3. Place each scallop between two sheets of waxed paper and gently pound to desired thinness. Reserve.
4. To make stuffing, in a 12-inch skillet, heat oil and 1 tablespoon butter. Over medium heat, sauté onion, shallots and garlic until translucent, about 5 minutes. Add chopped mushrooms and 1 tablespoon flour and stir to dissolve flour. Add Marsala and cream and cook over high heat until liquid evaporates, 5 to 8 minutes. Season with salt and pepper to taste. Cool.
5. Lightly dust veal in remaining flour, shaking off any excess. On each slice of veal place 1 heaping tablespoon of mushroom mixture. Top with 1 slice of prosciutto, 1 slice of mozzarella and 1 sage leaf or a pinch of dried sage. Season lightly with salt and pepper. Roll up scallops and secure with toothpicks.
6. In 1 or 2 ovenproof pans large enough to hold veal rolls in one layer, melt 4 tablespoons butter and brown veal rolls over medium heat. Sprinkle with Parmesan cheese and dot with remaining 2 tablespoons butter.
7. Transfer to oven and bake about 10 minutes, or until cheese and butter have melted.
8. To serve: Remove toothpicks and place 2 veal rolls on each heated serving plate and spoon butter sauce over. Serve immediately.

To Prepare in Advance: Through #5.

Freezing Instructions: Do not freeze.

Suggested Wine:
Italian: Young CHIANTI, a light red wine from Tuscany
American: GAMAY BEAUJOLAIS

VEAL SCALLOPS WITH MARSALA
Scaloppine al Marsala

Scaloppine refers to boneless, thin slices of meat, usually veal. The choicest cuts come from the loin, tenderloin and round. The sauces may vary, but *scaloppine* is served everywhere throughout Italy. **Serves 4**

1 pound veal, cut into 8 slices	Salt
2 tablespoons cooking oil	Freshly ground white pepper
¼ cup (½ stick) unsalted butter	½ cup dry Marsala
¼ cup all-purpose flour	

1. Place each slice of veal between two sheets of waxed paper and gently pound to flatten. (Veal should be thin but not paper thin.)
2. In a 12-inch skillet, heat oil and 2 tablespoons butter.
3. Dust scallops lightly with flour, shaking off any excess.
4. Over medium heat, slide the scallop into the pan and sauté about 1 minute per side. When scallop is done, remove to a platter and season with salt and pepper. Continue with remaining scallops. (No more than 2 or 3 will fit in the pan at one time.)
5. Discard grease from pan and add Marsala, stirring to scrape up bits from the bottom of the pan. Turn heat to high and cook about 1 minute, or until sauce starts to thicken.
6. Turn heat to low and whisk in the remaining 2 tablespoons butter.
7. Return scallops and any juices that may have accumulated on platter back to the pan. Turn to coat both sides of the veal and just heat through.
8. Place 2 scallops on each of 4 heated plates. Pour sauce over scallops and serve immediately.

To Prepare in Advance: Through #1.

Freezing Instructions: Do not freeze.

Variation: 1. A boneless chicken breast may be substituted for the veal and prepared the same way.
2. Sauté thinly sliced mushrooms in butter. Season with salt, pepper and fresh lemon juice to taste. Add to pan in step #7 and heat through with scallops.

Suggested Wine:
Italian: VINO NOBILE, a red wine from Tuscany
American: PINOT NOIR, 3 to 4 years old

VEAL WITH TUNA SAUCE Vitello Tonnato

This excellent cold veal is found in all parts of Italy. It is perfect for a buffet, especially during the warm weather. Leftover sauce makes a delicious dip for raw vegetables. This must be prepared a day ahead. **Serves 6**

1	2-pound veal roast, leg or round	1	tablespoon unsalted butter
	Salt	1	small carrot, peeled and diced
	Freshly ground pepper	1	small celery stalk, strings removed, diced
2	garlic cloves, chopped	½	small onion, diced
	Leaves of 1 sprig fresh rosemary	1	7-ounce can of tuna in oil, drained
1	bay leaf		

2   anchovy filets
2   egg yolks
1¼ to 1½ cups oil (half olive, half
    safflower)

Fresh lemon juice
Capers for garnish

1. Preheat oven to 325°F.
2. Season veal with salt and pepper to taste. Rub with garlic and sprinkle with rosemary. Lay bay leaf on top and dot with butter. Roast about 1½ hours, or until meat is tender and registers 170°F on meat thermometer. Do not brown.
3. Remove from oven and let cool, reserving juices.
4. Pour reserved juices, plus enough water to make ½ cup liquid, into a small saucepan and, over medium heat, cook carrot, celery and onion until tender and liquid is absorbed (amount of time depends on size of the diced vegetables).
5. Transfer vegetables to a food processor fitted with steel blade. Add the tuna and anchovy filets and process until puréed. Add the egg yolks and process just to combine.
6. With machine running, slowly pour oil through feed tube, making a very thick mayonnaise. Add lemon juice to taste.
7. Refrigerate veal and sauce, separately, overnight.
8. To serve, cut veal into thin slices and arrange on platter. Cover with sauce and garnish with capers.

To Prepare in Advance: Through #7.

Freezing Instructions: Through #3. Defrost overnight in refrigerator and continue with recipe.

Suggested Wine:
Italian: TIGNANELLO, a robust red wine from Tuscany
American: Heitz CABERNET

POTTED RABBIT WITH MUSHROOMS AND OLIVES
Conserva di Coniglio con Funghi ed Olive

This dish is found in the countryside of Piedmont and Liguria, where olives are plentiful. Not usually found in restaurants, the dish is prepared by country people who raise rabbits. This recipe was given to me by Roland Flexner and is a specialty of his mother, Aspezzia Bianconi. Any sauce that remains can be served over pasta. **Serves 4**

Marinade
- 1 bottle (750 ml) dry white wine
- ½ cup olive oil
- 1 medium carrot, peeled, thinly sliced
- 1 medium celery stalk, strings removed, thinly sliced
- 2 garlic cloves, minced
  Bouquet garni (1 bay leaf, pinch of thyme, 8 whole peppercorns, 2 parsley sprigs tied in cheesecloth)

- 1 rabbit, 3 to 3½ pounds, cut into 8 pieces (reserve liver and kidney)

- 2 tablespoons olive oil
- ¼ pound pancetta or unsmoked bacon, cubed
- 2 tablespoons all-purpose flour
- 2 large onions, thinly sliced
- 2 tablespoons unsalted butter
- ½ pound mushrooms, quartered
- 2 tablespoons chopped parsley
- 1 garlic clove, crushed
- 1 cup unpitted green olives
  Salt
  Freshly ground pepper

1. *For marinade:* In a large bowl, combine all marinade ingredients and marinate rabbit in refrigerator for 12 hours. Drain rabbit and pat dry with paper towels. Reserve marinade.

2. In a heavy 6-quart flameproof casserole or Dutch oven, heat olive oil. Over medium heat, sauté pancetta until lightly colored, about 5 minutes. Remove pancetta and reserve.

3. Dust rabbit with flour and over low heat brown pieces on all sides. Remove rabbit and reserve.

4. In same casserole, over low heat, sauté onions until translucent, 10 to 15 minutes. Return rabbit and pancetta to casserole.

5. In a 10-inch skillet, melt butter. Over medium heat, sauté mushrooms, parsley and garlic about 5 minutes. Add to casserole.

6. Pour marinade into casserole. Stir in olives and season with salt and pepper to taste. Simmer, covered, for 20 minutes, then uncover and continue to simmer until rabbit is tender, 40 to 50 minutes, stirring occasionally. Remove bouquet garni. Correct seasoning to taste.

7. To serve, arrange pieces of rabbit on plate. Pour sauce over and surround with vegetables and olives.

To Prepare in Advance: Through #6.

Freezing Instructions: Through #6. Defrost in refrigerator and warm over low heat.

Suggested Wine:
Italian: MERLOT DEL COLLIO, a red wine from the Veneto
American: Clos du Val MERLOT

Poultry and Game Birds

Chicken is economical, tasty and nutritious. It has an affinity for many different flavorings and sauces and can be served in a variety of ways. The best chickens in Italy, raised in Tuscany, are juicy and plump. Italians prefer grilling or broiling these succulent birds. Ideally, a charcoal or wood grill gives the best flavor, but an electric or gas broiler will also provide excellent results.

Game, too, is plentiful in many areas of Italy. The familiar methods of grilling and roasting are still observed, but newer, more original preparations are emerging from the Italian kitchen.

CHICKEN BREASTS WITH LEMON BUTTER
Petti di Pollo al Limone

Eating in Sostanza, a tiny restaurant in Florence, was like eating in a noisy kitchen—talking to people at neighboring tables, waiters shouting their orders. It was great fun and the food was superb. This is an adaptation of one of their special entrees. **Serves 6**

3	whole chicken breasts, boned, skinned and cut in half	1½	cups fine dry breadcrumbs
	Salt		Safflower or peanut oil
	Freshly ground pepper	6	tablespoons unsalted butter
2	tablespoons all-purpose flour		Juice of 1 medium lemon
2	eggs, beaten with 2 table-spoons heavy cream	6	thin lemon slices, optional

1. Trim breasts and remove tendon from filet with the tip of a knife.
2. Pat chicken dry with paper towels. Season on both sides with salt and pepper. Dust very lightly with flour, shaking off any excess.
3. Place egg mixture and breadcrumbs in separate bowls. Dip each chicken breast into egg mixture, coat heavily with crumbs and place on a plate or tray. Refrigerate for at least 30 minutes, or until ready to cook, to help crumbs adhere.
4. Heat 1 large or 2 small skillets large enough to hold the chicken without crowding. Add oil to ¼-inch depth and place over medium heat until moderately hot.
5. Carefully place chicken in the hot oil. Cook over medium heat 2 to 3 minutes on each side, or until chicken is golden brown; do not overcook. Remove and drain on paper towels. Place 1 chicken breast on each of 6 heated plates.
6. In a small saucepan, melt butter with lemon juice until bubbly. Spoon a little on each chicken breast and garnish with a slice of lemon, if desired. Serve immediately, passing additional lemon butter in a separate bowl.

To Prepare in Advance: Through #3.

Freezing Instructions: Do not freeze.

Suggested Wine:
Italian: A mature TAURASI, a robust red wine from Campania
American: Diamond Creek CABERNET SAUVIGNON

STUFFED CHICKEN BREASTS IN LETTUCE LEAVES
Petti di Pollo in Foglie di Lattuga

Ever frugal, the Italian cook will make a mousse out of an old, tough chicken and then enclose the mousse in chicken breasts. **Serves 6**

4 whole chicken breasts, boned, skinned and cut in half
   Salt
   Freshly ground white pepper
¼ cup (1 ounce) grated Parmesan cheese
2 teaspoons chopped chives
1 cup heavy cream, chilled
2 tablespoons truffle peelings, optional
6 or more large romaine lettuce leaves, blanched

4 cups Chicken Broth, heated (see page 48)

Sauce
2 shallots, chopped fine
1 cup Port
1 cup heavy cream
½ teaspoon red pepper flakes
2 tablespoons unsalted butter
   Salt
   Freshly ground pepper

1. Preheat oven to 350°F. Butter a 13 × 9 × 2-inch baking pan.
2. To prepare mousse for filling, cut 1 whole chicken breast (2 halves) into 1-inch pieces. Refrigerate along with bowl and steel blade of food processor. (Chilling will help prevent mousse from becoming grainy.)
3. Remove chicken pieces, bowl and blade from refrigerator and chop the chicken. Add ½ teaspoon salt, ¼ teaspoon pepper, the grated cheese and chives. With the machine running, pour the cream through the feed tube and process just until smooth; do not overprocess. Transfer mousse to a small bowl and fold in truffle peelings, if desired. Refrigerate until needed.
4. Lay remaining 6 breast halves on the work table, skin side down. Spread a sheet of waxed paper over breasts and gently pound to flatten and to enlarge. Remove paper and season lightly with salt and pepper. Divide mousse among breast halves. Fold both ends of chicken over filling and then roll up lengthwise, keeping the ends tucked in.
5. Completely wrap each half in 1 or more blanched lettuce leaves and arrange in a single layer in prepared pan. Pour in the broth and cover with aluminum foil.
6. Bake 30 minutes, or until chicken is firm to the touch. Remove chicken from pan and keep warm.
7. Meanwhile, to prepare sauce, combine shallots and Port in small saucepan. Over high heat, reduce until about 3 tablespoons remain. Add cream and reduce by about one third. Add ½ cup broth from the baking pan and red pepper and bring to a boil. Remove from heat and gradually whisk in butter. Season with salt and pepper to taste.

8. To serve, cut chicken into crosswise slices and arrange on plate. Pour sauce over and serve immediately.

To Prepare in Advance: Through #6, baking 15 minutes. Bring broth to a boil and continue with recipe.

Freezing Instructions: Do not freeze.

Suggested Wine:
Italian: GHEMME, a robust red wine from the Piedmont
American: A big PETIT SIRAH

CHICKEN BREASTS STUFFED WITH CABBAGE
Rollatini di Pollo e Cavolo

Another version of stuffed chicken breasts; here, cabbage and pancetta make a tasty and colorful stuffing. Serving on a blanched red cabbage leaf makes for an attractive presentation. **Serves 6**

1 pound green cabbage, hard core removed	3 whole chicken breasts, boned, skinned and cut in half
¼ cup olive oil	½ cup Chicken Broth (see page 48)
2 ounces pancetta, diced	¼ cup dry red wine
2 tablespoons pine nuts	¼ cup (½ stick) unsalted butter
Salt	Chopped parsley for garnish
Freshly ground white pepper	

1. To prepare the stuffing, julienne cabbage and blanch. (I find the easiest way to do this is to place the cabbage in a strainer or mesh basket and plunge into boiling salted water 1 to 2 minutes. Basket can then be removed and placed in ice water.) Dry cabbage thoroughly.
2. In a 12-inch skillet, heat 1 tablespoon oil. Over low heat, sauté pancetta briefly. Add cabbage and pine nuts and continue to sauté, stirring occasionally, until nuts are lightly golden and cabbage is tender, 10 to 12 minutes. Season with salt and pepper to taste. Cool completely.
3. Preheat oven to 450°F.
4. Lay chicken breasts on work table and carefully open each one lengthwise, holding knife parallel to table and cutting almost to opposite edge (do not cut through). Open each breast out to double its former size. Pound lightly to even thickness.

5. Divide cabbage mixture among opened chicken breasts. Fold ends over filling and roll lengthwise to enclose. Tie with string.

6. In an ovenproof skillet large enough to hold chicken in a single layer, heat remaining 3 tablespoons oil. Over medium heat, brown chicken on all sides. Transfer to oven and bake 10 to 15 minutes, or until tender. Transfer chicken to warm plate and cut away strings.

7. Discard grease from pan. Place pan on stove and deglaze with chicken broth and wine, scraping up bits remaining on bottom of pan. Over high heat reduce just until slightly thickened. Remove from heat and strain. Gradually whisk in butter.

8. To serve, cut each chicken breast crosswise into slices and arrange on plates. Ladle sauce over and sprinkle with parsley. Serve immediately.

To Prepare in Advance: Through #6, browning chicken only.

Freezing Instructions: Through #6, browning chicken only. Place chicken in covered pan and bake in preheated 425° oven for 10 minutes. Lower heat to 350°F and continue to bake 12 to 15 minutes longer. Pour a small amount of water into pan to prevent chicken from drying out.

Suggested Wine:
Italian: GRIGNOLINO, a very dry red wine with a delicate bouquet, from the Piedmont
American: BEAUJOLAIS

BROILED LEMON CHICKEN
Pollo Griglia al Limone

This Tuscan specialty is another example of a simple but delicious chicken preparation favored by the Italians. **Serves 2 to 4**

½ cup fresh lemon juice
¼ cup olive oil
1 garlic clove, mashed
Leaves from 1 sprig fresh rosemary *or* pinch of Italian Seasoning

1 teaspoon chopped parsley
Salt
Freshly ground pepper
1 3-pound chicken, cut into quarters

1. In a bowl large enough to hold chicken, combine lemon juice, olive oil, garlic, rosemary, parsley and salt and pepper to taste.

2. Marinate chicken pieces, turning to coat all sides, at least 2 hours, up to 8 hours.

3. Preheat broiler or grill. If using a grill, place heavy-duty aluminum foil on grill and brush with oil.

4. Broil or grill chicken 10 to 12 minutes on each side, depending on how close chicken is to flame. Brush with marinade every 5 minutes. Do not overcook.

5. Serve hot or cold.

To Prepare in Advance: Through #2 or #4.

Freezing Instructions: Through #4. Defrost overnight in refrigerator. Reheat, if desired, in hot oven. Pour a small amount of water into pan to prevent chicken from drying out.

Suggested Wine:
Italian: CHIANTI, a red wine from Tuscany
American: CARIGNANE

CHICKEN, HUNTER'S STYLE Pollo alla Cacciatora

Almost every Italian restaurant in the United States features *Pollo alla Cacciatora,* but too often the chicken is overpowered rather than flavored by the sauce. In the Umbria region, slivers of white truffle garnish the chicken, further enhancing the taste. **Serves 4**

1 **chicken, about 3½ pounds, cut into 8 pieces**	1 **cup dry white wine or white vermouth**
Salt	2 **medium tomatoes (½ pound), peeled, seeded and coarsely chopped**
Freshly ground pepper	
3 **tablespoons cooking oil**	
½ **medium onion, cut into ¼-inch slices**	½ **cup Chicken Broth (see page 48)**
2 **garlic cloves, minced**	2 **or 3 fresh basil leaves, minced *or* 1 teaspoon minced parsley**

1. Season chicken with salt and pepper to taste.

2. In a pan large enough to hold chicken in one layer, heat oil. Over medium heat, sauté chicken until golden brown on all sides, about 15 minutes. Remove chicken pieces as browned and set aside.

3. Add onion and garlic and sauté until golden, about 5 minutes. Discard grease.

4. Deglaze pan with wine, stirring with wooden spoon to scrape up all the particles on the bottom of the pan. Cook over medium heat about 5 minutes, or until slightly thickened. Add tomatoes and cook 10 minutes longer. Season with salt and pepper to taste.

5. Return chicken to pan and cook, covered, for 15 minutes, adding chicken broth as sauce evaporates.

6. To serve, arrange chicken on a platter. Spoon sauce over and garnish with minced basil or parsley. Serve immediately.

To Prepare in Advance: Through #4.

Freezing Instructions: Through #5. Defrost overnight in refrigerator. Warm over low heat.

Variations: 1. Garnish chicken with thinly sliced truffle.
2. Omit tomatoes in step #4 and broth in step #5. Pour in 1 cup Marinara Sauce (see page 61) and ¼ cup sliced black olives in step #4 and continue with recipe.

Suggested Wine:
Italian: Old BAROLO, a very robust red wine from the Piedmont
American: Beaulieu Vineyard CABERNET

CHICKEN WITH GARLIC AND PARSLEY
Pollo in Aglio e Prezzemolo

This is an adaptation of a recipe from Spago restaurant. If you are a garlic lover, this dish is for you. Blanching the garlic makes it sweeter and less pungent. **Serves 2**

15	to 20 garlic cloves, peeled	Salt
2	tablespoons chopped Italian parsley	Freshly ground pepper
		2 tablespoons unsalted butter
1	chicken, about 3 pounds, cut in half	Juice of ½ large lemon

1. Preheat grill or broiler. If using a grill, place heavy-duty aluminum foil on grill and brush with oil.
2. Blanch garlic in boiling water for 1 minute. Drain.
3. Mince garlic and combine with the chopped parsley. Gently slip your fin-

Gently slip your fingers under the skin of the chicken, lift the skin slightly and stuff.

gers under the skin of the chicken, lifting the skin slightly. Stuff half the garlic and parsley mixture under the skin of the chicken. Season the chicken with salt and pepper to taste.

4. Broil chicken approximately 10 to 12 minutes per side; do not overcook.

5. To prepare sauce, melt butter over low heat in a small skillet. Sauté the remaining garlic and parsley mixture for 1 to 2 minutes. Stir in the lemon juice and season with salt and pepper to taste. Keep warm until needed.

6. To serve, place each chicken half on a plate. Pour sauce over and serve immediately.

To Prepare in Advance: Through #3.

Freezing Instructions: Through #4. Defrost in refrigerator. Serve cold, or warm in preheated 375°F oven 10 minutes. Do not allow to dry out.

Suggested Wine:
Italian: SPANNA, a dry red wine from the Piedmont
American: Ridge ZINFANDEL

CHICKEN WITH HERBS Pollo alle Erbe

Chicken breast halves can be substituted for the whole chicken cut into pieces. Polenta or rice is an excellent accompaniment to this dish. **Serves 4**

1 3- to 3½-pound chicken, cut into 8 pieces	Leaves from 1 sprig fresh rosemary, chopped fine *or* pinch of Italian Seasoning (see page 12)
Salt	
Freshly ground pepper	2 garlic cloves, chopped
¼ cup olive oil	2 tablespoons tomato paste
¾ cup dry white wine *or* white vermouth	1 cup boiling water *or* Chicken Broth (see page 48)
Pinch of dried sage	Fresh sage *or* Italian parsley

1. Season chicken with salt and pepper to taste.

2. In a 12- or 14-inch skillet, heat oil. Arrange chicken in pan in one layer, skin side down. Over medium heat, brown the chicken on all sides, about 15 minutes. Remove chicken pieces as browned and reserve. Discard grease.

3. Deglaze pan with wine, stirring with wooden spoon to scrape up all the particles on the bottom. Stir in rosemary and garlic and cook until the wine reduces almost to a glaze.

4. Dissolve the tomato paste in water or broth and add to the pan. Return chicken to pan. Lower heat, cover and cook 15 to 20 minutes longer, or until chicken is tender.

5. To serve, place chicken on plate, spoon the sauce over and sprinkle with sage or parsley. Serve immediately.

To Prepare in Advance: Through #4. Reheat as necessary.

Freezing Instructions: Through #4. Defrost overnight in refrigerator. To reheat, place in preheated 350°F oven and bake about 15 minutes, adding more liquid if necessary. Do not allow to dry out.

Suggested Wine:
Italian: CHIANTI, a red wine from Tuscany
American: CARIGNANE

CHICKEN WITH RAW MUSHROOMS Pollo ai Funghi

In Italy this is served with paper-thin slices of white truffle. If you cannot get truffles, raw mushrooms are an excellent and practical substitute, but the mushrooms must be very fresh. **Serves 6**

3 whole chicken breasts, boned, skinned, and cut in half	2 tablespoons cooking oil
Salt	½ cup Chicken Broth (see page 48)
Freshly ground white pepper	¼ cup dry vermouth
¼ cup all-purpose flour	1 cup heavy cream
2 eggs, beaten with 2 tablespoons water	Juice of 1 medium lemon
	6 large mushrooms, caps only *or* 1 white truffle, thinly sliced
¼ cup (½ stick) unsalted butter	

1. Trim breasts and remove tendon from filet with the tip of a knife.
2. Pat the chicken dry. Season with salt and pepper to taste.
3. Place flour and egg mixture in separate bowls. Coat chicken lightly with flour, shaking off any excess. Dip into egg mixture, then coat with flour again.
4. In 1 or 2 skillets large enough to hold the chicken in a single layer, heat butter and oil until butter foams. Over medium heat, sauté chicken on both sides until golden brown, about 3 minutes on each side; do not overcook. Transfer to plate, cover and keep warm.
5. Discard grease from pan and deglaze with broth and vermouth, scraping up particles that stick to bottom of pan. Reduce liquid until it is syrupy. Add cream and reduce until it coats the back of a wooden spoon quite heavily. Season with salt, pepper, and lemon juice to taste.

6. While sauce is reducing, cut mushroom caps into very thin slices and toss with lemon juice. (If mushrooms are not absolutely perfect, peel them before slicing.)

7. Return chicken and any juices that may have accumulated on plate back to the pan, just to heat through.

8. To serve, spoon sauce onto each plate. Place a chicken breast in the center and top with sliced mushrooms. Serve immediately.

To Prepare in Advance: Through #2.

Freezing Instructions: Do not freeze.

Suggested Wine:
Italian: VALPOLICELLA, a sturdy red wine from Verona
American: GAMAY BEAUJOLAIS

CHICKEN WITH SAUSAGE Pollo con Salsiccia

From Lombardy, a tasty main dish. **Serves 4 to 6**

1 chicken, about 3½ pounds, cut into 8 pieces	½ pound (2 links) Italian sausage, sweet or hot
Salt	1 small onion, coarsely chopped
Freshly ground pepper	¼ pound pancetta, coarsely chopped
All-purpose flour	
3 tablespoons unsalted butter	1 cup dry white wine
2 tablespoons cooking oil	½ cup heated Chicken Broth (see page 48)

1. Season chicken with salt and pepper. Lightly dust with flour, shaking to remove any excess.

2. In a pan large enough to hold the chicken in one layer, heat the butter and oil.

3. Over medium heat, brown chicken on all sides. Remove and reserve.

4. Brown sausage and remove. Cut into bite-size pieces.

5. Sauté onion and pancetta until onion is golden, about 5 minutes. Discard grease.

6. Deglaze pan with wine, scraping up any particles that stick to the bottom of the pan, and bring to a simmer. Return the chicken and sausage to the pan and cook over medium heat, covered, until chicken is tender, 15 to 20 minutes. Pour in broth as necessary to keep chicken moist.

7. Serve immediately.

To Prepare in Advance: Through #6, returning chicken and sausage to the pan without cooking.

Freezing Instructions: Through #6. Reheat over low flame.

Suggested Wine:
Italian: VINO NOBILE DI MONTEPULCIANO, a red wine from Tuscany
American: CARIGNANE

MARINATED GRILLED CHICKEN Pollo alla Diavola

Grilling over wood or charcoal is the perfect preparation of the tender, meaty chickens found in Tuscany. The marinade not only adds flavor, but keeps the chicken moist. **Serves 2**

1 **chicken, about 2 to 2½ pounds**	8 **to 10 crushed white peppercorns**
3 **tablespoons olive oil**	⅛ **teaspoon red pepper flakes**
Juice of 1 small lemon	**Salt**

1. Cut the chicken in half, remove wingtips and press each half to lay flat.
2. In a glass dish large enough to hold the 2 halves, combine olive oil, lemon juice, crushed peppercorns, and red pepper. Let marinate 1 to 2 hours, turning chicken occasionally.
3. Preheat grill or broiler. If using a grill, place heavy-duty aluminum foil on grill and brush with oil.
4. Place chicken on grill skin side down and grill about 10 minutes, or until golden brown, brushing chicken with marinade as it grills. Turn and grill about 10 minutes longer. Season with salt to taste.
5. Serve immediately.

To Prepare in Advance: Through #2.

Freezing Instructions: Through #4. Defrost overnight in refrigerator and reheat in preheated 375°F oven about 10 minutes.

Suggested Wine:
Italian: NEBBIOLO, a red wine from the Piedmont
American: PINOT NOIR

CASSEROLE OF DUCK Stufato d'Anatra

Fresh duck is usually available from April through October; frozen duck can be purchased all year round. Ask your butcher for a firm, plump bird. Much of the duck served in Italy is wild; I prefer our domesticated variety, but either can be used. **Serves 4**

2 slices (2 ounces) thick bacon, diced	¼ cup (½ stick) unsalted butter
1 duck, about 5 to 5½ pounds, cut into 8 pieces	1 small onion, diced
Salt	½ cup dry white wine
Freshly ground pepper	1½ cups Chicken Broth (see page 48)

1. In 1 or 2 skillets large enough to hold duck pieces in one layer, sauté bacon over medium heat until golden, about 5 minutes.
2. Season duck with salt and pepper. Arrange in skillet and brown on all sides. Remove duck and reserve. Discard grease.
3. Melt butter in skillet. Add onion and cook, stirring occasionally, for 5 minutes. Pour in wine and let reduce to a glaze. Return duck to pan.
4. Pour in 1 cup chicken broth, lower heat and cover skillet. Cook about 40 minutes, or until duck is tender, turning duck once or twice. Add remaining ½ cup broth as needed to keep duck moist.
5. Serve hot, with risotto or fresh fettuccine.

To Prepare in Advance: Through #3.

Freezing Instructions: Through #4. Defrost overnight in refrigerator. Reheat in 375°F oven for about 10 minutes.

Suggested Wine:
Italian: MONTE VERTINE, a fruity red wine from Tuscany
American: Aged CABERNET

COLD SQUAB IN MINT GELATIN
Piccione alla Menta in Gelatina

This is a special occasion dish that proves the versatility of Italian cooking. It should be prepared the day before it is to be served, so that the sauce sets. **Serves 2**

2 squabs, 8 to 10 ounces each	Freshly ground pepper
Salt	⅔ cup dry white wine

2 tablespoons unsalted butter	1 medium celery stalk, diced
	10 mint leaves
Gelatin	¼ cup Marsala *or* Port
2½ cups dry white wine	
1 small onion, diced	8 mint leaves
1 small carrot, peeled and diced	

1. Cut each squab in half. Cut wings off at second joint. Remove breast bones and thigh bones, leaving leg bones intact. Reserve bones.

2. Place squab halves in a bowl. Season lightly with salt and pepper and pour the wine over. Marinate for 30 minutes.

3. Preheat oven to 400°F.

4. Remove squab from bowl, reserving wine. Dry thoroughly and arrange in a 9-inch-square baking dish. Dot with butter and bake 20 minutes.

5. Remove from oven and pour reserved wine over squab. Cool and refrigerate overnight.

6. *Meanwhile, to prepare gelatin:* Place reserved squab bones in a large saucepan. Add wine, onion, carrot and celery and cook over high heat until reduced by one third, about 20 minutes. Pour in 4 cups cold water and continue to cook over high heat 30 minutes longer.

7. Strain into a small saucepan and stir in the 10 mint leaves. Cook until 1 cup liquid remains, 20 to 30 minutes. Stir in Marsala and refrigerate overnight.

8. Arrange squab halves in the center of each of 2 plates. Divide sauce and pour over each serving. Refrigerate 3 to 4 hours.

9. To serve, decorate each squab half with 2 fresh mint leaves.

To Prepare in Advance: Through #7 or #8.

Freezing Instructions: Do not freeze.

Suggested Wine:
Italian: CABERNET Lazzarini, a light Cabernet
American: Trefethen PINOT NOIR

ROASTED QUAIL WITH RISOTTO
Quaglie con Risotto

A very simple and tasty dish from the Piedmont. Marinating the quail gives the dish wonderful flavor. **Serves 4 to 6**

1½ cups dry white wine	4 garlic cloves, minced
½ cup olive oil	8 fresh basil leaves, cut into julienne
1 medium onion, sliced	

	Pinch of sage		Salt
8	quail, ¼ pound each		Freshly ground pepper
1	recipe Risotto Milanese (see	2	tablespoons cooking oil
	page 99)	2	tablespoons unsalted butter

1. In a large bowl or pan, combine wine, olive oil, onion, garlic, basil and sage. Marinate quail, turning to coat all sides, 2 to 3 hours, or up to 8 hours.
2. Prepare risotto and keep warm.
3. Preheat oven to 450°F.
4. Pat quail dry and season lightly with salt and pepper. Truss with string.
5. In a large skillet, heat cooking oil and butter. Over high heat, sauté quail until golden brown on all sides, 8 to 10 minutes.
6. Transfer quail to roasting pan and roast 10 minutes.
7. To serve, remove string from quail and cut each one in half. Turn risotto out onto serving plate. Arrange the birds around and on top of risotto and serve immediately.

To Prepare in Advance: Through #1 or #4.

Freezing Instructions: Do not freeze.

Variations: 1. Soak 3 ounces dried porcini mushrooms in warm water to cover for 30 minutes. Drain and dry thoroughly. Cut into slices, stir into the risotto with the first addition of stock and continue with recipe.
2. Prepare Risotto with Asparagus (see page 100) and continue with recipe.
3. Split quail in half. Do not pat dry when removing from marinade. Grill until medium rare. Serve with risotto.

Suggested Wine:
Italian: CHIANTI, a red wine from Tuscany
American: Firestone PINOT NOIR

Frittatas and Egg Dishes

Egg dishes are very popular in Italy. Frittatas, the Italian version of an omelet, are very versatile. They can be filled with vegetables, meat, fish, cheese, or a combination, and eaten for lunch or supper; for dessert they can be filled with fruit.

Frittatas can be turned and cooked completely on top of the stove (best done by inverting onto a plate and then sliding back into the pan), or they can be placed under the broiler to complete, as recommended in the recipes. I find the latter a better procedure, guaranteeing a perfect frittata. Fillings that require cooking should be cooked first and then combined with the eggs.

APPLE FRITTATA Frittata di Mele

From Venezia Giulia, this can be served as dessert after a light meal, or for brunch with a variety of sausages. **Serves 2 or 3**

½ cup all-purpose flour
    Large pinch of salt
2 cups milk
6 extra large eggs, lightly beaten
2 tablespoons sugar
    Grated rind of 1 medium
      lemon

    Freshly grated nutmeg
¼ cup (½ stick) unsalted butter
1½ pounds Delicious apples,
      peeled, cored and cut into
      ¼-inch slices
    Powdered sugar

1. Preheat oven to 450°F.
2. In a large bowl, combine flour and salt. Gradually whisk in milk until smooth.
3. Whisk in beaten eggs, sugar, lemon rind, and nutmeg to taste. Let rest 20 minutes.
4. In a 10-inch ovenproof skillet, melt butter. Over medium heat, sauté apples until lightly golden, 8 to 10 minutes. Pour in egg mixture, lower heat and cook until eggs set, about 10 minutes, stirring eggs occasionally for even cooking.
5. Place skillet under the oven broiler until top puffs and frittata is lightly golden and firm to the touch, about 3 to 4 minutes; do not overcook. Frittata should still be moist inside.
6. Carefully slide onto warmed platter, sprinkle with sifted powdered sugar and serve immediately.

To Prepare in Advance: Through #3.

Freezing Instructions: Do not freeze.

BAKED ZUCCHINI FRITTATA Frittata di Zucchini

The baking causes this Tuscan frittata to puff almost like a soufflé. **Serves 8**

¼ cup olive oil
2 pounds zucchini, trimmed and
    thinly sliced
2 large onions, thinly sliced
¾ pound tomatoes, peeled,
    seeded and chopped

8 fresh basil leaves, cut into julienne
    Salt
    Freshly ground pepper
10 extra large eggs, beaten

1. Preheat oven to 350°F. Butter a 10-inch round cake pan.
2. In a 12-inch skillet, heat the olive oil. Over low heat, sauté the zucchini, onions, tomatoes and basil until the zucchini and onions are barely cooked, about 10 minutes. Season with salt and pepper and cool slightly. Transfer to prepared pan.
3. Season beaten eggs with salt. Pour over zucchini mixture and stir through, arranging vegetables decoratively throughout and on top of frittata.
4. Bake 45 to 55 minutes, or until firm to the touch.
5. Let rest 5 minutes and serve.

To Prepare in Advance: Through #3 or #5.

Freezing Instructions: Do not freeze.

CHEESE AND PARSLEY FRITTATA
Frittata di Formaggio e Prezzemolo

A simple, tasty omelet that can be served as a light supper. **Serves 6**

10 extra large eggs	Salt
1 cup (¼ pound) grated Parmesan cheese	Freshly ground white pepper
	Dash of Tabasco
Leaves from 3 sprigs parsley, chopped fine	¼ cup (½ stick) unsalted butter

1. Preheat oven to 500°F.
2. In a large mixing bowl, beat eggs until foamy. Whisk in the grated cheese, half the parsley, salt, pepper, and Tabasco.
3. In a 10-inch ovenproof skillet, melt butter. When foam subsides, pour in eggs and over low heat, cook until set, 10 to 12 minutes.
4. Place skillet under oven broiler until top puffs and frittata is lightly golden and firm to the touch; do not overcook. Frittata should still be moist inside.
5. Remove from oven and either serve directly from skillet or carefully slide frittata onto a warm serving plate. Sprinkle with remaining parsley and serve immediately.

To Prepare in Advance: Do not prepare in advance. However, leftover frittata can be served cold the next day.

Freezing Instructions: Do not freeze.

ONION, BACON AND TOMATO FRITTATA
Frittata di Cipolla, Pancetta e Pomodoro

From Lazio. **Serves 6**

3   tablespoons olive oil
1   large onion, thinly sliced
½   pound pancetta or bacon, blanched and cut into ½-inch pieces
2   medium tomatoes, peeled, seeded and chopped

10 extra large eggs
    Salt
    Freshly ground pepper
6   fresh basil leaves, cut into julienne

1. Preheat oven to 500°F.
2. In a 10-inch ovenproof skillet, heat the oil. Over medium heat, sauté the onion and pancetta for 2 to 3 minutes. Add the tomatoes and cook, stirring occasionally, 10 minutes longer.
3. In a large mixing bowl, beat eggs until foamy. Season with salt and pepper and stir in basil leaves.
4. Pour eggs into pan, lower heat, and cook until set, 10 to 12 minutes.
5. Place skillet under oven broiler until top puffs and frittata is lightly golden and firm to the touch; do not overcook. Frittata should still be moist inside.
6. Serve directly from skillet or carefully slide frittata onto a warm serving plate. Serve immediately.

To Prepare in Advance: Do not prepare in advance. However, leftover frittata can be served cold the next day.

Freezing Instructions: Do not freeze.

POTATO FRITTATA Frittata di Patate

The Italians are very adept at cooking with potatoes. This is like a potato pie or large pancake, and can be enjoyed with a roast or grilled meat. **Serves 6 to 8**

1½ pounds russet potatoes, peeled and cut into quarters
6   tablespoons unsalted butter
2   medium onions, chopped fine
4   eggs
¾   cup (3 ounces) grated Parmesan cheese

2   teaspoons chopped parsley
12 fresh basil leaves, chopped fine
    or ¼ teaspoon Italian Seasoning (see page 12)
    Pinch of dried sage
    Salt
    Freshly ground pepper

1. In boiling salted water to cover, cook potatoes until tender, about 20 minutes. Drain and mash (a food mill or ricer works very well).
2. In a 10-inch skillet, melt 3 tablespoons butter over medium heat. Sauté onions until golden, about 5 minutes. Combine with potatoes.
3. Preheat oven to broil.
4. In a medium mixing bowl, beat eggs. Add two thirds of the grated cheese, the parsley, basil and sage. Season with salt and pepper to taste. Pour into potato mixture and mix thoroughly.
5. In a clean 10-inch skillet, melt remaining 3 tablespoons butter. Spread potato mixture evenly in pan, sprinkle with remaining cheese, and cook over medium high heat until bottom has browned lightly and frittata has set.
6. Place skillet under the oven broiler until cheese melts and frittata is golden brown.
7. Slide out onto serving plate and serve immediately.

To Prepare in Advance: Through #3.

Freezing Instructions: Through #7. To heat, place in preheated 400°F oven and bake 8 to 10 minutes.

Suggested Wine:
Italian: BRUSCO DEI BARBI, a red wine from Tuscany
American: CABERNET FRANC

SALMON FRITTATA Frittata con Salmone

From Liguria, this is an excellent way to use leftover fish. However, for best results, the fish must not be overcooked. **Serves 6**

1 pound salmon, skinned, boned and patted dry	2 teaspoons chopped chives
Salt	1 garlic clove, chopped fine
Freshly ground pepper	2 tablespoons cooking oil
10 extra large eggs	1 tablespoon unsalted butter

1. Preheat oven to 400°F.
2. Cut salmon into thin scallops. Season lightly with salt and pepper, arrange in oiled baking pan large enough to hold scallops in a single layer and bake 2 to 3 minutes. Remove from oven and let cool.
3. In a large mixing bowl, beat eggs. Stir in chives and garlic and season lightly with salt and pepper.
4. In a 10-inch skillet heat oil and butter. Pour eggs into pan and cook over low heat until underside is lightly browned. Arrange salmon scallops over eggs.

5. Place skillet under the oven broiler and cook until eggs are set and top is golden; do not overcook. Frittata should still be moist inside. Serve directly from skillet or slide frittata onto a warm serving plate.
6. Serve immediately.

To Prepare in Advance: Through #2.

Freezing Instructions: Do not freeze.

BREAD AND CHEESE TIMBALES
Timballi di Pane e Formaggio

This is a noted Neapolitan dish. Bel Paese can be substituted for the mozzarella cheese. The sandwiches can be cut into bite-size pieces and served with cocktails. Make sure there are plenty of napkins for this and the next recipe! **Serves 6**

5 **eggs**	¾ **pound mozzarella cheese, thinly sliced**
3 **tablespoons heavy cream**	
Pinch of salt	½ **pound prosciutto, thinly sliced**
Freshly ground pepper	¼ **cup (½ stick) unsalted butter**
12 **thin slices white bread, crusts removed**	

1. In a medium bowl, whisk together eggs, cream, salt and pepper until blended.
2. Arrange slices of bread in one layer in a dish large enough to hold them. (You may have to use 2 dishes and divide the egg mixture.) Pour eggs over and let bread absorb the mixture, turning as necessary, 20 to 30 minutes.
3. Preheat oven to 375°F. Butter a 13 × 9 × 2-inch oven-to-table baking dish.
4. Arrange 6 slices of bread in one layer in prepared dish. Top with cheese and prosciutto, dividing equally among the bread slices. Cover with remaining 6 slices of bread and press the edges together. Dot with butter.
5. Bake 25 to 30 minutes, or until bread is golden and cheese is melted.
6. Serve immediately.

To Prepare in Advance: Through #2 or #4.

Freezing Instructions: Do not freeze.

FRIED SANDWICHES Cuscinetti

As in the previous recipe, Bel Paese can be substituted for the fontina, and the sandwiches can be cut bite-size and served as cocktail fare. **Serves 4**

2 teaspoons Dijon mustard, optional
8 slices French or Italian bread (not too thick)
½ pound Italian fontina cheese, cut into 4 slices
6 ounces baked or smoked ham, cut into 4 slices

3 eggs
2 tablespoons milk
Salt
Freshly ground pepper
Freshly grated nutmeg
½ cup cooking oil

1. Spread mustard lightly on the slices of bread, if desired. Prepare 4 sandwiches, arranging 1 slice of cheese and 1 slice of ham between 2 slices of bread. Press edges together to seal.
2. In a large bowl, beat together eggs and milk. Season lightly with salt, pepper and a pinch of nutmeg. Dip prepared sandwiches into the mixture, turning to coat all sides thoroughly.
3. In 1 or 2 skillets, heat oil. Arrange sandwiches in skillet(s) and, over medium heat, sauté on both sides until crisp and golden, about 5 minutes per side.
4. Drain on paper towels and serve immediately, cut into halves or quarters.

To Prepare in Advance: Through #2.

Freezing Instructions: Do not freeze.

Vegetables

No matter the city, outdoor vegetable stands flourish, the vegetables arranged decoratively, the colors vibrant. Italian vegetables are of the highest quality and are generally prepared very simply. They are usually served as a separate course rather than as an accompaniment to a main dish.

STEAMED ARTICHOKES Carciofi alla Romana

Artichokes, considered almost a staple in Italy, are prepared in many different ways. The small ones are eaten whole, the larger ones sliced and fried;
they are stewed and they are stuffed. In the marketplace, when artichokes
are in season they are artistically displayed as though they were flowers. **Serves 4**

4 large artichokes	6 mint leaves, minced
1 lemon, cut in half	¼ cup olive oil
6 tablespoons fresh breadcrumbs	Salt
3 garlic cloves, minced	Freshly ground pepper
Leaves from 2 sprigs fresh pars-	
ley, chopped fine	

1. Break off stems of the artichokes and trim away outer leaves. Cut artichokes about 1 inch from top and carefully pull or scoop out the "choke,"
using a small spoon, leaving a small cavity to be stuffed. Cut off tips of remaining leaves. As each artichoke is prepared, rub with cut half of lemon or
place in cold water with the juice of 1 lemon.
2. In a small bowl, combine the breadcrumbs, garlic, parsley, mint and 2 tablespoons olive oil. Season with salt and pepper to taste.
3. Divide stuffing among the cavities of the artichokes.
4. Arrange artichokes in a pan large enough to hold them in one layer. Pour
in the remaining olive oil and just enough water to cover the bottoms of the
artichokes. Season with salt and pepper, cover the pan tightly and cook over
low heat until the artichokes are tender, 40 to 45 minutes, adding water if
necessary. (Cooking time depends upon size and freshness of artichoke.)
5. Serve hot or cold.

To Prepare in Advance: Through #4.

Freezing Instructions: Do not freeze.

ARTICHOKES WITH PEAS Carciofi e Piselli

This Roman dish may or may not be flavored with mint. However, fresh mint
adds a delicate taste. **Serves 6**

4 large artichoke bottoms	1 garlic clove, minced
½ medium lemon	¼ pound prosciutto, chopped fine
¼ cup olive oil	1 pound peas, shelled, *or* 1
½ medium onion, chopped fine	10-ounce package frozen peas

¼ cup Chicken Broth (see page 48)   2 to 3 mint leaves, julienned, op-
   Salt   tional
   Freshly ground pepper

1. Break off the artichoke stems and trim flush with bottoms. Rub with lemon and cut into slices.

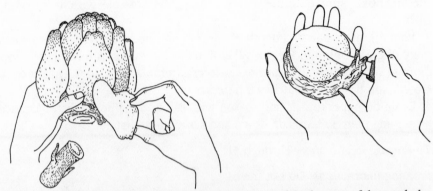

Trim away the outer leaves of the arti-   Trim around the bottom of the artichoke.
choke.

2. In a medium saucepan, heat olive oil. Over medium heat, sauté the onion, garlic and prosciutto until onion is translucent, about 5 minutes.
3. Add the artichokes and the fresh peas (if using frozen peas, add after 10 minutes). Pour in the broth, season with salt and pepper to taste, cover and cook over low heat until artichokes are tender, 15 to 20 minutes. Correct seasoning, adding mint leaves if desired.
4. Serve immediately.

To Prepare in Advance: Through #2. Reheat and continue with recipe.

Freezing Instructions: Do not freeze.

Variation: Green beans, cut into 1½-inch pieces, may be substituted for peas. Add beans with the artichokes.

FRIED ARTICHOKES Carciofi alla Giudia

The artichokes for this recipe must be very small ones, with no spikes. Cooking time depends upon the size of the artichoke. **Serves 4**

8 baby artichokes   **Salt**
   Juice of 2 lemons   **Freshly ground pepper**
   Cooking oil

1. Remove any rough outer leaves from the artichokes, leaving the stalk intact. Carefully scrape the stalk. Place the artichokes in a bowl with lemon juice and cold water to cover.
2. Drain thoroughly and dry well. Gently poke your finger into the center of the artichoke, spreading the leaves as much as possible without breaking them.
3. Pour oil into a pan to a depth of 2 inches and heat. (To test, place a small piece of green onion in the oil. When it turns brown, oil is ready.) Over medium heat, fry artichokes, turning as necessary to cook all sides. Do not overcrowd pan; fry in two batches if necessary.
4. Drain on paper towels and season with salt and pepper to taste. Arrange on serving platter stem side down and serve immediately.

To Prepare in Advance: Through #1.

Freezing Instructions: Do not freeze.

STUFFED ARTICHOKES Carciofi Ripieni

From Tuscany. **Serves 6**

6 large artichokes	2 tablespoons chopped Italian
1 lemon, cut in half	parsley
¼ pound pancetta or blanched	½ cup olive oil
bacon, chopped	Salt
2 garlic cloves, minced	Freshly ground pepper
2 teaspoons fresh breadcrumbs	2 cups Chicken Broth (see page 48)

1. Preheat oven to 375°F.
2. Break off the stems of the artichokes and reserve. Level the bottoms so that artichokes stand upright. Cut off the hard tips of the leaves with scissors. Gently pull the leaves to separate slightly. As each artichoke is prepared, rub with cut side of lemon.
3. Scrape the reserved stems and chop fine. Combine with the pancetta, garlic, breadcrumbs, parsley and 2 teaspoons oil. Season with salt and pepper to taste.
4. Press the stuffing between the artichoke leaves and arrange the artichokes in a baking dish large enough to hold them in one layer. Drizzle the remaining oil over and pour the chicken broth into the dish. Season lightly with salt and pepper.
5. Bake 1 hour, or until tender when pierced with the point of a sharp knife, basting every 10 to 15 minutes.

6. To serve, place 1 artichoke on each plate. Spoon a little of the cooking liquid over each one and serve hot or cold.

To Prepare in Advance: Through #4 or #5.

Freezing Instructions: Do not freeze.

ASPARAGUS PARMESAN Asparagi alla Parmigiana

The asparagus for this dish, which is from Emilia-Romagna, can be steamed or cooked in lots of boiling salted water. To ensure even cooking, open both ends of a coffee can (or similar size can) and place in boiling water halfway up sides. Stand the asparagus in the can, bottoms in the water. After a few minutes, depending upon the size of the asparagus, remove the can and let the entire stalk slip into the water. Continue to cook until tender. **Serves 4 to 6**

1½ pounds asparagus, scraped and trimmed (see Note)	¼ cup (½ stick) unsalted butter
1 garlic clove, mashed, optional	Salt
¼ pound Parmesan cheese, grated or thinly sliced	Freshly ground pepper

1. Cook asparagus in boiling salted water until al dente, 8 to 9 minutes for large spears. Plunge into ice water and dry on paper towels.
2. Preheat oven to 400°F.
3. Butter a 9 × 12-inch baking dish and arrange asparagus in one layer. Sprinkle with garlic, if desired, then sprinkle evenly with the cheese. Dot with butter and season with salt and pepper to taste.
4. Bake about 10 minutes, or until asparagus are heated through and cheese is golden.
5. Serve directly from dish.

To Prepare in Advance: Through #1 or #3.

Freezing Instructions: Do not freeze.

Variation: Trimmed broccoli can be substituted for asparagus.

Note: To scrape asparagus: holding tip, rest asparagus stem on work table. Using a peeler, gently scrape rough spots off stems. When all asparagus have been scraped, trim ends to a uniform size.

BEANS WITH GARLIC Fagioli all'Aglio

It is difficult to think of beans as a peasant dish when they are prepared by the Italians. The best Italian beans come from Lamon, in the Veneto.

All dried legumes are tastier if soaked before cooking. With the softer dried beans, 2 to 3 hours of soaking is sufficient; their volume will increase considerably after soaking. Discard any beans that float.

When this is served at room temperature, additional seasoning may be needed. **Serves 8 to 10**

1 pound Great Northern or small white beans	3 garlic cloves (1 peeled and whole, 2 peeled and minced)
1 cup Chicken Broth (see page 48) or 1 chicken bouillon cube dissolved in 1 cup boiling water (see Note)	2 teaspoons salt
	½ large onion, minced
	½ cup olive oil
	¼ cup minced parsley
1 bay leaf	Freshly ground pepper

1. Soak beans in water to cover 2 to 3 hours up to overnight.
2. Preheat oven to 350°F.
3. Drain beans and place in a bean pot or large casserole.
4. Add chicken broth, bay leaf and enough hot water to cover beans by 2 inches. Cover pot and bake for 1 hour.
5. Add whole garlic clove and salt, replace cover and bake 1 hour longer, or until beans are tender and liquid is nearly absorbed.
6. Remove from oven. Discard bay leaf. Add minced garlic, onion, olive oil, parsley and pepper. Correct seasoning to taste.
7. Serve warm or at room temperature.

To Prepare in Advance: Through #6.

Freezing Instructions: Through #6. Warm over low heat.

Note: When using bouillon cube use less salt in recipe; bouillon cubes contain a lot of salt.

BAKED LENTILS Lenticchie al Forno

The Italian lentil suitable for this dish is greenish-brown. The lentil remains whole when cooked and will not disintegrate as does the red variety. It can be found in Italian groceries as well as health food stores. **Serves 8**

1   pound lentils, washed
    Bouquet garni (pinch of thyme, 2 sprigs parsley, 1 bay leaf, 3 whole cloves tied in cheese-cloth)
1   small onion, peeled
1½ teaspoons salt
    Freshly ground pepper
1   tablespoon cooking oil

½ pound thick bacon, cut into thin strips
1   garlic clove, diced
2   small or 1 large shallot, chopped fine
4   eggs
1   cup (¼ pound) grated Parmesan cheese
¼ cup (½ stick) unsalted butter

1. In a medium bowl, cover lentils with cold water and let soak 2 hours. Drain.
2. Place lentils in a 6-quart saucepan. Add bouquet garni to lentils with whole onion. Season with salt and pepper.
3. Pour in 6 cups cold water and bring to a boil. Over medium heat, cook lentils until tender, 25 to 30 minutes. Drain thoroughly, removing bouquet garni and onion.
4. Meanwhile, in a small skillet, heat oil. Add bacon and cook over low heat 1 to 2 minutes. Stir in garlic and shallot and cook until golden. Drain.
5. Preheat oven to 400°F. Butter a 13 × 9 × 2-inch ovenproof baking dish.
6. In a large bowl, beat eggs. Stir in drained lentils, bacon mixture and half the cheese and combine well.
7. Arrange lentil mixture in prepared dish. Sprinkle with remaining cheese and dot with butter.
8. Bake 15 to 20 minutes, or until lentils are hot.
9. Serve immediately.

To Prepare in Advance: Through #7.

Freezing Instructions: Through #8. Reheat in preheated oven.

SAUTÉED CABBAGE Cavolo Fritto

This is from Trentino, a region influenced gastronomically by its proximity to Austria. Vegetables eaten here are of the coarser variety, including red and green cabbage.

Cabbage is a traditional accompaniment to *zampone* and *cotechino*, large Italian sausages. The sausage is cooked whole, then sliced and served with cabbage, potatoes or lentils, or a combination. **Serves 4 to 6**

1 small napa or savoy cabbage, about 1½ pounds	¼ pound bacon, diced
Salt	2 garlic cloves, minced
2 tablespoons unsalted butter	Freshly ground pepper

1. To clean cabbage, remove all tough outer leaves, cut cabbage in half, core and then cut into thin strips. Sprinkle with salt and let drain in colander for 10 minutes. Rinse thoroughly in cold water.
2. In a 4-quart saucepan, bring enough salted water to a boil to cover cabbage. Add cabbage and cook over high heat until tender, about 7 or 8 minutes. Drain thoroughly and reserve.
3. In the same saucepan, melt butter. Over medium heat, sauté bacon and garlic until bacon is golden, about 5 minutes. Lower heat, add the cabbage, season lightly with salt and lots of pepper and cook, stirring frequently, 5 to 10 minutes, or until cabbage is thoroughly coated with the bacon and butter. Correct seasoning to taste.
4. Serve immediately.

To Prepare in Advance: Through #2.

Freezing Instructions: Do not freeze.

GRILLED EGGPLANT Melanzane alla Griglia

Eggplants come in a variety of colors and sizes. In the United States, we are most familiar with the purple, oval eggplant, the smaller superior to the larger ones. Eggplant has been part of the Italian menu since the 15th century. This is one of the less involved preparations. **Serves 6**

1 1-pound eggplant	Salt
½ cup cooking oil	Freshly ground pepper
Juice of 2 large lemons	

1. Cut eggplant into ¼- to ½-inch slices. (For large eggplant, halve lengthwise, place cut side down and slice crosswise.)
2. Dip each slice into oil. Pour lemon juice over and season with salt and pepper to taste.
3. In a 12-inch skillet, over medium heat, sauté eggplant until lightly browned on one side, about 1 to 2 minutes. Turn and brown other side about 1 to 2 minutes. Use remaining oil as necessary. Or cook on preheated grill about 1 or 2 minutes per side. Drain on paper towels.
4. Serve hot.

To Prepare in Advance: Through #2 or #3. Keep warm in low oven.

Freezing Instructions: Do not freeze.

SAUTÉED PORCINI MUSHROOMS Funghi Porcini

Umbria produces a wide variety of mushrooms. The porcini mushroom, similar to the French *cèpe*, is grown in this region. For a delicate pasta sauce, reduce the cream by only about one third. **Serves 6**

3 tablespoons unsalted butter	Pinch of dried sage
12 medium porcini mushrooms *or* shitaki mushrooms, each cut into 3 or 4 slices	½ cup heavy cream Salt
1 garlic clove	Freshly ground pepper

1. In a 12-inch skillet melt the butter. Add the mushrooms, garlic and sage and cook over medium heat 3 to 4 minutes, stirring to coat the mushrooms. Remove the garlic.
2. Add the cream, turn the heat to high, and cook 5 to 6 minutes longer, or until most of the cream is absorbed. Season with salt and pepper to taste.
3. Serve immediately.

To Prepare in Advance: Through #2, cooking 2 minutes.

Freezing Instructions: Do not freeze.

GRILLED SHITAKI MUSHROOMS Funghi "Shitaki" alla Griglia

The red ovoli mushroom cannot be duplicated. But I have found a worthy substitute: a Japanese mushroom, the shitaki, that is now grown in California. It is spongy in texture and is brownish on top with a white underside.

This can also be served as an appetizer over a slice of toasted Italian bread. **Serves 4**

¼ cup olive oil
8 fresh shitaki mushrooms, stemmed (reserve stems to flavor soup or stocks) (see Note)
3 tablespoons red wine vinegar

¼ teaspoon chopped fresh rosemary leaves *or* pinch of Italian Seasoning
1 garlic clove, mashed but not chopped
Salt
Freshly ground pepper

1. Preheat broiler.
2. Pour olive oil over mushrooms, turning to heavily coat both sides.
3. Combine vinegar, rosemary and garlic in a broiling pan. Arrange mushrooms in pan, cap side up, and place on middle rack under broiler. Broil about 2 minutes, turn mushrooms cap side down, and broil 1 to 2 minutes longer. Season with salt and pepper to taste.
4. To serve, place mushrooms on plate. Remove garlic clove and pour sauce over mushrooms.

To Prepare in Advance: Through #2.

Freezing Instructions: Do not freeze.

Note: Dried shitaki mushrooms, available in Oriental groceries, can be used. Reconstitute by placing in a bowl large enough to allow them to double in size. Pour in warm water to cover and let soak 25 to 30 minutes. Drain. Cut off stems and proceed with recipe.

GLAZED PEARL ONIONS Cipolline Glassate

Tiny pearl onions grow in the Lake Como region. These onions are marinated in a vinegar sauce or glazed. For even cooking, select onions of the same size when possible. To peel onions more easily, blanch onions in boiling water 1 to 2 minutes. Drain and peel. This also reduces cooking time. **Serves 4 to 6**

¼ cup (½ stick) unsalted butter
1 tablespoon sugar

Pinch of dried sage

2 pounds pearl onions, peeled *or* small white boiling onions (see Note)	Pinch of salt ½ cup dry white wine ¼ cup Chicken Broth (see page 48)

1. In 1 or 2 skillets large enough to hold onions in one layer, melt butter. Stir in sugar, sage and onions. Over high heat, cook 3 minutes, stirring to coat onions.
2. Season with salt, pour in wine and continue to cook over high heat until wine is reduced by half. Add broth, lower heat and cover saucepan. Cook until onions are lightly colored and tender, stirring occasionally, about 5 minutes. Correct seasoning to taste.
3. Serve immediately.

To Prepare in Advance: Through #1.

Freezing Instructions: Do not freeze.

Note: If small white boiling onions are used, cooking time will be 10 to 15 minutes, depending on size of onions.

PEAS WITH ONIONS Piselli e Cipolline

Though the world generally recognizes the French *petits pois*, it was the Italian *piselli novelli* that were adopted by the French. Peas were imported into France from Genoa in the middle of the 17th century. If fresh peas are not available, frozen peas can be substituted, but never canned. Paper-thin slivers of prosciutto may be stirred in for extra flavor. **Serves 4**

1 tablespoon cooking oil ¼ pound bacon, cut into 2-inch pieces 1 small onion, diced	1½ pounds peas, shelled, *or* 2 10-ounce packages frozen peas ½ cup water Salt Freshly ground pepper

1. In a small saucepan, heat oil. Add bacon and onion and over medium heat, sauté until onion is wilted, about 5 minutes. Discard grease.
2. Add peas and water, cover and cook over low heat until barely tender, about 10 minutes. Season with salt and pepper to taste.
3. Drain and serve.

To Prepare in Advance: Through #1 or through #2, cooking 5 minutes.

Freezing Instructions: Do not freeze.

POTATO CROQUETTES Crocchette di Patate

Fritto misto is popular in all areas of Italy and can consist of a variety of deep-fried foods including these croquettes. They can be made with leftover chicken, meat or cheese. **Yield: 10 croquettes**

3	medium baking potatoes (1¼ to 1½ pounds)		Freshly ground pepper
¼	cup (1 ounce) grated Parmesan cheese		Freshly grated nutmeg
		4	to 5 ounces cooked chicken, chopped fine (¾ cup)
2	eggs	1	tablespoon chopped parsley or fresh basil
2	tablespoons unsalted butter, softened		
	Salt	1	cup fresh breadcrumbs
			Cooking oil
			Grated Parmesan cheese

1. Preheat oven to 450°F.
2. Bake potatoes until tender, about 50 minutes.
3. Remove the potato pulp and mash through a ricer into a large bowl. Beat in the cheese, eggs, butter, salt, pepper and nutmeg to taste, then chicken and parsley. Correct seasoning. Chill 2 to 3 hours to facilitate handling.
4. Form mixture into 10 sausage-shaped croquettes, 2½ inches long and 1 inch in diameter. Roll each croquette in breadcrumbs.
5. Pour oil into a deep saucepan to a depth of 3 inches and heat. Over medium heat, carefully place croquettes in the oil with a slotted spoon. Cook until golden brown on all sides, 2 to 3 minutes.
6. Drain on paper towels and transfer to a heated platter. Sprinkle lightly with additional Parmesan cheese. Serve immediately.

To Prepare in Advance: Through #4. Refrigerate until needed.

Freezing Instructions: Do not freeze.

Variations: 1. Substitute finely chopped cooked beef, lamb, pork or fish for the chicken.
2. Enclose a small piece of mozzarella, fontina or Bel Paese cheese in the center of each croquette. Roll in breadcrumbs and continue with recipe.

BAKED SPINACH Spinaci al Forno

Even such a basic vegetable as spinach tastes better in Italy. It becomes that much more interesting when baked, or as the main ingredient of a tart. This is from Emilia-Romagna. **Serves 8**

2½	pounds fresh spinach, washed and stemmed	1	cup fresh breadcrumbs
	Salt	½	cup (1 stick) unsalted butter
	Freshly ground pepper	1	cup Chicken Broth (see page 48)
½	pound Italian fontina, very thinly sliced		

1. Preheat oven to 350°F. Butter a 9-inch-square baking dish or a 6-cup soufflé mold.
2. In a large covered saucepan, over medium heat, cook washed spinach in water that clings to the leaves until wilted, about 5 minutes. Drain thoroughly and chop coarsely. Season with salt and pepper to taste.
3. Arrange one quarter of the spinach to cover the bottom of the prepared dish. Top with one quarter of the sliced cheese. Sprinkle with ¼ cup breadcrumbs and dot with 2 tablespoons butter. Continue to layer until all the ingredients are used, ending with breadcrumbs and butter (there should be 4 layers each of spinach, cheese, crumbs and butter).
4. Pour broth over and bake until cheese melts and crumbs brown slightly, about 20 minutes.
5. Serve immediately.

To Prepare in Advance: Through #3.

Freezing Instructions: Do not freeze.

SPINACH TART Pasticcio di Spinaci

From Emilia-Romagna, this makes a delicious light supper with a salad. **Serves 8**

½	pound Puff Pastry (see page 188) *or*	3	ounces pancetta or ham, diced
1	recipe One-Crust Pastry (see page 187)	½	medium onion, chopped
		1	garlic clove, chopped
2½	pounds fresh spinach, washed and stemmed	2	tablespoons all-purpose flour
		½	cup milk
3	tablespoons unsalted butter	2	eggs
		⅓	cup heavy cream

| Salt | Freshly grated nutmeg |
| Freshly ground pepper | 2 hard-cooked eggs, optional |

1. On a lightly floured board, roll out pastry and line a 9- or 10-inch pie plate (see Note). Trim edges. Refrigerate until needed.
2. Preheat oven to 350°F.
3. In a large covered saucepan, over medium heat, cook washed spinach in water that clings to leaves until wilted, about 5 minutes. Drain thoroughly and chop. Reserve.
4. Melt butter in a 10- or 12-inch skillet. Over medium heat, cook pancetta until lightly browned. Add onion and garlic and sauté until golden, 6 to 8 minutes.
5. Stir in flour using wooden spoon and cook about 1 minute. Add spinach and milk and stir until mixture thickens. Remove from heat.
6. Beat together 2 eggs and the heavy cream. Combine with the spinach mixture and season to taste with salt, pepper and nutmeg. Pour into prepared pastry shell and level.
7. Bake 40 minutes, or until firm to the touch.
8. Serve hot, sprinkled with chopped or sliced hard-cooked eggs if desired.

To Prepare in Advance: Through #6 or #7. Reheat as necessary.

Freezing Instructions: Do not freeze.

Note: Can be baked in individual dishes. Baking time will be reduced to 25 to 30 minutes.

SPINACH WITH RAISINS AND PINE NUTS
Spinaci alla Romana

A typical Roman dish. The spinach can be cooked in bacon drippings rather than butter. **Serves 4**

2 pounds fresh spinach, washed and stemmed	1 tablespoon pine nuts
¼ cup raisins	Salt
3 tablespoons unsalted butter	Freshly ground pepper
1 garlic clove, peeled	Freshly grated nutmeg

1. In a large covered saucepan, over medium heat, cook spinach in water that clings to its leaves until wilted, about 5 minutes. Squeeze dry and chop coarsely.

2. Plump raisins in warm water to cover. Drain and dry on paper towels.
3. In a 10- or 12-inch skillet, melt butter. Add garlic and pine nuts and cook over medium heat 1 to 2 minutes. Remove garlic.
4. Stir in raisins and spinach and cook until spinach is heated through, 3 to 4 minutes. Season with salt, pepper and nutmeg to taste.
5. Serve immediately.

To Prepare in Advance: Through #2.

Freezing Instructions: Do not freeze.

VEGETABLE CASSEROLE Verdure al Forno

It is not necessary to peel the potatoes and carrots, but do scrub them well with a vegetable brush. **Serves 6**

½ pound new potatoes, cut into ¼-inch slices	2 bay leaves, crushed
½ pound green beans, sliced in half lengthwise	2 pinches dried sage
½ pound carrots, cut into ¼-inch slices	½ cup (1 stick) unsalted butter
Salt	¼ cup Chicken Broth (see page 48)
Freshly ground pepper	¼ cup (1 ounce) grated Parmesan cheese

1. Cook the vegetables separately in boiling salted water, 3 minutes for the potatoes and green beans and 5 minutes for the carrots. Drain and reserve each vegetable separately.
2. Preheat oven to 350°F.
3. In a buttered 9- or 10-inch-square baking dish, arrange carrots in one layer. Season with salt and pepper to taste, a sprinkling of the crushed bay leaves and a pinch of sage. Dot with 2 tablespoons butter.
4. Repeat procedure with layer of potatoes and layer of green beans, omitting sage in the green beans and dotting with remaining butter. Pour in chicken broth.
5. Bake 30 to 40 minutes, or until vegetables are tender. Sprinkle with grated cheese and return to oven until cheese melts.
6. Serve immediately.

To Prepare in Advance: Through #4.

Freezing Instructions: Do not freeze.

FRIED ZUCCHINI Zucchini Fritti

Fritto misto is a combination of different ingredients, fried and then arranged on a serving plate. Fried zucchini can be one of the components. **Serves 8 to 10**

6 medium zucchini, about 1½ pounds
Salt
¾ to 1 cup all-purpose flour
2 to 3 eggs, beaten
Cooking oil
Grated Parmesan cheese

1. Wash and trim zucchini. Cut each zucchini in half crosswise, then cut each half into ¼-inch strips. Sprinkle strips with salt and let drain in colander 30 to 40 minutes. Pat dry.
2. Place flour and eggs in separate bowls. Coat each zucchini strip with flour, shaking off excess, dip into egg, then coat with flour again.
3. Pour oil into a deep saucepan to a depth of 3 inches and heat. Over medium heat, add zucchini a few strips at a time and cook until golden and crisp, 1 to 2 minutes.
4. Drain on paper towels, sprinkle with grated cheese and salt to taste. Serve immediately.

To Prepare in Advance: Through #1.

Freezing Instructions: Do not freeze.

STUFFED ZUCCHINI Zucchini Ripieni

There are as many versions of stuffed zucchini as there are cooks preparing them. The Ligurians not only are partial to fresh vegetables, they like to stuff them. This is usually served as a first course. It can be assembled early in the day and baked as needed. **Serves 6**

3 zucchini, about 1½ pounds (see Note)
6 slices white bread, crusts removed
½ cup milk
3 tablespoons grated Parmesan cheese
1 egg, lightly beaten
1 tablespoon chopped parsley
Pinch of dried marjoram
Salt
Freshly ground pepper
2 teaspoons olive oil

1. Preheat oven to 350°F. Lightly oil baking pan large enough to hold zucchini in a single layer.

2. In a medium saucepan, blanch zucchini in lightly salted water about 3 to 4 minutes. Drain and plunge into ice water to stop cooking process.

3. Cut each zucchini in half lengthwise. Carefully scoop out the pulp so that the outer skin is not pierced. Chop the pulp fine and place in a medium mixing bowl.

4. Soak bread in milk for 10 minutes. Squeeze very dry, chop fine and add to mixing bowl.

5. Stir in grated cheese, egg, parsley and marjoram and season to taste with salt and pepper.

6. Divide mixture among the zucchini shells. Drizzle a little oil over the top.

7. Arrange the stuffed zucchini in the prepared pan. Bake about 30 minutes, or until stuffing is lightly browned. Serve immediately.

To Prepare in Advance: Through #6.

Freezing Instructions: Do not freeze.

Variation: In step #7, after 15 minutes baking time, sprinkle stuffing with chopped walnuts or bits of crisp bacon and continue with recipe.

Note: If zucchini are very large, cut in half crosswise in step #3, then halve lengthwise and continue with recipe.

Breads and Doughs

Each region of Italy has its own bread and each region believes its bread to be the best. Bread is still made in the home by many housewives, and in some kitchens it is claimed to be the same recipe prepared generations ago.

The bread is coarser in texture than ours and a very important part of the Italian diet, whether the familiar round or long loaf, the flat bread, or the pizza and calzone, the Italian version of our sandwich, to be picked up by hand and eaten.

COUNTRY BREAD

Without some form of leavening, bread would remain flat. Yeast is the most widely used leavening agent, usually activated by dissolving in warm water. It is very important that the yeast be fresh to ensure proper action.

A common method of making bread is to begin with a "starter," a combination of yeast, water and flour. Once the starter begins to ferment, additional flour and water are added to make a "sponge," which is then kneaded and allowed to rise, usually until double in bulk. This is best determined by pressing down into dough with your knuckle. If the indentation remains, the dough is ready. Kneading of dough can be done with a dough hook attachment on a mixer or by hand.

This recipe can be doubled, making 2 loaves or 1 large loaf. **Yield: 1 loaf, 1½ pounds**

1	package active dry *or* fresh yeast	Pinch of salt
3	to 3½ cups all-purpose flour	1¼ cups water

1. To make the starter, in the large bowl of an electric mixer, combine the yeast, ½ cup of the flour, salt and ½ cup of lukewarm (82° to 84°F) water. Mix together to make a very soft dough.
2. Pour 2½ cups flour over the mixture, cover with a towel and let the sponge rest in a cool spot for 30 to 45 minutes.
3. Insert the dough hook into the mixer and on low speed, slowly add ¾ cup cold water and the remaining ½ cup flour as necessary. Knead until dough clumps around the dough hook and pulls cleanly from the sides of the bowl. Dough should be smooth and satiny.
4. Transfer dough to a greased large bowl, turning to grease all sides. Cover with a damp towel and let rise in a warm spot until doubled in bulk, about 1 hour.
5. Punch down, turn out onto a lightly floured board and knead for 1 or 2 minutes. Shape into a round or a long loaf. Sprinkle with flour and place on a baking sheet. Lightly cover with a cloth or plastic wrap and again let rise in a warm spot until doubled in bulk, about 30 minutes.
6. Preheat oven to 400°F.
7. Bake 35 to 40 minutes, or until golden brown and bread sounds hollow when lightly tapped.
8. Cool and serve as needed.

To Prepare in Advance: Through #7.

Freezing Instructions: Through #7. Defrost wrapped. Or bread can be sliced and slices toasted as needed.

To make bread by hand, follow directions through step #2, using a wooden spoon to combine ingredients. In step #3, slowly add the water and flour as necessary, using the spoon or your hand to form a solid mass. Turn out on lightly floured board or work table and knead dough. Fold the dough in half and, using the palm or heel of your hand, push down hard, sliding the dough forward. Repeat the procedure of folding, pushing and sliding until the dough is smooth and satiny, about 10 to 15 minutes, adding flour only as necessary.

Note: For best results, your oven should be lined with baking tiles, which can be purchased in most cookware stores. If you cannot obtain tiles, invert a heavy baking sheet on the rack on which you're baking the bread. Place baking sheet with bread on top.

COUNTRY BREAD WITH SAUSAGE

A sausage or cheese filling adds flavor to the Country Bread and makes for a substantial snack. **Yield: 1 loaf, about 2 pounds**

1 recipe Country Bread (see page 176)
½ pound (2 links) sweet or hot Italian sausage
1 egg, lightly beaten, for egg wash
½ teaspoon coarse salt

1. Prepare Country Bread recipe through step #4.
2. If using links, remove casing and crumble sausage meat. In a small skillet, over medium heat, sauté sausage meat until brown, stirring occasionally, about 10 minutes. Discard grease and cool sausage to room temperature.
3. Turn dough out onto a lightly floured board and roll into a rectangle approximately 8 × 14 inches. Spread sausage meat on dough to within 1 inch of all sides. Starting from a 14-inch side, roll up jelly roll fashion, tucking ends in as dough is rolled. (See illustrations, page 178.)
4. Sprinkle a 12 × 15-inch baking sheet lightly with flour and place bread on sheet. Cover with a damp cloth and let rise in a warm spot until doubled in bulk, about 30 minutes.
5. Brush with egg wash and sprinkle with coarse salt.
6. Bake 45 to 50 minutes, or until golden brown and bread sounds hollow when tapped.

Spread the sausage meat on the bread dough to within 1 inch of all the sides.

Starting from the 14-inch side, roll the bread over the sausage meat, jelly roll fashion, tucking the ends in.

7. Cool and slice as needed.

To Prepare in Advance: Through #6.

Freezing Instructions: Through #6. Defrost wrapped. Or bread can be sliced and slices toasted as needed.

Variation: Grate ¼ pound mozzarella cheese and combine with 8 minced fresh sage leaves *or* ¼ teaspoon of crushed dried sage leaves. Continue with recipe as above, substituting cheese for the sausage.

FLAT BREAD Focaccia

Focaccia is one of the old, traditional dishes of Italy. It is a bread that is eaten for breakfast as well as for a snack and is perfect for picnics. It can be plain, topped with onion, with sage, or stuffed. **Yield: 1 12 × 16-inch flat bread**

1 package active dry *or* fresh yeast	¼ cup olive oil
¼ cup warm water (105° to 115°F)	¾ to 1 cup warm water (105° to 115°F)
3 cups all-purpose flour	
Pinch of salt	1 tablespoon coarse salt

1. In a food processor fitted with steel blade, dissolve yeast in ¼ cup warm water (see Note).
2. Add flour, a pinch of salt and 2 tablespoons olive oil to bowl and process just to combine.
3. With machine running, slowly pour ¾ to 1 cup warm water through the feed tube. Stop when a mass begins to form on the blade; do not use any more water than is necessary.

4. Turn out dough onto a lightly floured board, and knead for 1 to 2 minutes. Form into a ball and place in an oiled bowl, turning to grease all sides. Cover with a damp towel and let rise in a warm spot until doubled in bulk, about 1 to 1½ hours.

5. Punch down, knead gently on a lightly floured board and shape into a rectangle about 12 × 16-inches.

6. Place dough on a greased 12 × 16-inch baking tray, sprinkle very lightly with flour, and cover with towel. Let rise in warm spot for 1 hour.

7. Preheat oven to 400°F.

8. Using your knuckle, poke some indentations over the surface of the dough. Sprinkle with coarse salt and the remaining 2 tablespoons oil.

9. Bake 20 to 25 minutes, or until golden. Serve warm.

To Prepare in Advance: Through #9, returning to oven to warm.

Freezing Instructions: Through #9. Defrost, wrapped, at room temperature. Warm before serving.

Note: To prepare by hand, in a small bowl dissolve yeast in ¼ cup warm water. Mound the flour and pinch of salt on a board, forming a well in the center. Pour olive oil, ¾ cup water and dissolved yeast into the well. Whisk lightly with a fork, gradually pulling flour into the center. Using the tips of your fingers, add remaining ¼ cup water as necessary to form a solid mass. Knead dough for about 10 minutes, or until smooth. Continue with recipe in step #4.

FLAT BREAD WITH ONIONS Focaccia con Cipolle

A variation of Flat Bread, flavored but not overpowered by the onions. **Yield: 1 12 × 16-inch flat bread**

1 recipe Flat Bread (see page 178)	2 tablespoons olive oil
1 medium onion, cut in half	1 teaspoon sea salt or coarse
Boiling water	salt

1. Prepare recipe for Flat Bread through step #6.

2. Cut onion into very thin slices and place in bowl. Pour boiling water over onion and let stand 2 to 3 minutes. Drain and cover with ice water. Drain and dry thoroughly. (This process will make the onion much sweeter.)

3. Preheat oven to 400°F.

4. Using your knuckle, poke indentations over surface of dough. Distribute onions as evenly as possible over dough and sprinkle with olive oil and salt.

5. Bake 20 to 25 minutes, or until golden. Serve warm.

To Prepare in Advance: Through #5, returning to oven to warm.

Freezing Instructions: Through #5. Defrost, wrapped, at room temperature. Warm before serving.

FLAT BREAD WITH SAGE Focaccia con Salvia

A Genoese favorite, sage lends a distinctive aromatic flavor to Flat Bread. Dried sage leaves can be substituted for fresh sage when it is not available. **Yield: 1 12 × 16-inch flat bread**

1	recipe Flat Bread (see page 178)	2	tablespoons olive oil
12	to 14 fresh sage leaves, minced, or 1 tablespoon dried sage leaves, crumbled	2	teaspoons coarse salt

1. Prepare recipe for Flat Bread through step #4.
2. Preheat oven to 400°F.
3. Punch dough down and knead gently, kneading sage into the dough. Cover with towel and let rest 20 minutes.
4. Shape dough into a rectangle about 12 × 16 inches or into an 11-inch circle.
5. Brush with olive oil and sprinkle with salt.
6. Bake 20 to 25 minutes, or until golden. Serve warm.

To Prepare in Advance: Through #6, returning to oven to warm.

Freezing Instructions: Through #6. Defrost, wrapped, at room temperature. Warm before serving.

STUFFED FLAT BREAD Focaccia Ripiena

Enjoyed by the shepherds of Apulia, this humble dish makes a very satisfying snack. **Serves 4 to 6**

Dough

1	package active dry *or* fresh yeast
3	tablespoons warm water (105° to 115°F)
1¾	cups all-purpose flour
1	teaspoon salt
2	tablespoons cooking oil
¼	cup water

Filling

¼	cup olive oil plus additional for brushing
1	pound onions, chopped fine
¾	pound tomatoes, peeled, seeded and chopped fine
7	ounces black olives, pitted and cut in half
1	tablespoon capers, drained
3	anchovy filets, chopped
¾	cup (3 ounces) grated Parmesan or pecorino cheese
	Pinch of salt, if needed

Grated Parmesan cheese

1. *To make dough:* In a small bowl, dissolve yeast in 3 tablespoons warm water.

2. On a work table or board, combine flour and salt. Make a well in the center and pour oil, ¼ cup water and dissolved yeast into the well. Gradually work flour into the mixture with your fingertips and then knead until dough is pliable, about 10 minutes, forming a ball. Place in large greased bowl, turning to grease all sides. Cover with moist towel and let rise in warm spot until doubled in bulk, about 1 to 1½ hours.

3. *While dough is rising, make filling:* In a 12-inch skillet, heat ¼ cup olive oil. Over medium heat, sauté onions until lightly golden, about 10 minutes. Add tomatoes, olives, capers and anchovy filets and cook until most of the liquid evaporates, about 10 minutes.

4. Remove from heat and stir in cheese. Correct seasoning to taste, adding salt only if necessary. Reserve.

5. Punch down dough and turn out onto board. Roll or stretch into a 15-inch square. Place on baking tray and brush with olive oil. Spread filling on half the dough, fold other half over and trim edges. Carefully roll edges to secure. Cover and let rise in warm spot for 30 minutes.

6. Preheat oven to 400°F.

7. Brush dough with oil and bake about 25 minutes, or until golden brown.

8. Brush lightly with oil, sprinkle with Parmesan cheese and serve immediately.

To Prepare in Advance: Through #4.

Freezing Instructions: Through #8. Warm before serving.

$\mathbf{P}$izza, a Neapolitan creation, was originally a poor man's meal, a simple topping over a large piece of dough. In this country, the toppings have become very creative; only the crust remains the same.

"Making pizzas can be as much fun as eating them," says Wolfgang Puck, owner and chef of Spago restaurant in Los Angeles. Under his tutelage, I kneaded, pinched and finally presented him with dough worthy of a Spago pizza. The toppings can be as varied as taste and imagination allow, with a combination of ingredients such as prosciutto, fontina, mozzarella, blanched or raw chopped garlic, sliced artichoke hearts, sausages, tomatoes, duck, fish, chopped sautéed eggplant, and even cream cheese and smoked salmon. To ensure good texture, the yeast should be fresh. I recommend using stone tiles in the oven and laying the pizza directly on the tiles. In Italy, the pizzerias have wood-burning ovens placed in a prominent spot so that part of the dining pleasure is watching the pizzas being made. Spago has adopted the same concept.

PIZZA DOUGH

Yield: 4 7- or 8-inch pizzas, 6 ounces each

1	package active dry *or* fresh yeast	1	teaspoon salt
1	teaspoon honey or sugar	2	tablespoons olive oil plus additional for brushing
¾	cup warm water (105° to 115°F)	1½	cups topping of your choice for each 7- or 8-inch pizza
2¾	cups all-purpose flour		

1. In a small bowl, dissolve yeast and honey in ¼ cup warm water, stirring as needed.
2. In a mixer fitted with dough hook, combine flour and salt. Add 2 tablespoons oil. When the oil is completely absorbed, add dissolved yeast.
3. Add remaining ½ cup water and knead on low speed about 5 minutes.
4. Turn out onto board and knead 2 to 3 minutes longer; dough should be smooth and firm.
5. Let rise in a warm spot, covered with a damp towel, about 30 minutes. (Dough will stretch when lightly pulled.)
6. Divide dough into 4 equal balls. Work each ball by pulling dough down and tucking under bottom of ball. Repeat 4 or 5 times. Then, on a smooth surface, roll ball under palm of hand until dough is smooth and firm, about 1 minute.
7. Cover with damp towel and let rest 15 to 20 minutes. At this point, balls can be loosely covered with plastic wrap and refrigerated for 1 to 2 days.

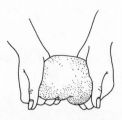

Work each ball of pizza dough by pulling down and tucking under the bottom of the ball.

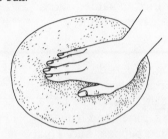

Press down on the center of the pizza dough, spreading it into a 7- or 8-inch circle.

8. Preheat oven to 525°F.

9. To prepare pizza, place a ball of dough on a lightly floured board (see Note). Press down on the center, spreading dough, or rolling, into a 7- or 8-inch circle; if dough breaks, brush torn area with beaten egg and patch with a small piece of dough. Brush lightly with olive oil and arrange topping over top, leaving a small border around the edge of the pizza.

10. Bake 15 to 20 minutes, or until pizza is nicely browned.

To Prepare in Advance: Through #7. Bring back to room temperature and continue with recipe.

Freezing Instructions: Through #7. Defrost, wrapped; bring back to room temperature and continue with recipe.

Note: To make a larger pizza, place one flattened ball of dough on top of another and press or roll into a 12-inch round or square.

SUGGESTED PIZZA TOPPINGS

(Use 1½ cups for each 7- or 8-inch pizza *or* 1 cup to fill each calzone. Season with salt and pepper to taste.)

I.
Tomatoes, peeled and thinly sliced
Mozzarella cheese, grated
Hard-cooked egg, chopped
Salami, thinly sliced
Fresh basil leaves
Oregano
Anchovy filets

II.
Tomatoes, peeled and crushed
Blanched garlic, chopped
Fontina cheese, thinly sliced
Mozzarella cheese, grated
Sausages, sliced
Cilantro, chopped

III.
Tomatoes, thinly sliced
Artichoke hearts, sliced
Eggplant, sliced and sautéed
Mozzarella cheese, thinly sliced
Parmesan cheese, grated
Thyme, fresh or dried

IV.
Pesto (see page 64)
Roasted peppers, sliced (see page 34)
Tomatoes, peeled and crushed
Onion, chopped
Scallops

V.
Cooked ham, slivered
Mozzarella cheese, thinly sliced
Parmesan cheese, grated
Sun-dried tomatoes, sliced
Basil leaves, julienned

VI.
Onion, chopped
Pecorino cheese, grated
Prosciutto, slivered
Olives, pitted and halved
Roasted peppers, sliced (page 34)

VII.
Shrimp, peeled
Tomatoes, peeled and crushed
Capers, drained
Parmesan cheese, grated
Mozzarella cheese, grated
Parsley, chopped

VIII.
Green onions, thinly sliced
Mushrooms, sliced
Sun-dried tomatoes, chopped
Garlic, blanched and chopped
Smoked ham, slivered
Yellow squash, sliced

Note: Stir 1 teaspoon red pepper flakes into 1 cup olive oil. Brush pizza or calzone dough with oil for spicier toppings. As with bottled olive oil, cover container with cheesecloth.

CALZONE

Eating pizza by hand is easier when the crust is folded over the topping—thus the Neapolitan *Calzone,* a folded pizza. It can be baked or fried in oil. **Yield: 4 4-inch calzone**

1 recipe Pizza Dough (see page 182)
   Topping of your choice (see page 184)
3 tablespoons olive oil

¼ cup (1 ounce) grated Parmesan cheese
4 small sprigs fresh rosemary or thyme

1. Prepare pizza dough through step #8.
2. To prepare each calzone, pull or roll each ball of dough as for pizza to form a 7- or 8-inch circle. Brush half the circle with oil and place 1 cup filling on one half of the dough. Fold dough over filling, pressing edges together. Trim as necessary.

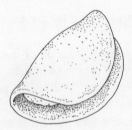

Fold the dough over the calzone filling, pressing the edges together.

Crimp the edges of the calzone with the tines of a fork to enclose the filling completely.

3. Brush top lightly with oil and crimp edges with tines of a fork to enclose filling securely.
4. Bake 15 to 20 minutes, until calzone are nicely browned (see Note).
5. Brush lightly with oil, sprinkle with grated cheese and decorate each with a sprig of rosemary or thyme. Serve immediately.

To Prepare in Advance: Through #1.

Freezing Instructions: Through #1. Defrost wrapped, bring back to room temperature and continue with recipe.

Note: To fry calzone, pour cooking oil into pan to a depth of ½ inch. Heat oil. Place calzone in oil and cook until golden brown, turning to brown both sides. If oil is very hot, this will take 2 to 3 minutes per side. Drain on paper towels, sprinkle with cheese and decorate with fresh rosemary or thyme.

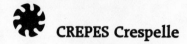

CREPES Crespelle

Crepes are easy to prepare and they freeze well. Try stirring bechamel into your leftover meat, fish or vegetables; wrap a crepe around the leftovers, spoon bechamel over and heat through in the oven. You will have an elegant meal out of what might have been a very ordinary one. This recipe can be doubled. **Yield: About 18 5½-inch crepes**

3 large eggs	2 tablespoons unsalted butter,
1 cup milk	melted
½ teaspoon salt	2 or 3 tablespoons cooking oil or
1 cup sifted all-purpose flour	softened butter

1. In a food processor fitted with steel blade, or a blender, combine eggs, milk and salt (see Note).
2. Add flour and process or blend until smooth.
3. With machine running, pour melted butter through the feed tube (or whisk in).
4. Transfer to bowl, cover and refrigerate at least 1 hour for lighter, more tender crepes.
5. Heat a 6-inch crepe or omelet pan and brush lightly with oil or butter (if using a nonstick pan, no oil or butter is necessary). Over medium heat, using a 1-ounce measure (2 tablespoons), ladle batter into pan. Quickly tilt pan so that the batter thinly coats the entire bottom of the pan, returning any excess batter to the bowl. Cook about 30 seconds, or until edges pull away slightly from pan. Turn crepe and cook 15 to 20 seconds longer. (Use your fingers and spatula to grasp the edges of the crepe and turn it over. This works better than a spatula alone.) Turn out onto a plate and continue making crepes until all the batter is used, stacking them as they are cooked. Brush pan as necessary with oil or butter.
6. Use as needed.

To Prepare in Advance: Through #5.

Freezing Instructions: Through #5, wrapping desired quantity in aluminum foil packages. Defrost, wrapped, in refrigerator.

Note: To prepare by hand, in a mixing bowl, whisk together egg, milk and salt. Gradually whisk in flour until smooth.

ONE-CRUST PASTRY Crostata

This is a very versatile pie crust that can be used with either a sweet or savory filling. The pastry can be rolled, fitted into a pie plate, trimmed and frozen. If using glass plate, be sure to bring to room temperature before baking. **Yield: 1 9- or 10-inch shell**

1 cup all-purpose flour	6 tablespoons unsalted butter, chilled and cut into small pieces
½ teaspoon salt	2 to 3 tablespoons ice water

1. In a food processor fitted with steel blade, combine flour, salt and butter and process until mixture resembles coarse meal (see Note).
2. With machine running, slowly pour ice water through the feed tube just until a mass forms on the blade.
3. Turn dough out onto a lightly floured board and pat into a 6-inch circle (to facilitate rolling out dough later). Wrap in plastic wrap and refrigerate at least 30 minutes before rolling.
4. Use as needed.

To Prepare in Advance: Through #3.

Freezing Instructions: Through #3. Defrost in refrigerator and roll into desired shape.

Note: To prepare by hand, in a small bowl, using a pastry blender or 2 knives, cut butter into flour and salt until mixture resembles coarse meal. Slowly add ice water just until dough holds together. Press into a 6-inch circle and continue with recipe.

CREAM PUFF PASTE Pasta Soffiata

These puffs can be filled with any number of savory fillings—crostini with chicken livers, cheese, etc. **Yield: 60 small puffs**

1 cup water	1 cup all-purpose flour
½ cup (1 stick) unsalted butter, cut into 6 pieces	4 large eggs
¼ teaspoon salt	1 egg, lightly beaten, for egg wash

1. Preheat oven to 400°F. Butter 2 large baking sheets and sprinkle with cold water, pouring off excess.
2. In a medium saucepan, combine water, butter and salt and bring to a rolling boil. When butter is completely melted, remove pan from heat and add the flour all at once, stirring vigorously with a wooden spoon until flour is ab-

sorbed. Return to low heat and cook for 1 to 2 minutes, stirring all the while, until dough comes away from the sides of the pan and forms a ball. Transfer to a food processor (see Note).

3. With machine running, add eggs all at once and process until the dough is very smooth and shiny, scraping down the sides as necessary.

4. Spoon dough into pastry bag fitted with plain ¼-inch round tip. Pipe 1½-inch rounds of dough onto prepared baking sheets 1 inch apart. Brush with egg wash and smooth any peaks that may have formed.

5. Bake 10 minutes, lower heat to 350°F and continue to bake 45 minutes longer, or until puffs are golden brown and sound hollow when lightly tapped. Cool.

6. Fill with desired filling.

To Prepare in Advance: Through #5.

Freezing Instructions: Through #5. Defrost for 30 minutes and reheat in preheated oven.

Note: To prepare by hand, remove pan from heat and add eggs one at a time, stirring vigorously with a wooden spoon after each addition until dough is very smooth and shiny.

PUFF PASTRY Pasta la sfogliatella

A flaky, rich pastry used primarily in the northern regions of Italy. **Yield: 2¼ pounds**

Pastry
1½ cups all-purpose flour
1 cup pastry flour (see Note)
1 teaspoon salt
¼ cup (½ stick) unsalted butter, chilled and cut into small pieces
¾ cup ice water

Butter block
1¼ cups plus 2 tablespoons (2¾ sticks) unsalted butter, removed from refrigerator 30 minutes before using, cut into 1-tablespoon pieces
½ cup all-purpose flour

1. *To prepare pastry:* In a food processor fitted with steel blade, or in an electric mixer fitted with dough hook, combine all-purpose flour, pastry flour, salt and butter and mix until texture resembles coarse meal.

2. With machine running, slowly add water until dough begins to form a ball. Turn out onto a very lightly floured board and pat into a small square. Lightly score to relax elasticity. Wrap tightly in plastic wrap and refrigerate for 1 hour.

3. Place rolling pin in refrigerator to chill.

4. *To prepare butter block:* In a clean bowl, food processor or mixer, combine butter pieces and flour just until butter masses into one piece; do not overwork. Remove from bowl, place between 2 pieces of waxed paper, and roll or press into a 6-inch square. Wrap securely in plastic wrap and refrigerate about 30 minutes.

5. On a lightly floured board, roll out the pastry into a 10-inch square. Place butter block in the center of the pastry, at an angle (see illustration), and using

Place the butter block in the center of the pastry, at an angle.

your knuckle, poke indentations in the butter to ensure puffier pastry. Cover butter completely with the ends of the pastry, meeting in the center like an envelope, and pinch together any opening in the pastry.

6. Turn pastry seam side down, and on a lightly floured board, roll out to a rectangle approximately 8 × 18 inches. Do not press down on the dough; you want to flatten butter between the layers of dough without allowing it to ooze through. Starting with the 8-inch side in front of you, fold dough into thirds.

7. Turn dough so that seam is on your right and again roll out to the same size rectangle, sprinkling board and pastry with flour as needed to prevent sticking. Using a large, dry pastry brush, brush away excess flour *before* and *after* folding. With your rolling pin, block pastry as it is being rolled. So that it keeps its shape. Again fold dough into thirds. You have just completed two turns. Using your knuckle, lightly press two indentations into the dough

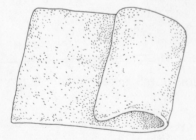

Starting with the 8-inch side in front of you, fold dough into thirds for the first turn.

After the second turn, make two light indentations in the dough with your knuckles.

to remind you of the number of turns you have made and repeat as you continue your turns. Wrap securely in plastic wrap and refrigerate for 30 minutes.

8. Repeat this procedure until you have completed six turns, refrigerating after each set of two. Puff pastry is now ready to be used.

To Prepare in Advance: Through #8.

Freezing Instructions: Through #8. Defrost, wrapped, overnight in the refrigerator, then roll into desired shape and use as needed. Pastry can be cut in half and frozen in separate packages. Or pastry can be fitted into pan, frozen and baked directly from freezer.

Note: Pastry flour can be obtained in health food or specialty food stores.

 ## SWEET PASTRY Pasta Frolla

This soft dough must be refrigerated before using for best results. The recipe can be doubled, then the dough divided in half and frozen for future use. The dough may break as it is rolled and pressed into the pan; if this happens, patch with bits of dough. **Yield: 1 8- or 9-inch shell**

1 cup all-purpose flour	1 egg yolk
6 tablespoons unsalted butter, cut into 6 pieces	Grated rind of ½ small lemon
	Pinch of salt
2 tablespoons sugar	1 teaspoon ice water

1. Using a food processor fitted with steel blade, combine flour, butter, sugar, egg yolk, lemon rind and salt and process until mixture resembles coarse meal (see Note).
2. Add water and process until dough forms a mass on the blade and leaves the sides of the work bowl.
3. Turn dough out and pat into a 6-inch circle to facilitate rolling out later. Wrap in plastic wrap and refrigerate at least 2 hours.
4. Use as needed.

To Prepare in Advance: Through #3.

Freezing Instructions: Through #3. Defrost in refrigerator, then roll into desired shape and use as needed.

Note: The food processor simplifies the making of pastry, but it can be done by hand. On a board, heap all the dry ingredients with the grated lemon rind in a mound, making a well in the center. Melt the butter and cool slightly. Pour into the well with the remaining ingredients and whisk lightly with a fork. Gradually pull the flour into the center, using the tips of your fingers. When a mass of dough begins to form, bring in all the flour and press into a 6-inch circle. Then proceed with recipe as above.

Desserts and Pastries

Pastry making is a recognized art in all regions of Italy, each region having its own specialties. There is an infinite variety of tarts, cakes, cookies and sweet pastries. In any large town, you can find groups gathered in a café drinking coffee and eating rich cakes.

On my last trip to Italy, my sons told me all the best ice cream spots to visit, and it was a gastronomic experience. It is a common sight to see a vendor behind a row of canisters filled with various flavors of ice cream. I have included some of my favorite flavors, starting with the basic vanilla. The sherbets, too, are luscious, the flavors intense.

I find that ice cream is at its best when served within 24 hours of preparation. For best results, transfer to refrigerator 20 minutes before serving to soften slightly.

I have sampled many desserts representative of Italian *cucina*, and I have selected recipes that can be easily and successfully prepared, recipes that you will enjoy making and be proud to serve.

If you want to serve wine with any of these desserts, I suggest Moscato (either Italian or American), a sweet white wine, sparkling or still.

ALMOND COOKIES Biscotti di Mandorla

Italians love to dip these hard cookies in wine. The cookies will keep for weeks in a tightly closed tin or jar. **Yield: About 52 cookies**

2	cups all-purpose flour		Grated rind of 1 lemon
1	teaspoon baking powder	1	teaspoon almond liqueur
	Pinch of salt	2½	cups (½ pound) almonds,
3	large eggs		coarsely chopped
1	cup sugar	1	egg, lightly beaten, for egg
1	tablespoon fresh lemon juice		wash

1. Preheat oven to 350°F. Butter a large baking sheet.
2. Sift together flour, baking powder and salt. Set aside.
3. Using a wire whisk or rotary beater, beat eggs and sugar until mixture is pale yellow and ribbons form when whisk is lifted from bowl. Stir in lemon juice, lemon rind and almond liqueur.
4. Add sifted ingredients and blend until incorporated. Stir in almonds, using hands to mix thoroughly. Dough will be sticky.
5. Flour your hands lightly and form 2 loaves, each 14 inches long and 2 inches wide, and place on prepared baking sheet. Brush with egg wash.
6. Bake 20 to 25 minutes, or until lightly golden.
7. Remove from oven. Using a serrated knife, immediately cut diagonally into ½-inch slices. Cool. Store in tightly covered container. The cookies harden as they stand.

To Prepare in Advance: Through #7.

Freezing Instructions: Through #7. Defrost, wrapped, at room temperature.

Suggested Wine:
Italian: ASTI SPUMANTE, a sweet, sparkling, straw-colored wine from the Piedmont
American: Martini MOSCATO AMABILE

ALMOND MACAROONS Amaretti

Almond macaroons or *amaretti* originated in Italy and can be found in a variety of shapes and forms. **Yield: About 46 macaroons, 1½ inches each**

1 cup blanched almonds, ground fine
1 cup sugar

2 egg whites
1 teaspoon almond extract

1. Preheat oven to 375°F. Butter and flour 2 baking sheets.
2. In the bowl of an electric mixer fitted with a whip, combine the almonds and sugar. On slow speed, add the egg whites and almond extract. When thoroughly combined, increase the speed to high and beat for 3 minutes.
3. Spoon batter into a pastry bag fitted with a #6 round tip. (Pastry will be runny.) Pipe into 1-inch rounds, 1 inch apart, on the prepared baking sheets. Let rest at least 1 hour.
4. Bake 12 to 15 minutes, or until golden brown (longer if you prefer your cookies browner).
5. Cool cookies on racks.

To Prepare in Advance: Through #5.

Freezing Instructions: Through #5. Defrost wrapped.

Variation: Spread Chocolate Cream on the bottom side of half the cookies. Sandwich with the remaining cookies. To make Chocolate Cream, cut 6 ounces semisweet chocolate into small pieces and place in a small heatproof bowl. Bring 6 tablespoons heavy cream to a boil and immediately pour over the chocolate. Stir until melted and smooth. Cool to spreading consistency.

LADYFINGERS Savoiardi

This recipe can be doubled if desired. If stored in airtight containers, ladyfingers will keep quite well. **Yield: 26 to 30 Ladyfingers**

1 whole egg
3 large eggs, separated
⅓ cup plus 1 tablespoon sugar

1 teaspoon vanilla extract
½ cup sifted cake flour
Sifted powdered sugar

1. Preheat oven to 350°F. Line two 12 × 14-inch baking pans with parchment paper.
2. Using a wire whisk or rotary beater, combine whole egg, egg yolks and

⅓ cup sugar and beat until mixture is very thick and pale yellow, about 5 minutes. Stir in vanilla.

3. Gently fold flour into egg mixture. Reserve.

4. With a clean whisk or rotary beater, whip egg whites to soft peaks. Add the remaining 1 tablespoon sugar and whip until stiff but not dry. Stir one quarter of the whites into the reserved mixture to lighten. Gently but quickly fold in the remaining whites.

5. Spoon batter into pastry bag fitted with #6 or #7 round tip. Pipe out ladyfingers, about 4 inches long, 1 inch wide and 1 inch apart, on prepared pans. Dust lightly with sifted powdered sugar.

6. Bake 15 to 18 minutes, reversing baking pans after 7 to 8 minutes for even baking; ladyfingers should be golden.

7. Remove from pans with spatula and cool on racks.

To Prepare in Advance: Through #6.

Freezing Instructions: Through #6. Defrost, wrapped, at room temperature.

FIG TART Banda di Fichi

The fig has been eaten, fresh or dried, for thousands of years. Figs are a delicacy, whether in Italy or the United States, and are harvested from July through October. The figs should be very ripe and bursting with flavor. If not available, ripe peeled peaches can be substituted. This tart is a specialty of the Hotel Hassler in Rome. **Serves 12**

1 pound Puff Pastry (see page 188)	**Pastry cream**
1 egg, lightly beaten, for egg wash	2 large eggs
	⅓ cup sugar
	¼ cup all-purpose flour
	Pinch of salt
6 large fresh figs (½ pound), peeled and cut into ⅛-inch slices	1 cup milk
	1 teaspoon vanilla extract or liqueur of your choice
	1 cup heavy cream, whipped

1. Roll out pastry into a 9½ × 13½-inch rectangle. Carefully cut a ¾-inch strip from each of the 4 sides, leaving an 8 × 12-inch rectangle. Reserve strips.

2. Place on baking sheet and brush around edges with egg wash, being careful that egg does not drip down sides. Place the 2 long strips on the 2 12-inch

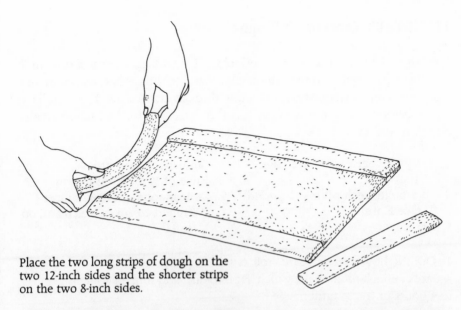

Place the two long strips of dough on the two 12-inch sides and the shorter strips on the two 8-inch sides.

sides and the shorter strips on the 2 8-inch sides (see illustration). Refrigerate at least 30 minutes.

3. Preheat oven to 400°F.

4. Brush side strips with egg wash. Using the tines of a fork, carefully prick all over the inside of the rectangle to prevent the dough from rising. Bake 20 to 25 minutes, or until pastry is golden. Cool on rack.

5. *To make pastry cream:* In a mixing bowl, whisk together the eggs and sugar. Add flour and salt and whisk until very smooth.

6. In a medium saucepan, bring milk to a boil. Slowly whisk into egg mixture.

7. Return to saucepan. Over medium heat, cook until thickened and smooth, whisking all the while, about 5 minutes. Transfer to bowl and cool.

8. Stir in vanilla or liqueur. Fold in the whipped cream, taste and add more flavoring if desired.

9. Fill inside of pastry with pastry cream and level with a rubber spatula. Arrange sliced figs in rows, reversing direction for each row, on top of the cream. Refrigerate until needed.

10. Cut into desired slices and serve.

To Prepare in Advance: Through #4, #8 or #9.

Freezing Instructions: Do not freeze.

PLUM TART Crostata di Prugne

Lunching in a small restaurant overlooking Lake Maggiore was a treat in itself. Ending a meal with this simple plum tart still brings back warm memories. Plums are available from early July through late August. If you chill the pastry before baking, there will be less shrinkage. **Yield: 1 9-inch-square *or* 8-inch round tart**

1 recipe Sweet Pastry (see page 190)	1 tablespoon all-purpose flour Juice of ½ medium lemon
4 to 5 large fresh plums (1 pound) (see Note)	2 tablespoons unsalted butter Whipped cream or ice cream, optional
¼ cup sugar	

1. On a lightly floured board, roll out pastry large enough to fit a 9-inch-square or 8-inch-round baking dish. Fit into dish and trim edges. Refrigerate 3 to 4 hours or freeze until needed.
2. Preheat oven to 350°F.
3. Cut each plum into 6 to 8 slices, removing pit. Place in a bowl and toss with sugar and flour.
4. Arrange plums on pastry in rows (or in circles, if using round dish), slightly overlapping the slices. Alternate the direction of each row of plums. Sprinkle lemon juice over and dot with butter.

Arrange the plum slices in a round or square baking dish, overlapping them slightly.

5. Bake 35 to 45 minutes, or until the crust is golden brown and plums are tender.
6. Serve warm or cold. Softly whipped cream or ice cream can be served on each slice, if desired.

To Prepare in Advance: Through #1. Or through #5, warming when ready to serve.

Freezing Instructions: Through #1. Fill directly from freezer and continue with recipe.

Note: Ripe peeled pears may be substituted. Rub peeled pears with cut side of lemon, slice, and continue with the recipe.

GOLDEN BREAD Pandoro di Verona

If one food were to be designated representative of Verona, it would be *pandoro*, meaning "bread of gold." *Pandoro* can be found in almost every bake shop in Verona. It is served plain or used as the base for other desserts. Special *pandoro* pans can be purchased at gourmet cookware shops. **Serves 8 to 10**

1	package fresh *or* dry yeast	2	teaspoons vanilla extract
¼	cup warm water (105° to 115°F)		Grated rind of 1 medium
¼	cup sugar		lemon
	Pinch of salt	2½	cups all-purpose flour
½	cup (1 stick) unsalted butter, melted	½	cup (1 stick) butter, softened
3	whole large eggs		Powdered sugar, sifted
3	egg yolks		

1. In a food processor fitted with steel blade, dissolve yeast in warm water and let sit for 10 minutes. (Or blend using two on/off turns to help yeast dissolve.)
2. Add sugar, salt, melted butter, whole eggs, egg yolks, vanilla, grated lemon rind and 1 cup of the flour. Process until well combined. Add the second cup of flour and process until incorporated. Finally, add the remaining ½ cup flour and process just until incorporated (dough will be quite soft).
3. Transfer dough to a well-buttered large mixing bowl, turning to coat all sides. Cover tightly with plastic wrap and let rise in a warm spot until more than doubled in bulk, 2 to 2½ hours.
4. Punch dough down to remove all air pockets. Turn out onto a well-floured board and knead until very smooth and shiny, 3 to 4 minutes.
5. Lightly dust plastic wrap with flour and wrap dough securely. Refrigerate for 30 minutes.
6. On a lightly floured board, roll out dough into a 12-inch square. Spread softened butter evenly over surface of dough, leaving a 1-inch border all around.
7. Fold dough into thirds, with the seam side nearest you (see illustration).

Fold the dough into thirds, as for puff pastry.

Turn dough so that seam is on your right and again roll out to a 12-inch square, sprinkling board with flour as needed to prevent sticking. Wrap in plastic wrap and refrigerate 30 minutes. You have now completed two turns.
8. Repeat the folding procedure, completing two more turns. (If dough becomes too soft, refrigerate between turns.) Refrigerate 30 minutes.
9. Generously butter a 12-cup tall ovenproof mold. Dust with flour, shaking out any excess.
10. On a lightly floured board, roll out dough into a 12-inch square. Fold in half (dough will now be 6 × 12 inches) with the 6-inch side nearest you. Tightly roll up dough. Place in prepared pan, rolled end up, and cover loosely

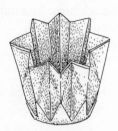

Starting with the 6-inch side in front of you, roll up the dough, jelly roll fashion. Place in the prepared mold.

with plastic wrap. Let rise in warm spot until it fills two thirds of the pan, about 1 hour.
11. Preheat oven to 350°F.
12. Bake 40 to 50 minutes, until cake is golden brown and sounds hollow when tapped.
13. Turn out on rack to cool.
14. When ready to serve, warm slightly and dust heavily with sifted powdered sugar.

To Prepare in Advance: Through #13.

Freezing Instructions: Through #13. Defrost, wrapped, at room temperature. Warm before serving.

Suggested Wine:
Italian: PICOLIT, a gold-colored wine that can be compared to French Sauternes, from Friuli-Venezia Giulia
American: Freemark Abbey EDELWEIN

AMARETTI TORTE Torta di Amaretti

A delicious chocolate cake flavored with amaretto. **Serves 8 to 10**

18 to 20 Almond Macaroons (see page 193) (packaged amaretti can be substituted)
½ pound semisweet chocolate, cut into small pieces
½ cup (1 stick) unsalted butter
5 large eggs, separated
⅔ cup sugar
Powdered sugar, sifted
1 cup heavy cream
1 tablespoon amaretto *or* kirsch, optional
8 to 10 strawberries

1. Preheat oven to 350°F. Butter a 10-inch round cake pan and sprinkle with sugar, shaking out any excess.
2. Process amaretti to a powder in a food processor fitted with steel blade, in a blender or with a rolling pin; you should have about ½ cup. Reserve.
3. In a metal bowl or the top of a double boiler, combine chocolate and butter. Place over simmering water until chocolate is melted.
4. In a large bowl, using a wire whisk or rotary beater, whip egg yolks. Add sugar, reserving 2 tablespoons, and whip until pale yellow in color and ribbons form when whisk is lifted from bowl.
5. Slowly whisk chocolate into egg yolk mixture. Stir in the powdered amaretti.
6. Using a clean whisk or rotary beater, whip egg whites until soft peaks form. Add reserved 2 tablespoons sugar and continue to whip until stiff and shiny. Stir one quarter of the egg whites into the chocolate mixture to lighten, then gently fold in the remaining egg whites. Pour into prepared pan.
7. Bake 50 to 60 minutes, or until toothpick inserted in center comes out clean. Turn out onto rack lined with parchment or waxed paper and let cool. Dust lightly with sifted powdered sugar.
8. Whip cream until it holds soft peaks. Flavor with amaretto, if desired.
9. To serve, cut cake into wedges, top with whipped cream and garnish each slice with a strawberry.

To Prepare in Advance: Through #7.

Freezing Instructions: Through #7. Defrost, wrapped, at room temperature.

LIFT-ME-UP CAKE Tiramisù

Though people think of this as a Veneto dessert, it is really from Milan and has become *the* dessert of northern Italy. It is considered a poor man's dessert because it is a mixture of ingredients with no classic, historical background. **Serves 6 to 8**

16 Ladyfingers (see page 193)	½ pound mascarpone cheese, softened
1 cup rum *or* liqueur such as amaretto or Frangelico	2 to 3 tablespoons unsweetened cocoa, sifted, *or* coarsely grated bittersweet chocolate
5 large eggs, separated	
1⅔ cups powdered sugar	

1. Arrange ladyfingers on the bottom of an 8-cup rectangular or oval serving dish that is not too deep. Pour rum over ladyfingers.
2. In a large bowl, using a wire whisk or rotary beater, combine egg yolks and powdered sugar and beat until mixture turns pale yellow and ribbons form when beater is lifted. Carefully stir in mascarpone until completely incorporated.
3. With a clean whisk or rotary beater, whip egg whites until stiff. Stir one quarter of the whites into the mascarpone mixture to lighten. Gently but quickly fold in the remaining whites.
4. Pour mixture over the ladyfingers and smooth with a rubber spatula. Sprinkle with cocoa and refrigerate, covered, for 1 to 2 hours.
5. Serve directly from serving dish.

To Prepare in Advance: Through #4.

Freezing Instructions: Do not freeze.

Suggested Wine:
Italian: MOSCATO DI PANTELLERIA, a sweet dessert wine, sparkling or still
American: Late harvest JOHANNESBURG RIESLING

FESTIVE SICILIAN SPONGE CAKE WITH CHOCOLATE FROSTING Cassata

Cassata, a Sicilian pastry customarily served at Easter, is now baked for other holidays as well as for family celebrations. Brushing the layers with liqueur moistens the cake and adds to the flavor. **Serves 8**

Cake
4 large eggs
½ cup sugar
⅔ cup sifted all-purpose flour
7 tablespoons clarified unsalted butter
1 teaspoon vanilla extract *or* grated rind of ½ medium lemon

Filling
1 pound ricotta cheese
¼ cup heavy cream
2 tablespoons sugar
¼ cup candied fruit, coarsely chopped
3 ounces bittersweet chocolate, coarsely chopped

Frosting
½ cup sugar
¼ cup cold water
2 ounces bittersweet chocolate
1 tablespoon strong coffee
1 large egg
1 cup (2 sticks) unsalted butter, cut into 16 pieces, softened

¼ cup Frangelico, amaretto or other liqueur of your choice

1. *To prepare cake:* Preheat oven to 350°F. Butter and flour an 9 × 5 × 2-inch loaf pan, shaking out excess flour.
2. In a stainless steel bowl set over hot but *not* boiling water, whisk eggs. Gradually whisk in sugar and whisk until eggs begin to get foamy and thicken slightly.
3. Transfer to electric mixer and beat at high speed until thick, 5 to 7 minutes.
4. Remove bowl from mixer and fold in flour, then butter and vanilla.
5. Pour into prepared pan, gently tapping pan on work surface to level.
6. Bake 25 to 30 minutes, or until golden, turning pan in oven as necessary for even baking.
7. Cool on rack for 15 minutes. Turn out onto waxed paper to cool completely.
8. *To prepare filling:* In a food processor fitted with steel blade or an electric mixer, whip ricotta until smooth. Gradually add cream and sugar and whip until completely incorporated. Fold in the fruit and chocolate. Reserve.
9. *To prepare frosting:* In a small pan, combine sugar and cold water. Cook over high heat until syrup spins a thread (230° to 234°F), 5 to 7 minutes.
10. In a metal bowl or the top of a double boiler, combine chocolate and coffee. Place over simmering water until chocolate is melted. Cool.

11. In an electric mixer, at high speed, beat egg until it thickens. With machine running, gradually pour sugar syrup into egg and continue to beat until bowl is slightly warm to the touch.

12. Add butter one piece at a time, letting each piece be absorbed before adding the next one. Stir in melted chocolate and reserve.

13. *To assemble:* Cut sponge horizontally into 4 even layers. Place first layer on plate and brush lightly with liqueur. Spread one third of the filling evenly over and cover with second layer. Repeat until last layer is set on top, making 3 layers of filling and 4 layers of cake. Refrigerate for 30 minutes.

14. Trim cake so that the sides are even. Frost sides and top of cake with a thin layer of frosting, using a metal spatula. Using a pastry bag fitted with serrated tip, decorate the cake as desired with remaining frosting. Refrigerate 2 to 3 hours.

To Prepare in Advance: Through #7 or #14.

Freezing Instructions: Through #7. Defrost, wrapped, at room temperature.

Variation: Coarsely chopped walnuts or blanched almonds may be added to filling. Finely chopped nuts may be pressed against sides of cake after frosting.

Suggested Wine:
Italian: MOSCATO DI PANTELLERIA, a sweet dessert wine, sparkling or still
American: Late harvest JOHANNESBURG RIESLING

WALNUT TORTE Torta di Noci

Walnuts are found throughout Italy, used in sauces as well as sweets. This is an adaptation of a cake served at Da Franco in Milan. **Serves 10 to 12**

1	pound Sweet Pastry (see page 190)		Grated rind and juice of 1 medium lemon
1	pound Walnut Paste (see page 203)	⅓	cup cornstarch, sifted
		2	tablespoons sugar
2	whole large eggs	½	cup (1 stick) unsalted butter, melted and cooled
4	eggs, separated		
2	tablespoons Marsala	1	cup heavy cream, whipped
		10	or 12 perfect walnut halves

1. On a lightly floured board, roll out pastry to a 12-inch circle and line a 10-inch cake pan. Trim edges. Refrigerate until needed.

2. Preheat oven to 350°F.

3. In a food processor fitted with steel blade, combine walnut paste, whole eggs, egg yolks, Marsala, lemon rind and juice and blend until smooth, scraping down sides of bowl as necessary.

4. Transfer to a large mixing bowl and gently stir in cornstarch.

5. Using a wire whisk or rotary beater, whip egg whites until soft peaks form. Add sugar and continue to whip until stiff and shiny.

6. Carefully stir one quarter of the whites into the batter to lighten. Gently fold in remaining whites; do not overmix.

7. Stir 1 cup of batter into the melted butter, then fold butter mixture back into batter; do not overmix.

8. Pour into pastry shell. Bake 50 to 55 minutes, or until cake is firm to the touch and is golden brown.

9. Let cool 10 minutes, then carefully invert on cake rack. Immediately place serving plate over cake and again invert.

10. When ready to serve, cut into wedges, top with a spoonful of whipped cream and garnish with walnut halves.

To Prepare in Advance: Through #1 or #8.

Freezing Instructions: Through #1, filling directly from freezer. Through #8. Defrost, wrapped, at room temperature.

Suggested Wine:
Italian: MOSCATO, a lightly sweet white wine, sparkling or still
American: MOSCATO

WALNUT PASTE Pasta di Noce

Like almond paste, walnut paste can be stuffed into dried fruits and the fruit dusted with sifted powdered sugar. **Yield: About 1¼ cups**

1½ cups walnuts	1 large or extra large egg white
1⅔ cups powdered sugar, sifted	

1. In a food processor fitted with steel blade, chop walnuts fine.

2. Add powdered sugar and continue to process until combined, scraping down sides of bowl as necessary.

3. Add egg white and process until a mass begins to form on the blade.

4. Turn out of the bowl and wrap securely. Refrigerate and use as needed.

To Prepare in Advance: Through #4. Walnut paste will keep up to 1 week.

Freezing Instructions: Through #4. Defrost, wrapped, in refrigerator.

FRUIT COMPOTE Macedonia di Frutta

In Italy, fresh fruit is a favorite dessert. The fruit is picked young, with emphasis on taste rather than size. Almost any combination of fruit will make this simple dessert elegant enough for your most formal dinner. **Serves 6**

1 bottle (750 ml) dry red wine	½ small unpeeled lemon, cut into small dice
1 cup sugar	
½ vanilla bean, split lengthwise	½ medium unpeeled orange, cut into small dice
½ inch piece cinnamon stick	
1 whole clove	1 pint raspberries
1 pint strawberries, hulled	4 mint leaves
¼ pound red currants	Whipped cream, optional

1. In a 2½-quart saucepan, combine the wine, sugar, vanilla bean, cinnamon and clove. Cook over medium heat until reduced by half.
2. Remove from heat and stir in strawberries, currants, diced lemon and orange.
3. When almost cool, gently stir in raspberries and mint leaves. Remove vanilla bean. Refrigerate.
4. To serve, divide compote among 6 shallow bowls. Pipe rosettes of whipped cream over each portion, if desired.

To Prepare in Advance: Through #3.

Freezing Instructions: Do not freeze.

Variation: To make fruit sherbet, prepare recipe through #3 and purée mixture in a food processor fitted with steel blade. Strain and freeze in an ice cream maker according to manufacturer's directions.

POACHED PEARS WITH ZABAGLIONE
Pere Affogate allo Zabaione

This is an elegant dessert that is delicate and not too rich. If desired, the pears can be poached through step #2 and served cold with whipped cream instead of zabaglione. **Serves 6 to 8**

4 ripe, firm, medium pears	2 strips orange rind, cut into julienne
½ medium lemon, rind removed in strips and cut into julienne	
	4 egg yolks
4 cups Madeira	¼ cup sugar

1. Peel, core and halve each pear lengthwise. Immediately rub with cut side of lemon to prevent discoloration.
2. In a saucepan large enough to hold the pears, bring Madeira and julienned lemon and orange rinds to a boil. Over medium heat, gently slide in pears and poach until tender but still slightly firm, 8 to 10 minutes. (If the pears are hard, it may take a bit longer.) Turn pears with rubber spatula to avoid bruising.
3. Using a slotted spoon, remove pears, dry with paper towel and arrange rounded side up in a 10-inch ovenproof serving dish.
4. Turn heat to high and reduce poaching liquid until ¾ cup remains. Strain, reserving rinds and liquid separately.
5. In a large stainless steel or copper mixing bowl, combine egg yolks and sugar using a wire whisk. Whisk in the poaching liquid and set bowl over hot but *not* boiling water.
6. Beat eggs until they begin to thicken and turn pale yellow, about 10 minutes.
7. Pour sauce over pears and decorate with the julienned peels. Place under the broiler to glaze, 2 to 3 minutes; watch carefully so that sauce does not burn.
8. Serve immediately, or serve at room temperature.

To Prepare in Advance: Through #3 or #7, if serving at room temperature.

Freezing Instructions: Do not freeze.

STRAWBERRIES IN RED WINE
Fragole al Vino Rosso

The wild strawberries of Italy cannot be surpassed. In some villages, strawberry festivals herald the berry harvest. This simple dish is served in the home. If there is any left over, purée and freeze into a sherbet. **Serves 6**

3	cups dry red wine	6	tablespoons sugar
1½	quarts strawberries		Whipped cream, optional

1. In a large enamel saucepan, bring wine to a boil over high heat. Lower heat and cook about 10 minutes, reducing by half.
2. Hull, rinse and dry berries. Place in serving bowl and gently toss with sugar.
3. Pour wine over and refrigerate for 2 hours.
4. Serve in red wine goblets with a dollop of whipped cream, if desired.

To Prepare in Advance: Through #3.

Freezing Instructions: Do not freeze.

Variation: Peeled, sliced fresh peaches may be substituted and make a favorite dessert when peaches are in season.

BAKED RICE PUDDING Dolce di Riso al Forno

In Bologna, a typical rice pudding would have almonds and perhaps candied fruit folded in. Layering apricots between layers of rice adds flavor and texture. This dessert can be served warm or cold. **Serves 6 to 8**

¾ cup Arborio rice (see Note)
2 cups milk
   Pinch of salt
2 large eggs, separated
⅓ cup sugar
¼ cup (½ stick) unsalted butter, cut into small pieces
½ teaspoon vanilla extract

Grated rind of 1 medium lemon
Pinch of freshly grated nutmeg
1 1 pound can peeled apricots, drained and dried (reserve syrup)
2 tablespoons Apricot Glaze (see next page)
   Whipped cream, optional

1. Preheat oven to 400°F. Butter a 6-cup baking or soufflé dish. Sprinkle with sugar, shaking out any excess. Refrigerate.
2. In a 4-quart saucepan, combine rice, milk, and salt. Bring to a boil over medium high heat, lower heat, and cook, stirring occasionally, until all the milk has been absorbed and rice is tender, about 15 to 20 minutes.
3. Remove from heat. Stir in sugar (reserving 1 tablespoon), butter, egg yolks, vanilla, lemon rind and nutmeg. Mix well.
4. With a wire whisk or rotary beater, whip egg whites until soft peaks form. Add reserved 1 tablespoon sugar and continue to whip until stiff and shiny.
5. Stir one quarter of the egg whites into the rice to lighten, then gently but quickly fold in the remaining whites.
6. To assemble pudding, spread one third of rice in prepared dish. Arrange apricot halves cut side down over rice; reserve 1 apricot half for garnish. Cover with second third of rice, the remaining apricot halves and finally the remaining rice.
7. Bake 25 to 30 minutes, until pudding is firm to the touch and begins to shrink from the sides of the baking dish. Remove from oven and let rest 5 minutes.

9. Run knife or spatula around edge of pudding and unmold onto serving plate. Brush with apricot glaze. Decorate top with reserved apricot half.
10. Serve warm or cold. If desired, pass a bowl of whipped cream.

To Prepare in Advance: Through #7 or #8. Serve cold.

Freezing Instructions: Do not freeze.

Variations: 1. Omit fruit from pudding and serve with thinned apricot glaze, reducing syrup by one third.
2. For individual molds, butter and sugar 6 ½-cup molds. Half fill with pudding, arrange 2 or 3 apricot or peach slices over and cover with remaining pudding. Bake about 20 minutes.

Apricot Glaze

Reserved apricot syrup   3   tablespoons apricot preserves

In a small saucepan, reduce syrup by half. Stir in preserves and cook 1 minute longer. Strain.

Note: To make pudding with regular long-grain rice, bring 2 cups of water to a boil with a pinch of salt. Stir in rice and boil for 5 minutes. Drain and continue with recipe from step #2.

BRANDIED MASCARPONE Crema al Mascarpone

Originally from Lombardy, this rich cream cheese can now be found in many other regions. Mascarpone is generally eaten as a dessert, combined with fruit and liqueur. It is usually saved for special occasions and served with a simple cookie or two. **Serves 6 to 8**

4   large eggs, separated   ¼   cup brandy
1   cup sugar   12   large strawberries, sliced
¾   pound mascarpone cheese

1. In a large bowl, using a wire whisk or rotary beater, combine the egg yolks and sugar and beat until mixture turns pale yellow and ribbons form when whisk is lifted.
2. Add the mascarpone and brandy, stirring until smooth.
3. With a clean whisk or rotary beater, whip the egg whites until stiff. Stir one quarter of the whites into the cheese mixture to lighten. Gently but quickly fold in the remaining whites.
4. Fold in the sliced strawberries.

BRANDIED MASCARPONE, continued

5. Heap into a large glass serving bowl or divide among 6 to 8 individual glass cups or dishes. Refrigerate at least 1 hour.
6. Serve cold.

To Prepare in Advance: Through #5.

Freezing Instructions: Do not freeze.

Suggested Wine:
Italian: MOSCATO D'ASTI, a sweet dessert wine from the Piedmont
American: Late harvest JOHANNESBURG RIESLING

TRIFLE Zuppa Inglese

Zuppa Inglese is neither soup nor English. It is a favorite Roman dessert, but I sampled a most delicious version in Verona, at the 12 Apostles restaurant. The Veronese *pandoro* was its base, but any good dry cake can be used.
Serves 8 to 10

8 egg yolks	2 cups heavy cream
½ cup sugar (see Note)	4 cups bite-size pieces of Golden
½ cup Marsala	Bread (Pandoro) (see page 197)
Rind of 1 medium lemon, minced	Grated bittersweet chocolate, optional

1. In a large stainless steel bowl, using a wire whisk or portable electric mixer, whisk together the egg yolks, sugar, Marsala and lemon rind for about 2 minutes.
2. Place over hot but *not* boiling water and continue to whisk until mixture thickens and turns pale yellow.
3. Remove from heat and cool to room temperature.
4. Whip cream until stiff. Stir one quarter of the cream into the egg yolk mixture, then fold in the remaining cream.
5. To assemble, alternate layers of the cream mixture and pandoro in a straight-sided 2-quart glass serving bowl, beginning and ending with the cream mixture. Sprinkle with grated chocolate, if desired. Refrigerate until needed.

To Prepare in Advance: Through #5.

Freezing Instructions: Do not freeze.

Variations: 1. Make Poached Pears with Zabaglione (see page 204). Cut pears into slices and fold whipped cream into the sauce. To assemble, alternate layers of zabaglione, sliced pears and pandoro, beginning and ending with zabaglione. Decorate top with julienned orange peel.
2. Add fresh raspberries or strawberries between layers.
3. Substitute Sherry or Port for Madeira, adjusting quantity to taste.

Note: If the pandoro has been heavily sprinkled with sugar, reduce sugar in recipe to ⅓ cup.

ZABAGLIONE Zabaione

Zabaione (the usual Italian spelling) is enjoyed as much in the United States as in Italy. It is frequently served warm, but is quite good cold. It can also be spooned over other desserts, as in Poached Pears with Zabaglione. **Serves 2**

4 **egg yolks**
4 **teaspoons sugar**
¼ **cup Marsala**

1. In a stainless steel or copper mixing bowl, using a wire whisk, blend egg yolks and sugar. Stir in Marsala.
2. Place bowl over a pan of hot but *not* boiling water and whisk until very thick.
3. Pour into serving glass and serve at room temperature.

To Prepare in Advance: Through #2.

Freezing Instructions: Do not freeze.

Variation: Fold whipped cream into chilled zabaglione. Layer bottom of serving glass with fresh raspberries, strawberries, or sliced peaches, pour in zabaglione and top with fruit.

Suggested Wine:
Italian: RECIOTO SOAVE, a gold-colored dessert wine, sparkling or still, from the Veneto
American: Late harvest JOHANNESBURG RIESLING

VANILLA ICE CREAM Gelato alla Vaniglia

Yield: About 1½ quarts

1 vanilla bean (see Note)	1 cup sugar
3 cups milk	8 egg yolks
1 cup heavy cream	1 teaspoon cold water

1. Split vanilla bean in half lengthwise and place in 4-quart saucepan with milk and cream. Bring to a boil.
2. Stir in sugar, cover and let steep 15 minutes.
3. In a large bowl, using a wire whisk or rotary beater, whip egg yolks and water.
4. *Slowly* whisk hot milk mixture into egg. Pour back into pan and, *stirring constantly* with a wooden spoon, cook over medium heat until mixture lightly coats back of the spoon. Chill. (At this point, mixture may be refrigerated overnight.) Strain.
5. Freeze in ice cream maker according to manufacturer's directions.

To Prepare in Advance: Through #4 or #5.

Freezing Instructions: Through #5.

Variations: 1. To make Ginger Ice Cream, finely chop 3 or 4 tablespoons crystallized ginger. Stir into ice cream after straining. Freeze as above.
2. To make Chocolate Ice Cream, in step #2, stir in ¾ pound chopped bittersweet chocolate. Continue with recipe.

Note: If you cannot obtain a vanilla bean, add 1 teaspoon vanilla extract after mixture coats the back of the spoon (step #4). Continue with recipe.

CARAMEL ICE CREAM Gelato Caramellato

The addition of a few drops of lemon juice to the caramel keeps the sugar from crystallizing and also cuts the sweetness, enhancing the flavor. **Yield: About 1½ quarts**

Ice cream base	*Caramel sauce*
2 cups milk	1 cup sugar
2 cups heavy cream	½ cup water
1 vanilla bean, split lengthwise	½ teaspoon fresh lemon juice
8 egg yolks	6 tablespoons unsalted butter, cut
¾ cup sugar	into small pieces

Sifted unsweetened cocoa, op-
   tional

Orange-Caramel Sauce (see page 217)

1. *To prepare ice cream base:* In a 4-quart saucepan, combine milk, cream and vanilla bean and bring to a boil.

2. In a large bowl, using a wire whisk or rotary beater, beat egg yolks. Gradually whisk in sugar and continue beating until mixture is pale yellow and ribbons form when whisk is lifted.

3. *Slowly* whisk hot mixture into egg yolks. Return to saucepan and, over low heat, cook, *stirring constantly* with a wooden spoon, until mixture heavily coats the back of the spoon.

4. *To make caramel sauce:* In a medium saucepan, combine sugar, water and lemon juice. Bring to a boil and cook over medium heat until a dark caramel color, 12 to 15 minutes. Do not stir. As necessary, brush down sides of pan with pastry brush dipped in cold water.

5. Add butter to sauce 1 tablespoon at a time and stir through.

6. While still warm, whisk in the milk mixture. Strain.

7. Freeze in ice cream maker according to manufacturer's directions. Transfer to freezer until needed.

8. To serve, set 1 or 2 scoops of ice cream in a rounded bowl. Sprinkle with sifted cocoa or top with Orange-Caramel Sauce, if desired.

To Prepare in Advance: Through #7.

Freezing Instructions: Through #7. Scoop servings directly from freezer. If too solid, refrigerate for 20 minutes before serving.

CHOCOLATE TRUFFLES Tartufi

This is for chocolate lovers in any language. The truffles should be made at least a day before serving and will keep in the freezer for up to one month.
Serves 6 to 8

9 ounces bittersweet chocolate
3 egg yolks
½ cup sugar

½ cup water
1 cup heavy cream
   Amaretto or Frangelico liqueur, optional

1. Grate 3 ounces chocolate. Reserve.

2. Using a wire whisk or portable electric mixer, whip egg yolks until thick.

3. In a small saucepan, over high heat, bring sugar and water to a boil until

syrup spins a thread (230° to 234°F); large shiny bubbles will form, and syrup will thicken.

4. Immediately remove syrup from heat. Slowly beat into yolks; take care not to pour syrup onto whisk or beaters, as this spins the syrup onto the walls of the bowl instead of into the eggs. Continue to beat until mixture is cooled and very thick.

5. Cut remaining 6 ounces of chocolate into small bits and melt in metal bowl or top of double boiler placed over simmering water. Add to the yolks. Mixture will be stiff.

6. Gradually pour in cream, beating at medium to high speed as needed to blend smoothly.

7. Flavor with liqueur to taste.

8. Freeze, covered, until firm enough to shape into balls, 3 to 4 hours. Shape into 6 to 8 balls or shape into smaller balls and set in small paper cups. (For convenience, dip 2 tablespoons into warm water. Scoop out tartufo with 1 spoon and shape with the other.) Roll in reserved grated chocolate and return

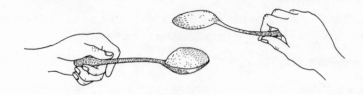

Shaping truffles with 2 tablespoons.

to freezer. Freeze overnight. Transfer to refrigerator 30 minutes before serving.

To Prepare in Advance: Through #7 or #8.

Freezing Instructions: Through #7 or #8.

ESPRESSO ICE CREAM I Gelato all'Espresso

Decaffeinated or flavored espresso beans can be used in this ice cream.
Yield: About 2 quarts

2 cups heavy cream	10 egg yolks
2 cups milk	1½ cups sugar
1½ cups espresso beans, coarsely crushed	Orange-Caramel Sauce (see page 217)

1. In a 4-quart saucepan, combine cream, milk and coffee beans. Bring to a boil. Turn off heat and let steep 30 minutes.
2. Using a wire whisk or rotary beater, combine egg yolks and sugar, beating well until mixture turns pale yellow and ribbons form when whisk is lifted from bowl. Whisk some of the hot milk mixture into the egg mixture and return to the pan, whisking all the while.
3. Over low heat, *stirring constantly*, cook until mixture coats the back of a wooden spoon and a candy thermometer reads 180°F. Pour into a chilled bowl and chill over ice. Refrigerate overnight, if desired, for stronger coffee flavor.
4. Strain into an ice cream maker and freeze according to manufacturer's directions.
5. To serve, scoop into shallow bowls and top with Orange-Caramel Sauce.

To Prepare in Advance: Through #3 or #4.

Freezing Instructions: Through #4.

Suggested Wine:
Italian: VIN SANTO, a sweet white wine
American: Schramsberg CRÉMANT

ESPRESSO ICE CREAM II Gelato all'Espresso

No ice cream maker is necessary to prepare this recipe. However, the ice cream should be taken out of the freezer and refrigerated for one hour before serving to soften. **Yield: 2 quarts**

4 eggs, separated	2 to 3 tablespoons instant espresso
⅓ cup sugar	2 cups heavy cream, whipped

ESPRESSO ICE CREAM II, continued

1. Using a wire whisk or rotary beater, whip egg yolks and sugar until pale yellow and ribbons form when whisk is lifted from bowl.
2. Stir in instant espresso to taste. Fold in whipped cream.
3. In a clean bowl, using a whisk or rotary beater, beat egg whites until soft peaks form. Stir one quarter of the egg whites into the batter, then quickly but gently fold in the remaining whites.
4. Pour into a glass bowl, cover tightly and place in the freezer for 2 hours. Whip again and return to freezer.
5. To serve, scoop out ice cream into individual bowls.

To Prepare in Advance: Through #4.

Freezing Instructions: Through #4.

PUMPKIN ICE CREAM Gelato di Zucca

This is particularly appropriate during the holiday season and an ice cream maker is not necessary.

Remove from freezer and refrigerate for one hour before serving to allow ice cream to soften to the right consistency. **Yield: 2 quarts**

4 large eggs, separated	¼ teaspoon freshly grated nutmeg
⅓ cup sugar	⅛ teaspoon mace
3 tablespoons canned pumpkin purée	2 cups heavy cream, whipped

1. Using a wire whisk or a rotary beater, beat egg yolks and sugar until pale yellow and ribbons form when whisk is lifted from bowl.
2. Stir in pumpkin purée, nutmeg and mace. Fold in whipped cream.
3. Using a clean whisk or rotary beater, whip egg whites until soft peaks form. Stir one quarter of the egg whites into pumpkin mixture, then quickly and gently fold in remaining whites.
4. Pour into glass bowl, cover and freeze for 2 hours. Whisk again and return to freezer; ice cream should be soft.
5. To serve, scoop out balls of ice cream into individual bowls or serve directly from glass bowl.

To Prepare in Advance: Through #4.

Freezing Instructions: Through #4.

RASPBERRY ICE CREAM Gelato di Lamponi

Strawberries may be substituted for raspberries; flavor to taste with Grand Marnier or framboise. Remove from freezer and refrigerate for one hour before serving to allow ice cream to soften to the right consistency. **Yield: About 2 quarts**

1 cup raspberries	4 large eggs, separated
1 tablespoon raspberry syrup, optional	⅔ cup sugar
	2 cups heavy cream, whipped
1 tablespoon Chambord liqueur	Raspberries for garnish

1. In a food processor fitted with steel blade, or a blender, purée berries. Add syrup and Chambord and process just to combine. Strain, if desired, and reserve.
2. Using a wire whisk or rotary beater, beat together egg yolks and ⅓ cup sugar until mixture turns pale yellow and ribbons form when whisk is lifted from bowl. Stir in raspberry purée. Fold in whipped cream.
3. In a clean bowl, using a whisk or rotary beater, whip egg whites until soft peaks form. Sprinkle in remaining ⅓ cup sugar and whip until stiff and shiny.
4. Stir one quarter of the egg whites into the raspberry mixture, then quickly but gently fold in remaining whites.
5. Pour into glass bowl, cover tightly and freeze for 2 hours. Whisk again and return to freezer.
6. To serve, scoop into individual bowls and sprinkle with additional raspberries.

To Prepare in Advance: Through #5.

Freezing Instructions: Through #5.

Suggested Wine:
Italian: BRACHETTO, a sweet red wine, sparkling or still
American: Schramsberg BLANC DE NOIR

MINT ICE CREAM Gelato alla Menta

A very refreshing dessert. Try piping over a mixture of fresh fruits. **Yield: About 1½ quarts**

4 cups half and half	3 to 4 sprigs mint
6 egg yolks	Chocolate Sauce (see page 217)
1 cup sugar	Mint leaves for garnish, optional

1. In a 4-quart saucepan bring half and half to a boil.
2. Using a wire whisk or rotary beater, combine egg yolks and sugar, beating well until mixture turns pale yellow and ribbons form when whisk is lifted from bowl.
3. *Slowly* whisk the hot half and half into the egg mixture. Return to saucepan and, over low heat, cook, *stirring constantly* with a wooden spoon, until mixture heavily coats the back of the spoon. Stir in mint and cool by placing bowl over ice. Mixture can be refrigerated at this point. Strain.
4. Transfer mixture to ice cream maker and freeze according to manufacturer's directions.
5. To serve, scoop 1 or 2 balls into a shallow bowl and top with Chocolate Sauce. Garnish with mint leaves, if desired.

To Prepare in Advance: Through #4.

Freezing Instructions: Through #4.

ORANGE SHERBET Granita all'Arancia

The origin of frozen desserts in Italy dates back to the early Romans, who ate iced fruit juices. Today, granita is usually eaten as refreshment on a warm afternoon. I find it a delightful dessert to end a filling meal. **Serves 6**

1¼ cups sugar	Juice of 1 medium lemon
2 cups fresh orange juice	4 large eating oranges, peeled

1. In a small saucepan, over medium heat, dissolve sugar in orange juice. Stir in lemon juice.
2. Freeze mixture in an ice cream maker according to manufacturer's directions. Transfer to chilled container and place in freezer until needed.
3. Cut oranges into individual sections.
4. To serve, arrange orange sections on plate and top with 1 or 2 scoops of sherbet (see Note).

To Prepare in Advance: Through #2.

Freezing Instructions: Through #2.

Note: Sherbet can be served in scooped-out orange shells after juicing. Place shells in freezer until firm, pack with sherbet and return to freezer. Serve directly from freezer. If bottom of orange is not level, carefully cut away a thin slice so that orange rests on the plate.

CHOCOLATE SAUCE Salsa di Cioccolata

A rich chocolate sauce that can be flavored with the liqueur of your choice. You can use any semisweet or bittersweet chocolate, but it must be real chocolate: the better the chocolate, the better the sauce. Serve over ice cream.
Yield: About 2 cups

1 cup heavy cream
1 vanilla bean, split lengthwise
½ pound semisweet chocolate, coarsely chopped

1 teaspoon instant coffee, optional
   or 1 teaspoon Grand Marnier, optional

1. In a small saucepan, over medium heat, bring cream to boil with vanilla bean. Lower heat and simmer 1 minute.
2. Place chocolate in a mixing bowl. Pour hot cream and vanilla bean over chocolate to melt, stirring occasionally. Flavor with instant coffee or Grand Marnier, if desired.
3. Remove vanilla bean and transfer sauce to covered jar. Cool and refrigerate.
4. Use as needed.

To Prepare in Advance: Through #3. Sauce will keep for weeks refrigerated. It thickens as it stands; to thin, warm slowly over low heat.

Freezing Instructions: Do not freeze.

ORANGE-CARAMEL SAUCE
Salsa Caramellata all'Arancia

A delicate sauce, this complements most ice cream flavors. This was served at a small restaurant in the Borghese Gardens in Rome, down the street from the Hotel Hassler. **Yield: 1¼ cups**

Zest of 4 medium oranges
½ cup sugar
¼ cup water

½ cup fresh orange juice
½ cup Grand Marnier or other orange liqueur

1. In a small saucepan, combine orange zest and water to cover and bring to a boil. Drain and reserve.
2. In the same pan, bring sugar and water to a boil over medium heat. Cook to a dark caramel color, about 15 to 20 minutes; do not stir or whisk. As crys-

ORANGE-CARAMEL SAUCE, continued

tals form around sides of pan, brush down with pastry brush that has been dipped in cold water.

3. Remove from heat and add reserved orange zest, juice and Grand Marnier. Set over low heat and stir to dissolve caramel.

4. Serve warm, spooning over scoops of ice cream. Make sure that you spoon some of the zest over each serving.

To Prepare in Advance: Through #3. Sauce will keep 3 to 4 days refrigerated.

Freezing Instructions: Do not freeze.

Suggested Menus

BUFFET-BRUNCH

Potato Frittata
Onion Tart
Spinach Tart
Spicy Italian Sausage
Peppers, Tomatoes and Onion
Baked Rice Pudding
Assorted Fresh Fruit

Onion, Bacon and Tomato Frittata
Potato Croquettes
Crepes with Cheese
Walnut Torte
   Wines: Italian Sparkling Brut such as Ferrari, Ca'del Bosco or Contratto

INFORMAL LUNCH

Salad Valentino
Lasagne
   Wine: Young Chianti
Strawberries in Red Wine
Almond Cookies

Vegetable Soup with Pesto
Chicken with Sausage
   Wine: Rubesco Riserva
Apple Frittata

INFORMAL DINNER

Bread Salad
Casserole of Duck
Polenta with Sliced Sautéed Mush-
    rooms
    Wine: Salice Salentino
Mint Ice Cream
Almond Macaroons

Roasted Peppers
Straw and Hay with Fresh Vegetables
    Wine: Dolcetto or Fara
Chicken, Hunter's Style
Plum Tart with Whipped Cream

INFORMAL SUPPER

Leek Soup
Bread and Cheese Timbales
    Wine: Cabernet del Piave
Fruit Compote

INFORMAL PARTY

Bresaola
Roasted Peppers
Pasta Roll
Broiled Lemon Chicken
    Wine: Barbera or Refosco
Brandied Mascarpone with Fresh Fruit

TEENAGE PARTY

Variety of Pizzas, I, III, V
Lasagne
Vanilla Ice Cream
Caramel Ice Cream
Chocolate Sauce

FORMAL LUNCHEON

Mushroom Soup
Sea Bass with Butter and Parsley
    Wine: Verdicchio di Jesi
Pasta with Zucchini Sauce
    Wine: Chiaretto or Bardolino
Orange Sherbet with Sliced Oranges

Steamed Artichokes
Cold Squab with Mint Gelatin
    Wine: Tignanello Antinori
Fig Tart   *Wine:* Asti Spumante

FORMAL DINNER

Stuffed Zucchini Flowers with To-
    mato Sauce
    Wine: Ca'del Bosco, Dosage Zero
    Cortese di Gavi (La Scolca)
Roasted Quail with Risotto
    Wine: Barbaresco '71 vintage
    (Giacosa)
Asparagus Parmesan
Radicchio and Arugula with Warm
Goat Cheese
    Wine: Amarone '64 or '71 vintage
Poached Pears with Zabaglione
    Wine: Moscato di Pantelleria

Caponata Timbales with Red Pepper
Sauce   *Wine:* Antinori Nature
Pasta with Pecorino and Asparagus
    Wine: Pinot Grigio Felluga
Sautéed Veal Medallions
    Wine: Gattinara '70 vintage
Festive Sicilian Sponge Cake with
Chocolate Frosting   *Wine:* Picolit

DINNER FOR AN OCCASION

Semolina Gnocchi   *Wine:* Orvieto
Roast Suckling Pig   *Wine:* Barolo
Sautéed Porcini Mushrooms
Glazed Pearl Onions
Trifle

Italian Food Specialty Stores

Below is a list of selected stores throughout the United States that carry Italian foods and/or cookware. Those marked with an asterisk (*) have mail order service; those with a catalog are also noted. A few of each store's specialties are mentioned.

CALIFORNIA

WILLIAMS-SONOMA* P.O. Box 7456 San Francisco 94120-7456 (415) 982-0295

Catalog Available. Cookware, Olive oils, Vinegars, Flours, Rice, Sea salt, Dried herbs

HUGO'S 8401 Santa Monica Blvd. Los Angeles 90069 (213) 654-3993

Fresh veal, Sausages, Cheeses, Olive oils, Wild mushrooms, Dried tomatoes, Wines

BAY CITY IMPORTS 1517 Lincoln Blvd. Santa Monica 90401 (213) 395-8279

Sausages, Cheeses, Wines, Olive oils, Vinegars, Imported pastas

NEW YORK

ZABAR'S 2245 Broadway New York City 10024   (212) 787-2000

Catalog Available. Sausages, Cheeses, Olives, Olive oils, Vinegars, Pastas, Flours, Cookware

DEAN AND DeLUCA* 121 Prince St. New York City 10012 (212) 254-7774

Catalog Available. Cookware, Spices and Seasonings, Cheeses, Oils, Vinegars, Salamis, Sausages, Dried tomatoes and mushrooms

TODARO BROS.* 557 Second Ave. New York City 10016   (212) 679-7766

Cookware, Cheeses, Salamis, Pastas, Truffles, Flours

MANGANARO'S* 488 Ninth Ave. New York City 10012   (212) 563-5331

Pastas, Cheeses, Sausages, Rice, Truffles, Pancetta, Prosciutto

MICHIGAN

LOMBARDI FOOD CO. 2465 Twenty-Three Mile Rd. Utica 48087   (313) 254-3550

Catalog Available. Cookware, Flours, Sausages, Cheeses, Olive oils, Vinegars, Spices and Seasonings, Beans

ILLINOIS

CONTE-DI-SAVOIA 555 W. Roosevelt Chicago 60607   (312) 666-3471

Pastas, Pancetta, Sausages, Flours, Olive oils, Vinegars, Cheeses, Dried Tomatoes and mushrooms

COLORADO

P.C. MANCINELLI 3245 Osage St. Denver 80211   (303) 433-9449

Cheeses, Salamis, Sausages, Pastas, Olive oils, Flours, Vinegars, Cookware

Beside these specialty stores, some department stores are now opening food sections for the convenience of their customers: Macy's, Bloomingdale's, I. Magnin and Saks Fifth Avenue, to name a few.

Williams-Sonoma, described in the California listings, also has stores in Beverly Hills, Palo Alto, Costa Mesa, Dallas, Minneapolis, Washington, D.C., Los Angeles, Pasadena, Culertino, Denver, Stamford, Short Hills, Oakbrook.

Index

Knives, 2–3

Ladyfingers, 193–94
  lift-me-up cake, 200
Lamb:
  braised, chops, 114
  roast leg of, 115
Langostinos for fish soup,
  52–54
Lasagne, 82–83
  duck, 84–85
Leek soup, 54
Lemon:
  butter, chicken breasts
    with, 136
  chicken, broiled, 139–40
  fruit compote, 204
Lemon juice as salt
  substitute, 20
Lenticchie al Forno, 163
Lentils, 10
  baked, 163
Lettuce leaves, stuffed
  chicken breasts in,
  137–38
Lift-me-up cake, 200
Lima beans, 10
List of recipes, x–xiii
Liver(s):
  calves':
    with sage, 116–17
    Venetian style, 116
  chicken:
    Crostini with, 24–25
    pasta roll, 86–87
    sauce, 67

Macaroons, almond, 193
Macedonia di Frutta, 204
Mandoline, 5
  defined, 5–6
Marinade, marinated, 6
  grilled chicken, 145
  for potted rabbit, with
    mushrooms and
    olives, 132–33
Marinara sauce, 61–62
Marinate, defined, 6
Marjoram, 19

Mascarpone cheese, 16
  brandied, 207–208
  and gorgonzola puffs,
    31–32
  lift-me-up cake, 200
  pasta with four cheeses,
    88–89
Mayonnaise, 44
  mustard, sliced raw
    beef with, 36
Measuring cups and
  spoons, 2
Meat, see Beef; Lamb;
  Pork; Rabbit; Veal
Meat sauce, 63
Melanzane alla Griglia,
  164–65
Melt, defined, 6
Melted mozzarella,
  tomato and basil, 32
Mezzaluna, 3
Milk:
  baked rice pudding,
    206–207
  Béchamel sauce, 65–66
  crepes, 186
  fondue, 30
  semolina gnocchi, 95–96
Mince, defined, 6
Minestrone, see Spring
  soup; Vegetable soup
  with pesto
Minestrone al Pesto, 58
Mint, 19
  gelatin, cold squab in,
    146–47
  ice cream, 215–16
Mix, defined, 6
Mixing bowls, 2
Mortadella for salad
  Valentino, 43
Mortar and pestle, 64
Mound, defined, 6
Mozzarella cheese, 16
  bread and cheese
    timbales, 154
  crepes with cheese,
    81–82
  Crostini with, and
    anchovy, 25–26

lasagne, 82–83
  melted, tomato and
    basil, 32
  stuffed zucchini flowers,
    37–38
  veal rolls, 129–30
Mushroom(s):
  chicken with raw,
    143–44
  dried, 12
  grilled shitaki, 166
  pasta, 78
  potted rabbit with
    mushrooms and
    olives, 132–33
  risotto with, 101–102
  salad, 40–41
  sauce, 68–69
  sautéed porcini, 165
  soup, 55
  steak with porcini,
    grilled, 117–18
  straw and hay, with
    fresh vegetables,
    95
Mussels:
  fish soup, 52–54
  steamed, 110
Mustard mayonnaise,
  sliced raw beef with,
  36

Navy beans, 10
Noodles, baked, 79
Nutmeg, 19

Oil, 12
Olive oil, 12
Olives:
  pasta with tomatoes
    and black, 88
  potted rabbit with
    mushrooms and,
    132–33
  stuffed flat bread,
    180–81
One-crust pastry, 187
Onion(s):
  bacon and tomato

About the Author

Judy Gethers is the former director of Ma Cuisine, the cooking school of
Los Angeles's famed Ma Maison restaurant. Ms. Gethers brought to the
school such culinary guest stars as Maida Heatter, Julia Child, and Wolfgang
Puck. She is the author of several cookbooks, including
THE WORLD FAMOUS RATNER'S MEATLESS COOKBOOK and
THE FABULOUS GOURMET FOOD PROCESSOR COOKBOOK.
Ms. Gethers continues to teach and lecture in cooking schools around the
country, and lives in Beverly Hills, California.